The Transformation of the Supreme Court's Agenda

TRANSFORMING AMERICAN POLITICS
Lawrence C. Dodd, Series Editor

Dramatic changes in political institutions and behavior over the past two decades have underscored the dynamic nature of American politics, confronting political scientists with a new and pressing intellectual agenda. The pioneering work of early postwar scholars, while laying a firm empirical foundation for contemporary scholarship, failed to consider how American politics might change or to recognize the forces that would make fundamental change inevitable. In reassessing the static interpretations fostered by these classic studies, political scientists are now examining the underlying dynamics that generate transformational change.

Transforming American Politics will bring together texts and monographs that address four closely related aspects of change. A first concern is documenting and explaining recent changes in American politics—in institutions, processes, behavior, and policymaking. A second is reinterpreting classic studies and theories to provide a more accurate perspective on postwar politics. The series will look at historical change to identify recurring patterns of political transformation within and across the distinctive eras of American politics. Last and perhaps most importantly, the series will present new theories and interpretations that explain the dynamic processes at work and thus clarify the direction of contemporary politics. All of the books will focus on the central theme of transformation—transformation in both the conduct of American politics and in the way we study and understand its many aspects.

TITLES IN THIS SERIES

The Transformation of the Supreme Court's Agenda

FROM THE NEW DEAL TO THE REAGAN ADMINISTRATION

Richard L. Pacelle, Jr.

University of Missouri–St. Louis

Westview Press

BOULDER • SAN FRANCISCO • OXFORD

Transforming American Politics

Copyright © 1991 by Westview Press, Inc.

Published in 1991 in the United States of America by Westview Press, Inc., 5500 Central Avenue, Boulder, Colorado 80301-2847, and in the United Kingdom by Westview Press, 36 Lonsdale Road, Summertown, Oxford OX2 7EW

Library of Congress Cataloging-in-Publication Data
Pacelle, Richard L., 1954–
  The transformation of the Supreme Court's agenda : from the New
Deal to the Reagan administration / Richard L. Pacelle, Jr.
    p. cm. — (Transforming American politics)
  Includes bibliographical references and index.
  ISBN 0-8133-8376-5
  1. United States. Supreme Court—History. 2. Judicial review—
United States—History. 3. Political questions and judicial power—
United States—History. I. Title. II. Series: Transforming
American politics series.
KF8742.P3 1991
347.73'26—dc20
[347.30735]   91-22609
                                                                          CIP

Printed and bound in the United States of America

The paper used in this publication meets the requirements
of the American National Standard for Permanence of Paper
for Printed Library Materials Z39.48-1984.

10   9   8   7   6   5   4   3   2   1

To my parents,
Patricia K. Pacelle and Richard L. Pacelle, Sr.

Contents

Tables and Figures

TABLES

Acknowledgments

Many individuals were instrumental in making this project possible. Steve Flinn, James Woods, John Daniels, Robert Brown, Beth Hall, and especially Margaret Anderson helped me prepare the manuscript and tables. Professor Harold Spaeth made the Supreme Court Data Base available to me. Professors Lee Epstein, H. W. Perry, Roberta Herzberg, and Joseph Aistrup offered encouragement and important substantive suggestions. Professor Larry Dodd, the editor of this series, and Jennifer Knerr, Martha Leggett, and Christine Carson of Westview Press were patient, endured many odd questions, and suggested significant improvements. Jeanne Campbell did a thorough job copyediting and improving the manuscript. I have profited from their assistance.

I owe the greatest intellectual debts to Lawrence Baum, whose assistance throughout the genesis of this project has been invaluable. Choosing to study under his direction was among the best decisions I have ever made. I owe a great deal to Fenton Martin, whose help, moral support, care, and constant encouragement made this manuscript possible. The Supreme Court bibliography she coauthored was a valuable resource. I dedicate this book to my parents, whose constant love, support, and encouragement have always been appreciated. I hope whatever merit the book has reflects well on their child-rearing abilities.

Richard L. Pacelle, Jr.

1

The Supreme Court's Agenda and American Politics

The Constitution of the United States represents an attempt to fashion relations between the branches of government and between levels of government and the Bill of Rights defines the liberties of individuals. Both documents are composed in broad strokes--the language of many provisions is vague and open to many interpretations. The Supreme Court of the United States has responsibility for applying constitutional provisions to specific circumstances. In fact, the Court took this power for itself because Article III of the Constitution, which deals with the judiciary, is both brief and vague.

Through its decisions and its case selection policies, the Supreme Court interprets the Constitution and various statutes and thereby assists in the construction of policy in a number of areas. In addition, building an agenda through the selection of the cases on the docket and making decisions on the merits of cases define the role of the Supreme Court in the American governmental structure. Changes in agenda priorities and judicial doctrine are a function of institutional transformations and may reflect broader-scale changes occurring in the external political, social, and economic environment.

The analysis in this book focuses on the changes in the issues concerning the Supreme Court over the last half-century (1933-1988). Those changes have occurred in the context of significant changes in American politics that began with the New Deal and have continued through the efforts of President Ronald Reagan to reverse many of the policies that had created a large federal governmental infrastructure. The changes in the Supreme Court's priorities were initiated to effect a revision in the institutional role of the Court. Over the past half-century, that role has undergone a fundamental transformation, which has been implemented through changes in the Court's agenda and judicial doctrine.

In establishing the blueprint for our form of government, the framers of the Constitution were guided by historical precedent and political theory. Borrowing liberally from Montesquieu and Locke, the framers sought to establish a limited government controlled by separating legislative, executive, and judicial prerogatives while giving each branch some authority to check the other branches. Theoretically, this configuration divides the policy process into neat stages: public officials and external actors approach the governmental units in the agenda stage, Congress formulates a solution, the president and the bureaucracy implement the program. The Supreme Court may be asked to interpret provisions or assess their constitutionality. In reality, stages blur and the points of access serve multiple purposes.

The judiciary is a prime example of the reconceptualization and evolution of the policy process. The long-standing judicial myth held that judges did not make policy; they found law in existing precedents. The elected branches were to make policy, unelected judges were referees interpreting the Constitution and statutes. There is controversy over the proper role of the judicial branch and the extent to which courts should make policy, but it is evident that judges are important policymakers.

The role of the Supreme Court falls along a continuum defined by Alexander Hamilton and Alexis de Tocqueville. In arguing for the form of government established by the Constitution, Hamilton maintained that the judiciary was "the least dangerous branch of government."[1] A seemingly contradictory assessment was offered less than a half-century later by Tocqueville, a visitor and commentator on American society. Seeing greater potential in the power of the judiciary, he wrote, "scarcely any political question arises in the United States that is not resolved, sooner or later, into a judicial question."[2] Few would dispute that Hamilton underestimated the impact of the Supreme Court. As a policymaker, the Court is involved in most issues affecting society.

The constitutional system established under this framework created a form of government often referred to as pluralistic. A democracy presupposes that the preferences of the citizenry are addressed by duly elected or appointed officials. The notion of pluralism requires multiple points of access to the system for those seeking the assistance of government. The agenda stage is considered the ideal point in the process for that access.

The agenda is arguably the most critical stage of the policy process. It is the linkage stage during which citizens and groups approach government seeking redress for grievances. On a practical level, issues that do not survive the agenda stage are effectively denied further consideration. On a philosophical level, the agenda offers citizens the access to government that democratic theory promises. The agenda reflects problems that concern citizens and represents an important linchpin of a dynamic policy process. The evaluation of existing policy often reveals unanticipated consequences of the previous design. The agenda is the opportunity for readjustment to correct perceived problems.

There are two portions to the agenda stage: agenda setting and agenda building. The former refers to the "governmental agenda" and comprises all issues receiving some consideration, which is often limited and perfunctory. In a sense, agenda setting represents the universe of issues that citizens, organized groups, and governmental actors seek to bring to an agency's attention. The number of issues that exist as viable concerns far outstrips the capacity of a governmental agency to address them. From the mass of these petitions, the governmental body must select a fraction of the issues to consider for substantive attention. The process of culling the chosen issues is referred to as agenda building.

If a governmental body decides to consider an issue formally, that item is said to have achieved the institutional or decision agenda.[3] Regardless of the ultimate disposition, the governmental agency has granted the issue or appeal some legitimacy. This is a threshold that must be negotiated before further action can be propagated. Because there are more problems than government can address, the institutional agenda serves a very necessary gatekeeping function. The process of agenda building allows the institution to manage its workload.

If politics is indeed "who gets what, when, and how," then the concept of the agenda is crucial. Deciding which issues receive serious consideration is a stage in the ultimate allocation of resources. Any governmental agency that builds an institutional agenda, in effect, sets the conditions and environment for participation of citizens. The agenda is, in some senses, a bellwether for public policy writ large. The shape of the agenda should have some fundamental impact on the shape of policies emerging from various governmental agencies.

Although the notion of agenda building is important in and of itself, the nature and structure of agenda change also carry significant implications. The scope and pace of agenda change suggest the responsiveness of the governmental agency building an agenda and its ability to adapt to its environment. Empirically, changes in the Court's decision agenda can be compared to transformations occurring in U.S. politics and public policy. Existing problems, emerging issues, and changes in technology create demands on institutions charged with policymaking responsibilities. Agenda change may also be a function of the relative influence of external policy entrepreneurs and other governmental actors seeking the attention of the agency.

The present study analyzes the Court's agenda over the past half-century, an epoch marked by a transformation in American politics. The study examines the cases the Court has accepted in that period, and focuses on surges and declines in Court attention to a number of policy areas during the Hughes, Stone, Vinson, Warren, Burger, and early Rehnquist courts. The period began one month before Franklin Roosevelt was elected and ended in the waning days of Ronald Reagan's second term. This time frame represents a seminal period in American constitutional history. Changes in the agenda provided the Court with the opportunity to revise its institutional priorities. The trends of agenda change yield propositions about the factors and determinants that govern the building of the agenda and the dynamics that structure such changes.

THE SUPREME COURT AND ITS AGENDA

The U.S. Supreme Court has long been an active participant in the construction of national public policy. At times and in certain policy areas, the Court has assumed an interstitial secondary role in making policy. During other periods and in different domains, the Court has been the primary force. Regardless of the Court's relative prominence in the overall policymaking scheme, the notion of how an institution initiates policy change is critical. Analysts of the Court have long observed the development of judicial and constitutional doctrine.[4] Implicit in such analyses are the changes manifested in the Court's agenda.

The significance of the agenda may be most evident in the judicial branch in general and in the Supreme Court in particular. The Supreme Court is not a self-starter. The justices must wait for petitions to be brought before them. Annually the Court faces a flood of petitions, yet it can only hear a fraction of these cases. Thus, like any governmental body, the Court must build its agenda. The justices must winnow out frivolous demands, requests that cannot be met for a variety of reasons, and issues whose time has not yet arrived. Cases surviving this process constitute the Court's institutional agenda for the term.

In allocating the finite agenda space, the Court implicitly encourages certain types of cases and discourages others.[5] The choices that the Court makes in its agenda building and the decisions on the merits of the cases have an impact on subsequent agendas. Items arise because past policies fail to address certain problems, create new problems, or beget related issues. More broadly, the construction of the agenda affords the Court the opportunity to affect the policies responsible for changes in American politics.

This study concerns the scope and pace of Supreme Court agenda change and the factors that influence patterns of change. As a result, this research is guided by two basic questions. First, what is the nature of the change in the Supreme Court's agenda? This empirical question will be addressed by means of a longitudinal analysis of the Court's agenda in the 1933-1988 terms, during the most significant transformation in American politics and the Supreme Court. Second, what factors structure the scope and pace of agenda change? The goal is to develop propositions that can aid the construction of a conceptual framework to explain the dynamics of agenda change. The initial stage requires an analysis of the factors influencing the case-screening policies of individual justices and the procedures governing case selection. This analysis is a prelude to broader notions of institutional agenda building.

PROCESSES OF CASE SCREENING

Virtually all cases arrive at the Supreme Court as writs of certiorari, operating under the rule of four: If four justices want to hear a case, it is accepted for decision on its merits. The writ, if granted, orders the lower court to send the records of the case to the Supreme Court for review. The Supreme Court uses it as a discretionary device to choose the cases it wishes to hear. A denial of certiorari carries, according to the Court, no precedential value. The writ of certiorari is covered in Rule 10 of the Court's revised procedures, but the language gives little guidance as to the reasons this writ should be granted. The criteria are broad, general, and leave the Court virtually complete discretion. Such writs are to be granted only when there are "special and important reasons." Among such reasons recommended by Rule 10 for consideration are lower court conflicts, state decisions concerning federal questions, lower court decisions that conflict with previous Supreme Court precedents, or new issues the Supreme Court should consider. Ultimately, these decisions to accept the case depend on the votes of at least four justices.

The Court receives a wealth of petitions, approximately 4,500 in recent terms, but has the institutional capacity to attend to only about 300. About half of these accepted cases receive full consideration; the remainder are treated in a more perfunctory manner. The most common treatment of those cases that are accepted but do not receive full treatment is an unsigned, *per curiam* or memorandum decision. Normally, these are brief opinions referring to another decision that was more fully developed by the Court.

The writ of certiorari was created by the Judiciary Act of 1925. Prior to that time, the Court had mandatory jurisdiction--it had to hear every case that was properly brought to its docket. Since 1925, the Court's appellate docket has been composed of writs of appeal, which were mandatory, and writs of certiorari, which were discretionary. Although writs of appeal were presumably mandatory, justices had some ability to deny them. In 1988, Congress, which controls the Court's appellate jurisdiction, passed the Act to Improve the Administration of Justice restricting the Court's mandatory jurisdiction to cases decided by three-judge federal district courts and involving some antitrust matters, reapportionment, and cases arising under the Civil Rights and Voting Rights acts, and the Presidential Election Campaign Fund Act.[6]

The 1988 change appears to usher in a new era for case selection, but its effects on the agenda should be minimal. Writs of appeal have annually made up only a small percentage of the Court's docket. The justices also made liberal use of a number of tools designed to deny writs of appeal or treat them in a perfunctory manner. The Court could deny a writ as improvidently granted or could accept the writ and decide the issue without oral arguments through a brief *per curiam* or memorandum opinion. The most significant difference may be that justices can treat less important appeals like writs of certiorari and simply deny them without opinion or the expenditure of any time or energy.

Despite the growth in the number of certiorari petitions, the number of cases accepted remains basically unchanged. To facilitate the review of these petitions, the Supreme Court has institutionalized some procedures designed to structure the process of case selection and to develop some mechanisms or shortcuts allowing the justices to transact their business more efficiently.

On the broadest level, the cases brought to the Court fill two dockets. About half the petitions are "paid" cases, meaning that the filing fees have been paid by the litigant. The remainder of the cases are filed *in forma pauperis* by indigent persons. The preponderance of the *in forma pauperis* petitions are criminal cases brought by prisoners. The paupers' petitions have traditionally been treated in a different fashion from the paid cases. Although the processes of examination have converged, the acceptance rates are quite different: The vast majority of paid cases are denied, but an even larger percentage of paupers' cases (more than 99 percent) are denied. It is obvious that the status of the petition sends a message to the justices.[7]

One means of improving the agenda-building process is to reduce the number of petitions the justices must address systematically. The Court is unable to accept every important case or even a significant percentage of potentially major cases each term. Furthermore, a large number of the cases on the docket each term are trivial and deserve no attention. The creation of a "dead list" by a former chief justice marked an attempt to dismiss many cases immediately. The remainder of the cases would be discussed in conference. Chief Justice Warren Burger reversed the process by creating a "discuss list." Putting a petition on this list would signal the justices that the case would merit attention. A case failing to make the list is effectively killed unless another justice seeks to have it added to the discuss list, a rare occurrence.[8]

The use of the discuss list (and the dead list before that) was an attempt to find an institutional solution to a major procedural problem. It addressed part of the problem but has not mitigated the need for individual-level procedures that would help the justices cope with their own workloads. The Supreme Court has often been referred to as "nine little law firms."[9] The justices individually assess the merits of the petitions before them and then meet in conference to discuss and vote on whether to accept or reject the cases. Individual members of the Court make extensive, though varying, use of their clerks to assist in the process of reviewing the petitions. The modal use of the clerks seems to be as a funnel of sorts. The clerks read the petitions and issue a brief summary of the major issue and the precedents cited. Often these summaries contain recommendations to the clerk's justice whether to accept or deny the petition.

Some justices have taken this process even further through the creation of a "certiorari pool." Most of the current justices are members of this "cert pool" (Justices William Brennan and Thurgood Marshall were not a part of the pool before their retirements; Justice John Paul Stevens is a nonparticipant). Members of the pool divide the petitions among themselves and the recommendations of the clerks are circulated among the members. Each justice reviews these recommendations, but it is clear that some centralizing has occurred.[10]

In addition, the Court has been forced, due to the expansion of demand, to develop its own form of deficit spending. Because its agenda has only a finite amount of space each term, the Court has increasingly had to borrow time from next year's agenda by carrying over to the next term some of the cases it granted for decision or reargument.[11]

DETERMINANTS OF CASE SELECTION

These procedures have helped, but they are small measures to cope with an increasing problem. As a result, justices need to develop informal mechanisms for making the onerous task of case selection more manageable. Analysts have posited the existence of a number of perceptual shorthands that might aid members in paring the cases to accept from the mass of petitions. The assumptions underlying these propositions make a great deal of practical and theoretical sense. These various "theories" do not guarantee that certain cases will be accepted or rejected. Rather, they are based on the assumption that cases possessing certain cues, indices, or signals serve the function of raising a flag for the members of the Court. The presence of one or more of these cues encourages a justice to put the petition aside and give it a closer reading. Cases without any of the signals tend to be rejected out of hand.[12] Interviews with justices and clerks confirm the existence of such cues.

The cues identified as significant include the identity of the petitioner, including the U.S. government, the nature of the issue, and the existence of conflict between circuit or lower courts. Successful repeat players earn Court respect over time. As a result, petitions that bear the names of these repeat players' attorneys merit closer attention from the justices. Certain types of issues, recently those involving individual rights and liberties, also signal the justices to take a closer look. It is likely that the nature of the cues may change over time as issues rise or fall from judicial favor.

Analysts have long been concerned with the factors that lead justices to accept some cases and reject others. The Court's rules and procedures provide little guidance on this point. The preponderance of the existing literature concentrates on the individual cases as the unit of analysis. The case selection literature is important because it provides a framework for evaluating judicial behavior. Any broader notions of the agenda must acknowledge the propositions discovered at the individual level and remain consistent with those findings. At the same time, concerns for the individual case selection should not blind analysts to the possible existence of broader institutional dynamics that would ultimately structure the context for selecting individual cases.

The case selection literature suggests a number of propositions that can account for decisions on individual petitions and the rationale for justices in accepting or rejecting the cases before them. Synthesizing the findings provides a more complete picture of the factors that influence case selection and rejection.

Decisions to accept some cases and reject others are predicated on the same types of factors that govern decisions on the merits of the issues. Among the most important factors presumed to affect a justice's decisionmaking are the individual members' values and attitudes, which involve their ideological predispositions and are influenced by a variety of background variables (political party, religion, previous experience, age, and law school), the influence of small group dynamics, and the judicial role orientation.[13]

The most important factors at the ultimate decision stage are the values and attitudes of individual members. The preponderance of the case selection literature suggests that those factors are also the most critical determinants of the decision to select certain cases and reject other petitions. S. Sidney Ulmer identifies the decision to select a case as a first vote on the merits of issue.[14] As a consequence, cases are normally accepted to reverse decisions of lower courts. Because the Court can only accept so many cases, justices who support the lower court decision are likely to leave the favorable decision alone. H. W. Perry's research, based on interviews with a number of the members of the Court, confirms the significance of the values and attitudes of members of the Court at the case selection stage. Perry refers to this process as the "outcome mode" of decision.[15]

Some analysts suggest that the influence of values and attitudes goes even further. Glendon Schubert, for instance, posits a sophisticated rational-choice model of case selection. According to this study, justices start with their values and attitudes, but then take institutional patterns into account before making their ultimate determinations on whether to grant the petition. The major consideration for these members is whether they have the votes not only to have the case accepted, but whether they can build a majority to win on the merits. Justices are portrayed as rational actors with relatively complete information concerning their alternatives and the votes of their colleagues, who are primarily interested in furthering their policy goals.[16] Although many analysts dismiss a broadly based rational-choice model of case selection,[17] Perry's interviews suggest that under some circumstances in some cases, justices do act strategically in their selection decisions. It is not uncommon for justices to vote against hearing a case, even if they disagree with the lower court decision, because they fear that the ultimate decision on the merits would be contradictory to their values and attitudes. Justices refer to this practice as a "defensive denial."[18]

More recent analyses have incorporated the influence of the judicial role into the calculus of case selection. The judicial role assimilates notions such as consistency in the law, attention to precedent, and a need to keep order in the judicial system.[19] The responsibilities attendant to this role may induce members of the Court to select certain cases in order to resolve inconsistencies between lower courts. Studies confirm the fact that many cases are selected for the primary purpose of settling disputes between lower courts.[20] Perry's interviews substantiate these findings. A number of the justices and their clerks claimed that they needed to accept cases in order to correct lower court mistakes, clarify doctrine, investigate dissensus within a lower court, or resolve lower court disputes. Perry refers to this as the "jurisprudence mode" of decisionmaking.[21] Analysts posit or implicitly suggest that there is an interactive effect between the policy goals and individual role orientations of the members of the Court. These factors are responsible for the decisions to accept some cases and reject others.[22]

A few studies examine the influence of dynamics of the small group, mostly in implicit terms.[23] The numbers of cases that are accepted with the minimum four votes and those with only three votes are measures of the interactions between members. Unfortunately, analysts are seldom privy to the data needed to formulate such judgments. In fact, the basis of many of the propositions that provide the foundation for understanding case selection are derived from the papers of Justice Harold Burton, who served during a period of Court history that is far from representative. Studies derived from Justice William Douglas's papers, which cover a longer period of time and a more recent era, have begun to appear. One problem with data gathered from the papers of justices is that they may ignore the existence of long-term dynamics because of a focus on individual cases.

NOTIONS OF AGENDA BUILDING

Although the preponderance of the literature concentrates on individual case selection, a few studies have a broader perspective and focus on the agenda as an entity rather than on individual cases. Most of the agenda-building literature concentrates on the state courts and lower federal courts.[24] These studies are different in emphases but support the propositions that underlying social, political, and economic activities affect the complexion of the agenda and that the agenda has an independent empirical meaning. The plethora of jurisdictions and lower court judges makes the study of individual behavior at the lower levels a prohibitive enterprise. As a consequence, research concentrates on the institutional level. The ease of studying individual behavior has been an impediment to such macrolevel analyses at the Supreme Court level.

One study of the Court's agenda is similar to the research of the lower courts' agenda. Gerhard Casper and Richard Posner have examined the forces that affect agenda setting--the cases that get to the Court. They ascribe changes in the Court's agenda to the nature of underlying societal and economic conditions, to important Supreme Court decisions that create rights, and to the consistency, or lack thereof, of Court decisions in similar cases. The effects of such factors are conditional, however, and vary under certain circumstances. At some point, despite continued growth in the external environmental factors, litigation rates will peak and stabilize or decline.[25]

Most studies that concentrate on the agenda as an entity focus on the decision agenda, the cases the Court accepts, and the trends in agenda change. Gregory Caldeira examined criminal law cases and determinants of agenda change both internal and external to the Court. His results suggest that internal forces, such as the ideological composition of the Court, have a much greater impact on the Court's criminal law agenda than external forces such as the crime rate or public opinion.[26] Thomas Likens traced the variation in agenda trends across six policy areas. Although external forces had some effect, Likens confirmed Caldeira's results on the impact of internal determinants. Likens's analysis also substantiates some of the findings of Casper and Posner regarding the Court's ability to shape its future agendas.[27] The decisions issued during one term have an impact on future demand and the later selection of cases.

One recent study undertook a rigorous analysis of the Court's total docket in the 1982 term. Samuel Estreicher and John Sexton were concerned with the Court's role and proposals to create an intermediate federal court between the Courts of Appeals and the Supreme Court for the purpose of relieving the tremendous docket pressures on the latter. In examining the cases on the governmental agenda and those that survive, the authors made a number of recommendations designed to redefine the Supreme Court's role and its criteria for the selection of cases.[28]

These few studies of the broader agenda suggest that the Court's agenda merits further attention and that the institutional level is worthy of focus. Virtually none of the existing studies (except the Likens and the Estreicher and Sexton research) explicitly deal with the finite nature of the agenda. Implicitly, all analysts recognize the enormous time constraints upon the justices in screening cases and that only a small percentage of the petitions can be accepted each term. The assumption of finite limits to the agenda raises an additional issue: The fact that accepting some cases means other cases, which may be important and worthy, will need to be rejected.

My study examines the Court's agenda-building process by focusing on the apportionment of agenda space by policy area. It is unnecessary to study agenda building if either of two assumptions is accepted. First, if agenda space is unlimited, then studies of case selection alone are adequate because the choice of one case would have no effect on the acceptance or denial of other cases. Second, if the Court's agenda is a mere summation of the selection of individual cases, then agenda building has no independent empirical meaning. Neither of these assumptions is tenable, however. The Court's agenda space is decidedly finite and real choices must be made whereby important items are denied access in deference to other cases.

A NEW PERSPECTIVE ON AGENDA ANALYSIS

It is no surprise that the Supreme Court's agenda has undergone significant change in the last half-century. After all, the Court could hardly be isolated from the fundamental restructuring that was occurring in the sociopolitical and economic environment. There has been little systematic attention to the dimensions of the transformation of the Court's agenda or the determinants of its scope and pace. This book reveals the nature of changes in that agenda.

The subject is significant on a number of levels. Most specifically, this study fills a gap in the judicial literature. Judicial behavior research is dominated by studies that focus on the determinants of judicial decisionmaking. Studies related to the agenda stage tend to concentrate on the selection of individual cases. Such a focus obscures interrelationships between issues, the long-term process of agenda building, and ignores the finite nature of the Court's annual agenda. In addition, the interrelationship between the selection of cases and decisions on the merits is implicit in the research, but seldom addressed in a systematic fashion. Diachronic processes of judicial decisionmaking and doctrinal construction require long-term agenda building. In effect, the selection of individual cases in a given term is a function of past decisions and contributes to the ongoing process of doctrinal development.

This book approaches the study of the Supreme Court's agenda from a different perspective. It adopts a neoinstitutional focus, beginning with the assumption that the Supreme Court is a political, unitary actor and the variation in its behavior and policies over time can be explained systematically. Such policies carry the imprimatur of the Court's name and are stamped with its legitimacy.

The preponderance of the judicial research focuses on the behavior of individual justices[29] and the selection of individual cases.[30] Most of the propositions and testable hypotheses in public law have been derived from this research tradition. Such research provides the basis for many of the inferences found in this study. These microlevel analyses, while important, have inherent limitations. Such studies, for instance, reveal little about the trends of agenda change.

The significance of the range of substantive issues the Court considers and the importance of the Court as a policymaker do not suggest that microlevel analyses of behavior should be abandoned. They do, however, mandate increased attention to institutional concerns. A number of recent studies of the Supreme Court have begun to focus on this broader level of analysis.[31] Analyses of other governmental units, most notably Congress[32] and the bureaucracy,[33] have also profitably adopted a neoinstitutional perspective.

This neoinstitutional perspective maintains that institutional arrangements and rules structure the aggregation of individual preferences within a decisionmaking body. As a result, the agency's decisions are not merely the collective expression of the individual preferences of its members but are a function of a complex interaction of individual preferences and institutional structures and rules. Neoinstitutionalism also suggests that outcomes can differ as a consequence of different institutional contexts.[34] This perspective allows for the incorporation of individual concerns into an integrated framework for understanding the construction of the institutional agenda and ultimately institutional policymaking.

Concern with the institutional level is predicated on the assumption that there are a series of factors and dynamics governing the scope and pace of the Court's agenda change. This analysis seeks to identify these factors. The data derived from the Court's records are supplemented by the application of the theoretical propositions gathered from the judicial behavior literature, general policy studies of the agenda, and principles generated from neoinstitutional studies of the agendas of other branches.

This study also has implications for the burgeoning public policy literature, which tends to focus on the elected branches of government, most notably Congress, and the bureaucracy. This book will suggest possible parallels between the judicial branch and other governmental institutions. Issues appear to follow certain definable patterns in being accepted for the legislative, executive, and judicial agendas; they also seem to evolve in similar manners and usher related issues on to the agenda. The existence of similar processes in different institutional settings suggests the influence of the policy entrepreneurs, institutional rules and structures, and sets of similar dynamics. If parallels emerge, they may suggest alternative hypotheses and propositions that can be investigated to explain policymaking in other branches. In addition, the results of this analysis can suggest other avenues for building public-policy theory.

Ultimately, there are important historical dimensions to this analysis of the Supreme Court's institutional agenda. A Great Depression, a partisan realignment, a world war, a military action, an undeclared war, dozens of economic cycles, periods of domestic turmoil, and fourteen presidential elections were among the most consequential events that crowded the past half-century. The period included what may have been the most important transformation in American politics, and the Supreme Court participated in the transformation. The justices resisted some components of the change, abetted others, and were directly responsible for altering the nature of the transformation in some important ways.

THE PHILOSOPHICAL BASIS OF AGENDA CHANGE

The connection between diachronic notions of agenda building and policymaking has important implications for historical development, political theory, and recent nation building in the republic. The nature of agenda change was both a function of past historical events and an impetus for later trends and developments. The substantive nature of agenda and doctrinal change profoundly affected the nature of the American political system and the Constitution on which it is based.

The time frame of the analysis, the 1933-1988 terms, serves to make this important from an historical perspective. This reflects the period in which the Court has discretion over the cases it wishes to accept. Most importantly, this period represents a major epoch for the Supreme Court. It was the period of a fundamental transformation in the institution as a policymaker and in the types of issues that the Court confronted. The Court chose, in part because of external pressure, to limit its consideration of some issues and to become a forum for others.

The agenda trends are a vivid record of the Supreme Court and the policies that have dominated this half-century. The Hughes Court (1930-1940) was the transitional tribunal presiding over the decline of the *ancien regime* and ushering in the modern Supreme Court. The Stone (1941-1945) and Vinson (1946-1952) courts uneasily faced many new issues for the first time. The Warren Court (1953-1969) created a constitutional revolution that accelerated policy and agenda changes. The Burger Court (1969-1986) expanded some of the policies of the Warren Court, limited others, and opened new avenues of its own. The Rehnquist Court (1986-) appears poised to usher in a new series of dynamics that may alter the tone of policies emerging from the Court and may realign the agenda in fundamental ways. As a result of such periodic changes, the Court has shed the long-standing image of a neutral arbiter and an interpreter of policy. Rather, it is recognized as an active participant in making policy.

On the broadest level, this study has implications for democratic theory. The pluralist system is predicated on the notion of access for citizens and groups. The agenda provides that access. This is especially relevant for the Supreme Court, which has traditionally served as a point of access for groups and issues that are inappropriate for or denied access to the elected branches of government. The results of this study can suggest how responsive the agenda is to the demands of groups.

These notions of pluralism and democratic theory are, perhaps, particularly important for the U.S. Supreme Court. Since Chief Justice John Marshall wrote the opinions in *Marbury v. Madison* 1 Cranch 137 (1803), creating the power of judicial review, and *McCulloch v. Maryland* 4 Wheaton 316 (1819), which expanded the Court's authority to interpret the Constitution, the Court has been the legitimate agency for determining the meaning of its vague clauses. In assuming that role and contributing to the charting of national public policy, the Court has been referred to as the "schoolmaster of the republic."[35] As a result, the members of the Court can be seen as the modern political theorists of the polity.[36] In helping to divine the scope of power granted the central government, the divisions between the three branches of government, the relationship of business to government, and the connections between the sociopolitical infrastructure and the economic system, the Court has created a vision of constitutional democracy.

More recently, especially for the time frame of this study, the Court has assumed the dominant role in balancing the liberties of individuals and minorities with the police powers of the state. The Court's recent attention to civil liberties and civil rights required the justices to breathe new life into the Bill of Rights and the Fourteenth Amendment. In constructing doctrine to underpin these decisions, the Court had to fashion a brand of political theory that would guide other policymakers and determine the nature of relationships between institutions and individuals. The construction of the agenda was a means to that end. In addition, the Court needed to stamp its imprint on the changes in the role of the central government and the nature of intergovernmental relations left in the wake of the New Deal.

Symbolically, the nine robed individuals, insulated from the reach of public opinion and accountability, appear to represent a council of elders who decides fundamental questions defining societal relationships. In effect, the justices have the authority to "rewrite" the Constitution by interpretation. Because that document is the most important part of the theoretical basis of this form of government, the status of the Court confers the title of political theorist on the justices. Procedurally, this role may result from the fact that the Court offers extensive written justifications for its institutional decisions. Furthermore, complementary and competing views may also find their way into print in concurring and dissenting opinions. The written opinions of the justices represent their individual and collective judgments about the meaning of constitutional provisions and the state of social, political, and economic relationships. The long-term construction of doctrine suggests that the political theory emerging from the Court is cumulative and evolutionary in scope.

The notion of the Court's political theory is particularly important in its contribution to nation building. The Court was a vital participant in building the republic after the Revolution. After the Civil War tore the nation asunder, the Court's decisions, particularly those involving the Fourteenth Amendment, helped rebuild the structure of the republic. The growth of U.S. business could not have occurred without the intervention of the Court and several key decisions. The Court contributed to the development of economic liberalism in taking governmental restraints off business. Finally, when the depression wrought a national catastrophe, the Court ultimately abetted the new economic order. In doing so, the Court adopted a new role in determining the rights of individuals and insular minorities in a new social order. In its decisions, the Court approved of a twentieth-century liberalism: governmental regulation coupled with protection of individual liberties.[37]

RESEARCH DESIGN

There are a few different strands to weave together to describe the nature of the agenda conversion. The first step in identifying the critical factors affecting agenda building is to consider empirically the Court's actual agenda. As noted, Congress granted the Court the discretionary writ of certiorari in 1925. The 1933 term was the initiation point to allow the Court to adapt to its new procedures. This lag provided a few years for the Supreme Court to rid the agenda of the older items that were on the docket prior to 1925, when the cases before the Court were part of its mandatory jurisdiction.

The variation in the agenda across time is measured as a function of the variation in the relative shares of agenda space allocated to the different policy areas. The data base for this research is composed of all cases the Supreme Court accepted in the 1933-1988 period, and on which it issued an opinion longer than one page. These requirements yielded 7,688 cases, all but six of which were placed into one of fourteen general policy areas (Appendix 1 explains the composition of these policy areas).

The minimum of one page is designed to eliminate cases that the Court could decide with one sentence in light of an existing precedent. The theoretical rationale is borne out by the empirical reality; very few cases are decided by one page. Most of the decisions are full opinions, brief memoranda decisions published in the back of the *United States Reports*, or terse *per curiam* decisions. Longer *per curiam* and memoranda decisions are included because their length indicates their importance and substance.

No distinction has been made between cases that arose under writs of appeal and those that arrived by means of a writ of certiorari. There were formal differences between the writs, before appeals were abolished, but the Court had means of denying writs of appeal. Although some analysts disagree, it appears that cases are judged on their relative merit or importance rather than the nature of the writ.[38] If the appeal is considered trivial or unimportant, the Court dismisses it. The practical effect is equivalent to a denial of certiorari. A number of the appeals are also decided briefly, often in less than one page (which does not meet the requirements for my inclusion of the case).

Policy area is the most important variable under consideration. *The Supreme Court Reporter*, published by West, has its "key" system that labels the policy areas. I used these in the clearest cases, when all the keys listed the same policy area as controlling. In cases with multiple codings, I read the decisions to prioritize the issue areas. I coded each case in terms of the most important issue or policy area (the original codings preserved the three most important issues, but for the most of the analysis, the single most significant issue was used).

My original coding was based on the substantive policy issue of the case, such as search and seizure, labor relations, gender discrimination, libel, and free exercise of religion. I aggregated these subareas into fourteen broader areas, such as U.S. Regulation, State Regulation, Internal Revenue, Ordinary Economic, State and U.S. as Litigant (government liability), and Federalism. Theoretically and empirically, some of these fourteen issues cluster together into broader dimensions. For instance, Due Process, Substantive Rights, and Equality constitute a broader Civil Liberties dimension. Four smaller areas (Criminal Law, Government as Provider, Separation of Powers, and Foreign Affairs) constitute the remainder of the substantive policy areas. Although the fourteen intermediate areas are the primary focus of the analysis, attention is also directed to the summary dimensions and to many of the specific subareas that make up the fourteen policy areas.

The categories are a mixture of substantive policy areas and legal concepts or rights. Most are consistent with the factors identified by David Rohde and Harold Spaeth.[39] Glendon Schubert found fewer, broader dimensions in an earlier study of judicial decisionmaking.[40] As policy areas evolve, the increasing complexity of issues may account for the more refined subfactors found by later analysts. Many of the categories are directly parallel to the categories in the Supreme Court Judicial Data Base. There are a few differences in the codings, which will be noted where appropriate.

To supplement the agenda data, I utilitized the Supreme Court Data Base, which covers the 1953-1988 period and codes the Court's decisions across a number of variables.[41] Of particular interest for my analysis are the variables that measure the reason the Court granted certiorari, the bases of decisions, the direction of the decisions, and the votes of the Court and individual justices. Because the time frame for my analysis predates some of the Supreme Court Data Base, I collected additional data that measure reasons for granting certiorari, the Court's vote, the ideological direction of the decision, among other items, to complete the records, particularly since 1937. I attempted to adhere as closely as possible to the coding rules set out in the Supreme Court Judicial Data Base code book and documentation.[42]

I analyzed the empirical data in the context of existing institutional and individual behavioral studies and used the propositions and hypotheses of other studies to define the parameters of this analysis. A number of strands of research, including empirical studies of case selection and judicial decisionmaking, supplemented these findings. In addition, doctrinal analyses, historical studies, and judicial biographies, which are often ignored by behaviorists, provide a number of propositions and rich description that increase the understanding of diachronic change. Outside the judicial sector, institutional studies of other branches, particularly Congress, can also provide a framework for analysis. Finally, the public policy literature, specifically studies of agendas, provides theoretical propositions that can help explain the Court's agenda and the nature of change.

OUTLINE OF THE STUDY

The broader notions raised in this introduction will be developed throughout the substantive chapters. The analysis of agenda change proceeds on two levels: the trends in individual policy areas and in the agenda as a whole. Chapter 2 establishes a context for the analysis, identifying key actors and propositions that affect agenda building and agenda change. The conceptual framework, developed from individual and institutional studies of the Court and other relevant literature, will be used to evaluate the empirical and substantive results of the analysis.

Chapter 3 sets the historical context for the changes in the agenda and views the agenda as an entity. The goal is to provide a perspective for evaluating the overall pace of agenda change. Assessing the agenda and the interrelationships between the policy areas is a necessary prerequisite for identifying the factors that influence the empirical patterns of agenda change.

The results are analyzed in subsequent chapters, with attention to major policy areas such as the Economic issues (Chapter 4) that governed the early agenda, Regulation and Federalism issues, important elements of the transitional agenda (Chapter 5), and Civil Liberties, the staple of the modern agenda (Chapter 6). The analysis extends to many of the subareas that constitute these summary clusters of issues. Ultimately, the intent is to develop propositions that can contribute to a theory of agenda change. In addition, the nature of agenda trends is placed in the context of the transformation that was occurring in U.S. politics over the past half-century. The final chapter speculates on the future trends of agenda change.

2

A Theoretical Framework for Agenda Building and Change

This chapter seeks to establish a context that is consistent with notions of agenda building. The processes of institutional agenda building and agenda change are long term so simple explanations of individual case selection are inadequate. Rather, the explanations of processes must account for an institutional memory that allows the agenda to develop and evolve systematically over time. This chapter identifies the important actors in agenda building, propositions about the agenda and agenda change, the dynamics of the agenda, and the relationship of current decisions to subsequent agendas. In short, construction of the agenda and the process of agenda change must be placed in the context of the Supreme Court's policymaking processes. The study of judicial agenda building must integrate case selection with decisionmaking.

Models of the policy process are heuristic devices for understanding the actors and conditions that build or block policy outputs. In such a framework, the agenda is the first stage of the process. Once items reach the agenda they move through the formulation and legitimation stages and ultimately, the policies are implemented in some fashion.[1] In reality, the stages are not easily distinguished from one another except analytically. Furthermore, issues and items emerge at different junctures of this policy process. Results of policies at later stages of the process can structure and affect the shape of later agendas. For instance, a failure in the implementation stage of a policy may convince the Court to accept another case to send a clearer or more forceful message to recalcitrant or confused implementers.

In the Supreme Court, the policy process appears to resemble the ideal theoretical framework better than in the other branches. The stages of judicial policymaking appear considerably more distinctive from each

21

other. Litigants bring the cases to the docket, and justices decide, using the rule of four, whether to accept the cases. At the next stage, the attorneys for the two sides formulate the issues, and through their briefs and oral arguments urge a majority of the justices to accept their interpretations of the law and the Constitution. Individually and then collectively, the justices legitimate one of the proposed alternatives and issue a decision that serves as the law of the land and is binding on lower courts. At that point, the issue normally leaves the judicial bureaucracy and must be enforced or implemented by other actors.[2] To be sure, the nexus between case selection and decisionmaking suggests a blurring of these processes. The individual and institutional determinants of case selection and decisions on the merits of the cases are very similar. The decision to accept a case is often a first vote on the merits.

The construction of judicial policy and legal doctrine is a dynamic, diachronic process. One decision, no matter how consequential, seldom settles an area of law. Much of the Court's work has been compared to the building of a mosaic.[3] Court decisions create new questions and new interstices to be filled. As a positive process, the Court may seek to build or expand policy. As a result, the justices screen petitions for cases that will help them build doctrine and fill gaps. The tone of the Court's decisions may encourage litigants to bring additional cases in that policy area or in related areas. Some of the Court's influence is negative. Confusion in doctrine creates uncertainty for lower courts and litigants and generates subsequent rounds of cases aimed at resolving the uncertainties.

There appear to be important elements of rationality in the building of an agenda and the formulation of doctrine. Agenda change does not occur randomly. A number of general propositions need to be developed to provide a valid framework for examining the empirical trends.

Even though the propositions identified in this chapter are confined to the judicial sector, they must be viewed in the context of policy analyses and cross-institutional research concerning the agenda and agenda change. Properties discovered in the studies of other institutions, most notably Congress, appear to have analogues in the judicial sector. Many of the dynamics of the agenda exist outside an institutional framework. As a result, to supplement this exploratory analysis of the Supreme Court's institutional agenda, I adapted research concerned with the agendas of other policymakers to the judicial sector.

This framework must weave individual-level results with institutional-level concerns to yield theoretical propositions concerning the processes of judicial decisionmaking and agenda building. Establishing institutional processes of agenda building is a necessary prerequisite to understanding the scope and nature of agenda change. This, in turn, creates a context for examining the transformation of the Supreme Court and its agenda.

The framework begins with the notion that the justices of the Supreme Court are active policymakers whose decisions affect the course of American public policy, the decisions of other institutional actors at the national and subnational levels, and effectively shape or refine notions of constitutional interpretation. As unelected members of the nation's highest court, however, there are some important constraints on the Court's policymaking and the theoretical framework must account for these constraints. Members of the Court do not make policy in a vacuum; they need the assistance of organized litigants who sustain the process by bringing subsequent cases to the docket.

The theoretical framework must also conceptualize the agenda as an institutional entity rather than the summation of individual case selection. At the broadest level, the agenda is an integral part of the policymaking process. The decision of which cases to accept is an important prelude to the ultimate decisions on the merits. The framework must account for an agenda that reflects the Court's institutional responsibilities and its policymaking goals. The transformation of the Court's agenda should be a function of the transformation of the Supreme Court's role, its decisions, and the changes in the American political structure. How changes in the agenda reflect the transformation of the Court's role, its policies, and the external environment is the subject of this analysis.

SUPREME COURT JUSTICES AS POLICYMAKERS

On the broadest level, a theory of Supreme Court decisionmaking proposed by David Rohde and Harold Spaeth is applicable to this analysis of agenda change and policy development. Decisions of the Court are a result of three factors: goals, rules, and situations. Goals include the individual and collective values and attitudes of the members of the Court, traditionally seen as the most significant determinants of decisionmaking. Rules comprise the formal procedures, norms, and rule structures of the institution. Neoinstitutional analysis is particularly concerned with the effects of rules. Finally, situations or conditions can dictate or affect the decisions of the justices and the institution.[4] Rohde and Spaeth concentrate their analyses of the decisionmaking factors on the goals of individual members and the Court. In this study, all three of these factors are considered significant in agenda building and the process of policymaking.

The Supreme Court has long played an active role in charting the course of national public policy. In addition to drawing the boundaries between the branches of government and between levels of government, the Court assisted in buttressing the economic foundations that underpin the system.[5] More recently, the Court has been charged with the responsibility of balancing the rights of individuals with the responsibilities of government to keep order. The importance of the Court as a policymaker has long been recognized, but this has not always been translated to the individual level. For normative reasons, when vacancies occur on the Court, the president making the selection, the American Bar Association (which determines the fitness of the candidate), members of the Senate Judiciary Committee (who must confirm the prospective justice), and the nominee normally carry on an elaborate charade that paints the process and the nominee as nonpartisan. The implicit underlying assumption is that the individual will forsake his/her past values and attitudes and judge each case on its own merits with no preconceptions.[6]

Behavioral research has clearly demonstrated that notions of justices who decide every issue on the merits with no predispositions are at least exaggerated and probably just false. In fact, studies of judicial decisionmaking probably err in the opposite direction. Implicitly, such studies focus on the values and attitudes of the justices to the exclusion of other determinants of decisionmaking. The values and attitudes or goals of the individual members are probably the most important single determinant of decisions in most cases; however, they are not the sole rationale for decisions. The judicial role orientation sets an important context for decisionmaking of individual justices. The judicial role involves the rules of the institution in certain situations and mediates the impact of the goals of the justices.

The judicial role orientation is a crucial intervening variable. The responsibilities of being a judicial forum and the court of last resort place strictures upon the Supreme Court and its members. In this respect, the judicial role includes some of the institutional rules component raised by

Rohde and Spaeth. For individual justices, the judicial role may necessitate that members of the Court avoid certain cases to protect the legitimacy of the Court as an institution.[7] Protecting the institution may also dictate a certain substantive decision. For instance, during World War II, the justices supported the executive order that forced the internment of Japanese-Americans.[8]

The judicial role is often conceptualized in terms of judicial activism and judicial restraint. Advocates of judicial restraint believe that the Court should interpret law rather than make law. Because the justices are not elected and the Supreme Court is not a democratic organ, proponents of restraint feel that members of the Court should not exercise their values and attitudes in decisionmaking. Those who support restraint believe that policymaking is best left to the elected branches of government.[9]

Judicial activists, however, do not believe that the Court should abdicate its policymaking function. They are undeterred by the fact that justices are not elected and they believe that elections, in and of themselves, do not confer wisdom or additional legitimacy on the executive and legislative branches. Rather, these activists think that the Court has the authority to substitute its judgment for the elected branches when warranted and that for some issues the Court is the sole appropriate forum for decision. Civil liberties and civil rights, which are decidedly countermajoritarian, should not be left to the whims of the majority; the Court, befitting its insulation from public control, should be charged with the task of protecting insular minorities.[10]

In a sense, the judicial role can be seen as a suppressor variable or an interactive variable. For a restraintist, the judicial role serves to block the influence of values and attitudes.[11] For these justices, their endemic liberalism or conservativism is pushed aside and they defer to the elected branches of government. In a normative sense, this is traditionally seen as the ideal justice. Justice Felix Frankfurter is typically cited as the quintessential example of a judicial restraintist.[12] For the activist, the influence of the judicial role may be better viewed as having an interactive effect on a justice's decisionmaking.[13] In this fashion, the role does not inhibit the individual's values and attitudes; rather, the activist role encourages the use of policy goals as a determinant of decisions. Justice Hugo Black is frequently cited as an example of a judicial activist.[14]

Most of the literature on individual decisionmaking begins with the implicit or explicit premise that justices are primarily interested in pursuing their individual values and attitudes through their decisions. The present study views the determinants of decisionmaking more broadly. Justices are seen as important policymakers whose decisions are based on their personal values and attitudes and their individual conceptions of the judicial role. These factors are evident at both the case selection and decisionmaking stages. Using terms developed in the Rohde and Spaeth theory, goals mediated by rules are the most significant determinants of decisionmaking.

As noted, the primary determinant for the selection of individual cases by individual justices is the values and attitudes of the members. Cases are normally accepted to pursue personal policy interests. The normal tendency for justices is to take cases in order to reverse the decisions of the lower court.[15] On the other hand, the case selection literature also demonstrates the impact of the judicial role. Justices accept many cases primarily to settle a conflict between two or more lower courts. In different circuits similar cases may be decided differently. As a result, the law will vary across different regions of the country. The Supreme Court needs to intervene to achieve some consistency in the law and maintain a semblance of order in the judicial system. In fact, some justices regularly dissent from denials of certiorari in cases that raise lower court conflicts.[16]

In the same vein, the selection of individual cases may be predicated on dissent in the lower court.[17] When a lower court sits in a three-judge panel or *en banc* and one or more judges dissent from the court's decision, that sends a signal to the Supreme Court that may resemble a conflict between lower courts. The vast majority of lower court decisions are unanimous.[18] When a split decision is on the Supreme Court's docket it suggests that some lower court judges may be misinterpreting previous precedent, confused about the development of doctrine, or just in error. Granting the petition in such cases may be a preemptive measure designed to settle the issue before a conflict between two lower courts materializes. Alternately, the lower court dissensus may serve as a cue that the issue in the case is divisive and controversial.

Research on individual-level case selection supports the influence of the same determinants that are evident in the decisions on the merits. This applies to the institutional level as well. The Court's institutional goals are a function of the preferences of individual members mediated by individual and institutional conceptions of the judicial role. The agenda is the first stage of the process of decisionmaking, and judgments made at that stage will have important consequences for institutional policymaking. The first step is to conceptualize the Court's institutional agenda as an entity consistent with the case selection literature and with the individual and institutional research on decisionmaking.

INSTITUTIONAL CASE SELECTION: THE AGENDA

The process of institutional agenda building in the Supreme Court is a function of the individual case selection policies of the members of the Court. It is more than a mere summation of the work of the "nine little law firms," however. Because the agenda has a finite capacity and policymaking is a long-term process, the Court's agenda building and the pace of agenda change are evolutionary in scope. The selection policies of this term and the substantive decisions on the merits of the cases selected are a function and a reflection of past agenda policies and past decisions. At the broadest level, there are important static elements to the agenda. The choices made during one term will also have a profound impact on the case selection policies and the substantive decisions for the foreseeable future.

Microlevel examination of individual behavior provides an important foundation for devising a neoinstitutional framework for the analysis of the Court's agenda. The empirical results of case selection research have important implications for institutional research. At a minimum, the hypotheses proffered about institutional processes must be consistent with the empirical results of previous individual analyses. Perhaps the most important proposition that can be gleaned from the case selection literature is the fact that policy values and attitudes govern the selection of some cases, and the strictures imposed by the judicial role are responsible for the selection of other cases.

The Court's role induces it to expend precious agenda space that policy designs might well reserve for other issues that might be more significant. In short, the role of the Court appears to be an omnipresent limitation the Court imposes upon its agenda building, which affects long-term patterns of change. H. W. Perry's interviews with a number of Supreme Court justices and their clerks confirm the impact of judicial role. Each of the justices interviewed professed that they often used their values and attitudes to determine which cases to accept. Each justice also cited the need to accept other cases in order to correct lower court mistakes, clarify doctrine, or resolve lower court disputes.[19]

These limitations suggest that viewing the judicial agenda as a single entity might be misleading. It may be that the Supreme Court's agenda is actually bifurcated. In principle, the Court has almost complete discretion over the cases it wants to accept. In practice, the Court exercises its own restraint. To label portions of the agenda mandatory would be misleading, but to claim complete discretion would be minimizing the impact of judicial role. The judicial agenda is really two agendas. The first can be labeled the "exigent agenda." While not mandatory, many issues virtually require some attention to settle questions and resolve lower court disputes. Thus, institutional rules and norms structure the process of agenda building. The remaining cases make up the "volitional agenda."[20] The Court can build this portion of the agenda with cases that fulfill the policy designs or goals of its members.

In addition, these institutional rules may affect the goals of the members. First, because of the finite nature of agenda space, the need to attend to the exigent agenda places some limits on the size of the volitional agenda. Second, individual and institutional decisions on exigent agenda issues may be based on factors other than policy goals.

The empirical evidence substantiates this notion of a bifurcated agenda. In the 1938-1952 period, the stated reason for granting certiorari in 80 percent of the accepted Economic cases was to settle lower court disputes or because the resolution of the case was important to judicial administration. By contrast, less than 20 percent of the granted Civil Liberties petitions during the same period were accepted to resolve conflicting interpretations of lower courts.

The Court's current agenda also has a strong bifurcated component. U.S. Regulation cases appeared to migrate from the volitional portion of the agenda to the exigent agenda. Since the 1970s, an increasing percentage of Regulation cases accepted (over half in recent terms compared to less than 20 percent in the 1938-1972 period) have been granted to resolve lower court conflicts. In addition, decision coalitions and ideological patterns in Regulation cases have atomized in the last fifteen terms.[21] This fragmentation is a consequence of the transition to the exigent agenda: Justices accept and decide these cases not because of their substantive importance but to resolve differing interpretations between Courts of Appeals. The changes in the underlying determinants of case selection and decisionmaking corresponded with the systematic decline in the agenda space allocated to Regulation cases.

The scope and nature of agenda change are affected by the Court's need to balance the two components of its institutional agenda. To advance the volitional agenda, which had been dominated by U.S. Regulation and Civil Liberties issues for decades, the Court had to pare its exigent agenda, which had a strong Economic component. Subsequent analyses in this book will discuss the systematic processes by which the Court transferred issues from one portion of the agenda to the others (Chapter 5) as well as the tools used to reduce the exigent agenda (Chapter 4) and to expand the volitional agenda (Chapter 6).

It is the nature of the Court's agenda that issues may eventually migrate from one category to another. The Economic issues that are part of the exigent agenda were at one time part of the volitional agenda. Once an issue has been on the volitional agenda, its life may be extended long after the Court's interest in the issue has waned. Even though the Court is no longer concerned with that issue, the lower courts, which must hear the cases before them, will still be deciding remaining questions. If there are disagreements in the interpretations of different courts, the Supreme Court may need to intervene and settle the question.

This conceptualization of the Court's agenda provides a vehicle for evaluating the transformation of judicial concerns over time. The bifurcated nature of the agenda suggests constraints on the Court's ability to pursue its policy goals. When the Court makes an institutional decision to leave an area of law or to delegate responsibility to lower courts or administrators, it must temper its retreat with the strictures of the judicial role, which require the establishment of consistent decisions and guidelines. Similarly, the desire to pursue new areas of policy will be slowed by the need to attend to exigent issues and the limited nature of agenda space.

The bifurcated nature of the institutional agenda underlines the significance of the goals and rules of the Court. Yet the judiciary is not a self-starter and thus must rely on litigants to bring cases to the docket. Notions of policymaking and agenda building must incorporate the interactive influence of litigants and justices.

THE INFLUENCE OF POLICY ENTREPRENEURS

External policy entrepreneurs play an important role in the American political structure. By design, the Constitution created a fragmented policy process based largely on the principles of separation of powers and checks and balances. These philosophies have prevented tyranny, but at the cost of efficiency and the ability to construct coherent policy. The framers of the Constitution recognized that factions would benefit from the system.[22] Indeed, the power of interest groups in bridging the gaps created by the Constitution has been a central feature of the U.S. political structure.[23]

The significance of policy entrepreneurs certainly extends to the judicial arena. Indeed, the story of the recent Court reflects a dramatic increase in group litigation. Groups seek access that is denied elsewhere, use the courts because it is inappropriate to use the other branches, or to protect gains achieved in other fora.[24] The fact that the Court is not a self-starter maximizes the utility of groups.

The judicial process is not amenable to the coherent construction of policy without the assistance of groups that monitor policy, read the entrails of decisions, and sponsor or join subsequent litigation.[25] Successful groups can sequence cases to structure both the evolution of policy and the nature of judicial debate. Church-state litigation is an excellent example of this process. Three groups, working together, were involved in virtually all major litigation in the 1951-1971 period and were able to frame issues for the Court and specify alternatives.[26] The work of the National Association for the Advancement of Colored People (NAACP) in building up to the *Brown v. Board of Education* 347 U.S. 483 precedent provides the classic example of systematic, incremental litigation designed to pursue long-term goals.[27] The group attempted to distinguish its early cases involving graduate and professional school opportunities for minorities from *Plessy v. Ferguson* 163 U.S. 537 (1896), a hostile precedent that allowed separate but "equal" facilities for blacks and whites, but the NAACP never directly sought to overturn it until much later.

"Repeat players" pursue policy goals in the courts by litigating strong cases to achieve favorable precedents that will penetrate the judicial system and settling weak cases to avoid harmful precedents. Such groups tend to have impressive legal and financial resources, informal relations with institutional incumbents, and the ability to predict which cases have the best chance of creating the precedents they desire. Such groups are able to litigate strategically and rationally, although more recently, this task appears to be getting more difficult.[28] These systemic advantages mean the precedents and thus the law will often favor the repeat players.[29]

Even those groups with the most resources cannot hope to monitor or litigate every issue that concerns them. At the same time, such groups will be affected by a variety of decisions issued by the Supreme Court. Thus, repeat players need to keep a viable "presence" in a number of areas of law. Groups lacking sufficient resources can enter pending cases through an *amicus curiae* ("friend of the court") brief, which serves to inform the Court about the impact of a decision on a group that is not directly involved in the case. *Amici* briefs can frame the issues in a case in a different context and help specify alternatives to consider.[30] In effect, such briefs serve the same functions as organized group testimony before congressional committees: marshalling specialized opinion, providing both general and technical information, and providing an informal tally of public opinion.[31] The existence of an *amicus* brief has an impact at the case selection stage as well, making the granting of certiorari more likely.[32]

The most important repeat player, the solicitor general, has enormous influence in setting the Court's agenda. This presidential appointee has the authority to appeal almost all decisions the government has lost in the lower courts. Because the government is involved in so many cases, the solicitor general could flood the Court with petitions. Instead, under normal circumstances, the solicitor general carefully screens the cases and only brings the best cases forward.[33] As a result of this unique symbiotic relationship with the Court, the government is generally more successful having its cases accepted and winning on the merits than other litigants. The consequence is that the solicitor general will have a great influence over the framing of issues, the sequencing of cases, the Court's agenda, and ultimately over the construction of precedents and policy.

As a result, although the goals of litigants are the most important determinant of their decisions to pursue certain cases, the other components of the theory of decisionmaking are significant as well. First, the notion of the situation is critical. Litigants seek to bring the best cases at the appropriate time. Finally, although they have little control over the institutional rules, litigants attempt to use these rules to attain advantages that will yield policy goals. For instance, litigants will attempt to incorporate lower court conflict, real or feigned, in their petitions to attract judicial attention.

In an important sense, the justices of the Supreme Court are policy entrepreneurs, who seek to fulfill their policy goals through their case selection policies and their decisions on the merits of the issues. Justices

carry ideological baggage to the Court and pursue specific constitutional
and policy goals through their decisions. Certain justices are associated
with particular theories of jurisprudence and policy designs. Hugo Black
came to support absolutism in free speech and the total absorption of the
Bill of Rights to the states.[34] Felix Frankfurter favored judicial restraint
in civil liberties and economic issues.[35] William Rehnquist is a legal
positivist who values property rights over civil liberties.[36]

Justices must work in concert with the litigants who bring
subsequent rounds of cases. Members of the Court who desire to make
public policy may not have the proper cases necessary to make policy at
the appropriate time. In such instances, purposive justices can manipulate
cases before them to pursue their designs. This process, known as "issue
fluidity," mitigates the problems created by the fact that the Court is not
a proactive institution. Issue fluidity occurs when justices expand the
issue (issue expansion) or contract the issue (issue suppression) raised in
a litigant's brief.[37]

When the Court narrows an issue, it signals a desire to limit the
agenda resources granted that area. Shifting an issue from the volitional
to the exigent agenda means that it is no longer a vital concern. There
are behavioral expectations consistent with the process of issue
suppression. The Court must tread a fine line in deciding such cases. The
goal is not to create new policy initiatives but to settle existing confusion.
Deciding subsequent questions must be done with an eye to the
implications of the current decision. As a result, the Court must decide
the existing case narrowly to avoid reinstituting the issue as a viable
policy concern. Issue suppression refers to the process by which the
Court culls one narrow issue from the case at hand and avoids or simply
dismisses all of the other questions raised in the petition. The Court uses
this device to separate the question that caused a conflict between lower
courts from the remaining questions in the petition, which will be
ignored.

Issue expansion is often a function of the policy designs of the
majority of the Court. Justices interested in opening a new issue can take
an existing policy area and convert it to a new issue through a landmark
precedent. The usual pattern of issue expansion is that a case arrives in
the normal course of litigation for another area or presenting a narrow
question. The Court then converts the issue to a landmark in a different
issue area or expands the impact of the case beyond the narrow facts of
the specific dispute. *Mapp v. Ohio* 367 U.S. 643 (1960 term), for
instance, is cited as an example of issue expansion. The case reached the

Supreme Court as a narrow case questioning the legality of Ohio's obscenity law. On the basis of a suggestion in an *amicus curiae* brief, the Court turned it into a major policy pronouncement on search and seizure and the incorporation of a constitutional amendment to the states. *Gideon v. Wainwright* 372 U.S. 335 (1962 term) is an example of an issue that was expanded within the same framework. The case raised the issue of the right to counsel for indigents. The Court instructed the attorneys in the case to expand the case to address the issue of incorporation (the process by which the Court applies provisions of the Bill of Rights to the states).[38]

The expansion of an issue is consistent with the process of opening or expanding the agenda space granted that issue. A problem is perceived, a solution is found, and justices seek the proper vehicle for the coupling. If an ideal petition is not available, interested justices can adapt another case. Because issue expansion is a proactive process by which the Court directly intervenes in litigation, it is a reasonably clear indication that the issue affected is headed for increased attention and space on the volitional agenda.

Issue fluidity is an institutional-level manifestation of the Court's broader policymaking. Issue expansion is a function of the Court's dominant ideological values. Issue suppression also reflects the Court's ideology while incorporating elements of the Court's institutional role. In this way, the process of issue fluidity combines the goals of the Court with a use of institutional rules. Attempts to change the nature of the issues before the Court is also dependent on certain situations or conditions, the third component of the decisionmaking theory.

The long-term impact of issue fluidity gives the process an important institutional dimension. Restructuring the volitional agenda means changes in the exigent agenda are probably forthcoming. In addition, the advent of new issues or significant changes in existing issues, through issue expansion, portends a long-term process of agenda allocation for those specific policy areas.

On an institutional level, the ideology of the Court is a function of the values and attitudes of the individual members. Individual Courts are often reified in the name of the particular chief justice. The Warren Court is widely viewed as the most liberal Supreme Court in history, and it presided over a virtual constitutional revolution. The Burger Court is generally characterized as conservative, although analysts have shown that this is true only in relative terms.[39] In fact, the Burger Court was responsible for a number of decisions that protected individual rights and created new rights, such as abortion and affirmative action. The Rehnquist Court is still taking shape but appears to be moving in a more conservative direction.

The ideological predilections of the sitting Court provide a context for the litigants and groups that approach the Court with their problems and concerns. As the Court's ideology shifts and support for individual liberties and civil rights grows or declines, different litigants will be encouraged to use the courts. Other groups may retreat or modify their strategies in light of the Court's changes. In discussing the ebb and flow of the various issue areas in subsequent chapters, the ideological dispositions, decisions, and agenda priorities of the various Courts will be considered. The transformation of the Supreme Court's agenda should be some function of changes in the membership of the Court.

LANDMARK DECISIONS

Issue fluidity is often manifested in a landmark or seminal decision, which opens a new area of law or fundamentally changes, modifies, or reverses the nature of law or policy in a given policy area. Landmark decisions are important tools for justices to utilize in prospectively building future agendas and structuring the nature of agenda change. The transformation of the Court as an institutional actor and its agenda was accomplished through landmark decisions. Such decisions often further the goals of the Court and are dependent on certain situations. The doctrinal changes created by the landmark decision virtually assure the justices the opportunity to address similar types of cases in order to continue the development of doctrine in these recently changed areas.

Landmark decisions can be identified objectively. Studies of doctrinal development specify a number of significant cases that changed the nature of individual policy areas and American constitutional law, more generally. Decisions like *Brown v. Board of Education* 347 U.S 483 (1953 term) (school desegregation), *Roe v. Wade* 410 U.S. 113 (1972 term) (abortion rights), and *New York Times v. Sullivan* 376 U.S. 254 (1963 term) (freedom of the press and libel) are obvious and well-known examples of major landmarks. Other cases, such as *Monroe v. Pape* 365 U.S. 176 (1960 term), which expanded the use of Section 1983 of Title 42 of the U.S. Code to sue state officials who exceed legal bounds, and *Camara v. Municipal Court* 387 U.S. 523 (1967 term), concerning whether city public health officials needed to obtain a warrant before conducting administrative searches, also represent major extensions of judicial policy into new areas. The results of landmark decisions on the agenda can be measured empirically through changes in the levels of agenda allocation that can be ascribed to the landmark.

The sustained growth of Civil Liberties should be the result of a number of discrete landmark decisions in a number of areas of law. Early landmark decisions would be responsible for the initial growth of Civil Liberties. Later landmark decisions would abet the growth of individual rights on the agenda and change the allocation of agenda space in the individual areas that underlie the broader Civil Liberties dimension: Due Process, Substantive Rights, and Equality.

One of the issues to be investigated is the relationship between landmark decisions in different areas of law. We assume that justices are purposive actors interested in pursuing their personal constitutional philosophies and values and attitudes, so one landmark decision can be expected to lead to other seminal decisions in other, often related, policy areas. The dynamics of the agenda and the emergence of new issues suggest that there are connections between policy areas.

A landmark decision is a mechanism that allows the Court to circumvent (to a degree) some of the problems inherent in the reactive nature of the judicial process. In this way, under certain conditions and situations, the justices pursue their goals through the rule structure of the Court. This is particularly true when justices utilize issue expansion to create a landmark case from a petition that does not appear dramatic on its face. A landmark decision is a means by which justices create conditions inviting litigants to bring cases that will fill in the nascent doctrine or signaling litigants that such cases are no longer welcome. This is a specialized form of the process known as the "dynamics of the agenda," which can work to sustain or retard the pace of agenda change.

THE DYNAMICS OF THE AGENDA

The patterns of agenda change depend on both the members of the Court and organized litigants. In a sense, the long-term policy process is a cuing process that resembles a broadly based stimulus-response model. The Court's decisions answer some questions, but they raise others and may affect related areas of law. A crucial component in the process is the existence of repeat players who systematically monitor the decisions of the Court and respond by bringing the next round of cases. Policy-oriented groups will pay close attention to the Court's case selection policies and the tone and substance of the decisions on the merits. Often the Court will suggest future ramifications in the *obiter dicta* of its decisions. Groups will then attempt to raise the next set of questions that will continue to flesh out the emerging doctrine.[40] Additional cases may not be sequenced or arise so strategically, however. Furthermore, lower courts may disagree in their interpretations of the existing precedents and the Supreme Court may intervene to settle the issue.

This long-term cuing process is a part of the dynamics of the agenda. The "dynamics" of the agenda refers to the protracted process by which cases come to the Court, are accepted or denied, are decided on the merits, have various impacts, and create waves of subsequent cases. The agenda and demands for Court activity are frequently responses to earlier decisions. The Court's decisions percolate throughout the judicial system and beget later cases seeking to clarify, expand, or limit past precedents. In the broadest sense, the dynamics of the agenda can impede the emergence of new issues because the existing issues consume agenda space, and there are prohibitive start-up costs for new issues. These dynamics also serve to introduce an inertia that will keep existing issues on the Court's docket. The evidence suggests that the dynamics initially constrained the rate of agenda change but ultimately abetted the accelerated growth of Civil Liberties.

The dynamics of the agenda represent an interactive process between the two major entrepreneurs: organized group litigants and justices. The first component of these dynamics involves litigant demand. The conversion of the agenda requires a battery of proper cases to enable the justices to advance properties of individual rights and create precedents that would penetrate throughout the legal system.

The pace of agenda change is not simply a function of the mix of cases brought to the Court. The responsibility for the construction of policy is shared between the Court and litigants. The Court is an active participant in the process and possesses three institutional devices to signal litigants: extending or reducing the queueing process in case selection, the consistency of its substantive decisions in related cases, and the language of its decisions.

First, the Court's case selection policies send a message to litigants. Repeat players monitor the cases the Court accepts and rejects and respond to those cues. The evidence during this period substantiates this process. Filing cases, however, is a means to an end. The ultimate goal is victory on the merits of the cases. As a result, the pattern of the Court's substantive decisions can send a relatively clear message to litigants and groups. Finally, the legal experts for groups pay close attention to the actual language of opinions that affect their interests. The tone of the Court's opinion, dicta and any concurring and dissenting opinions carry a variety of messages.

These dynamics should take different forms that vary as a function of the nature of issues and which component of the agenda that issue occupies. To ensure this, justices may manipulate the petitions. For cases on the exigent agenda, cases should reach the Court in a less systematic fashion because the rationale for acceptance depends on conflicts between lower courts or dissensus within a lower court. Thus, the rules of the institution serve to govern the selection of these cases and the decision on the merits. In addition, justices will narrow the petition and concentrate on the question that spawned the lower court conflict. For volitional cases, however, the policy goals of members of the Court and the need to attend to the judicial role and the strategies of litigation should introduce some elements of coherence to the sequencing of cases. To assist this process, justices may convert the case before them to fit their goals or the gap that needs to be filled.

THE EMERGENCE AND EVOLUTION OF ISSUES

The dynamics of the agenda and the construction of judicial doctrine is a protracted process intertwined with notions of issue and policy evolution. The initiation and evolution of issues should affect patterns of agenda change. New issues tend to emerge from landmark decisions. Once new issues reach the agenda, they lay claim to future agenda space. As a result, significant agenda change is manifested a few terms after the seminal decision is announced.

Analysts maintain that the agenda tends to be inhospitable to new issues. Creative activity and wholly new ideas do not suddenly appear on the agenda; rather these "new ideas" tend to be recombinations of old ideas.[41] Casting new issues in terms that are familiar to policymakers serves two important purposes. First, it conserves precious agenda resources because new issues take more time to address and resolve than existing issues. If there are analogues from previous issues, the policymaker has a frame of reference in making the decision. Second, the difficulty of passing new issues can be mitigated by recasting the new issue in terms of other issues that have successfully navigated the policy process. If proponents of the "new" policy are successful, then the coalitions that passed the "old" issue can be reformed.

Policy construction in the Supreme Court can be conceptualized as an evolutionary process. A new issue results from a related existing area and takes on the color of that issue until it emerges in its own right. The new issue typically results from an ancillary issue in an existing domain or as a conscious effort on behalf of litigants or justices seeking to adapt success in other areas to the new area. At this stage, the new issue may be viewed in the context of the issue that spawned with it. The novel area may take a while to develop its own doctrinal identity. This suggests that despite the goals of the members, the emergence of a new issue depends on the existence of certain conditions and situations.

To achieve its own status, the new policy area must attract agenda space annually. The ability of the Court to take a number of cases concurrently and over time allows justices to isolate the new issue from its predecessor and to treat that issue on its own terms. To be sure, the emerging doctrine will bear a resemblance to a number of preexisting areas, but it will increasingly develop its own focus.

Substantively, these cases involve first-generation questions--the core questions of that policy area. These issues are unidimensional in scope, and there is an expectation that individual justices will come to evaluate these questions in a consistent manner. First, justices are policymakers with fixed preferences in a unidimensional space. Second, as members of the Court of last resort, justices have an institutional obligation to decide cases in a consistent manner so as to guide lower courts and the implementing population. This is consistent with the strictures of the judicial role and is affected by the rules.

The expectation of individual-level consistency in decision patterns should eventually translate (given stability in membership) to macrolevel issue stability. At some point, the Court should resolve the first-generation issues in a manner that will guide lower courts. At that point, the issue is expected to progress to more elaborative cases. This phase is marked by the increased difficulty of the questions being litigated. The original concerns having been settled, the question remains how much further the justices are willing to go. Lower courts are uncertain, and litigants supportive of the earlier decisions attempt to induce the Court to expand its previous decisions. It must be emphasized that these more difficult questions remain part of the original unidimensional space.

In the absence of membership change, policy is expected to evolve from the unidimensional or single-issue space. A multidimensional component may be added to the basic issue. The behavioral impact is instability in individual decisionmaking, coalitional patterns, and the decisions of the Court. Some members of the Court may decide the case on the basis of one dimension while their colleagues view a different dimension as controlling.

The need for order and consistency in decisions may induce the Court to separate the issues and address them individually. If that occurs, a new issue may emerge, while the Court returns to the original issue that has reverted to a unidimensional space. An issue does not emerge full blown in the Supreme Court. Rather, the inauguration of a new area is almost invariably the result of previous policies, mostly related but occasionally representing different issues.

The normal expectation, given stability in membership, is that the Court will establish consistency in its decisions. When membership does beget ideological changes, the evolution of policy may take a different avenue. A new ideological coalition may well limit or reverse the nature of policy in a given area. In terms of the framework of policy evolution, the Court may reevaluate or reverse previous decisions.

Search and seizure provides a good example of policy evolution. The cases arose from the general "fair trial" rules established by the Supreme Court to deal with criminal procedure cases. Its appearance on the agenda was neither systematic nor regular. *Mapp v. Ohio* raised the core issue of search and seizure and the exclusionary rule. Later cases like *Terry v. Ohio* 392 U.S. 1 (1967 term) presented more difficult situations, in this instance the legality of a patdown search. The search of a college newspaper office, in *Zurcher v. Stanford Daily* 436 U.S. 547 (1977 term), raised multidimensional disputes: freedom of the press and search and seizure. *See v. Seattle* 387 U.S. 541 (1966 term), a noncriminal administrative search of a warehouse, is also a case with multiple issues. More broadly, that case helped spawn an administrative due-process area of litigation. The growing hostility of the Burger and Rehnquist Courts toward defendants' rights has signaled a return to the core questions in the search-and-seizure area. The Court is increasingly deciding cases involving the need for warrants and procedures for their issuance that had seemingly been decided a generation ago.[42]

The emergence and evolution of judicial policies structure the scope and pace of agenda change. First, when a new issue arises, it will begin to proceed through the various stages of development. As a result, the new issue will be a part of the Court's volitional agenda for the foreseeable future. In addition, venerable issues may directly or indirectly lead to the emergence of other issues. As noted, new issues may be derivatives of existing issues. Less directly, work in one policy area may sensitize justices and litigants to proximate issues. These processes will further expand the volitional agenda and force the Court to reorganize existing issues to create more space. Older issue areas may no longer merit extensive Supreme Court attention and may be moved to the exigent agenda.

POLICY WINDOWS AND SPILLOVERS

As a result of the problems attendant to advancing new issues, certain conditions and situations must exist for the emergence of such issues, which will alter the dynamics of agenda change. Policy entrepreneurs prepare policy communities for their pet projects. The incremental nature of the policy process creates an inertia that tends to resist changes and new ideas. It is the role of the policy entrepreneur to break this cycle and create a favorable environment for the policy proposal. Policy entrepreneurs are responsible for initiating and continuing the processes of agenda change.[43] The influence of policy entrepreneurs is conditional. Policy advocates must await the situational occurrence of a "policy window," a propitious opportunity for action. A policy window opens as a result of a change in a political stream or because a problem reaches prominence. Changes in the political stream might include changes in the Court's membership or different strategies by repeat player litigants, particularly the solicitor general. Problems may reach prominence due to increased attention by lower courts, specialized publics in the legal community, or other governmental agencies.

New issues achieve institutional agenda status by moving through open policy windows. To do so, a problem may require the existence of a viable solution. To reach the decision agenda, a series of streams must be coupled. The convergence of solutions and policy alternatives needs to be attached to a problem. If that occurs, the problem is likely to find support in the political stream. If streams are not coupled, the window will close quickly.[44] Despite the goals of the members, a proper situational context must be present for the opening of a policy window and the introduction of a new issue to the agenda.

Similarly, if the proper conditions are not present, the policy window may never be opened. The Court's refusal to grant agenda space to the issue of homosexual rights is an example of a policy window that was left closed. Petitioners then sought entry through a variety of existing windows including criminal law, education, and public employment. The claims invoked equal protection, privacy, due process, and the First Amendment. Apparently, a majority of justices thought the nation was not ready for definitive rulings concerning homosexual rights.[45]

The issuance of landmark decisions is closely related to the notions of policy windows, which are representative of the "situations" that Rohde and Spaeth identify in their theory of decisionmaking. Policy windows set various agenda dynamics into motion. Many issues that emerge through a policy window are initially part of the volitional agenda. Once a policy window has been opened, that issue lays claim to agenda space for the foreseeable future. Even if the justices are no longer interested in this issue, its cases may still find their way to the Court's docket. Lower courts may disagree about the implications of later cases within that issue area. The Supreme Court must accept some of these cases to fulfill its judicial role. As a result, such cases may move the policy area from the volitional component of the agenda to the exigent agenda.

Agenda research notes the impact of "spillovers," whereby the success of one policy increases the probability that policy windows will open for other issues. The successful opening of a policy window pushes a specific issue on to the decision agenda. Perhaps more significantly, this success may serve as the impetus for other policy windows introducing related issues to the decision agenda.[46] In the wake of landmark decisions, the Court may graft tested constitutional principles to related issues. On one level (the expansion of concerns) the success in one summary area, like Economics, can be transplanted to another broad area, like Regulation. On the second level (the dispersion of attention) the decisions in one narrow area within a broad area can be used in adjacent or related subareas. For example, within the Due Process area, decisions in a subarea like search and seizure create an environment for a different issue, like right to counsel.

The phenomenon identified as the "expansion of concerns" confirms the proposition that an institution dealing with a collective issue will turn to other collective issues.[47] In general, the rise of an issue can create a recognition among justices and litigants that other areas merit attention. Initial successes generally cause the most powerful spillovers. Entrepreneurs are encouraged to rush to the next issue. Attempts to open subsequent windows are often marked by coupling similar solutions to emerging problems.

Procedurally, related issues can succeed if the coalition that constructed the initial program can be reformed. Policy change establishes new principles that entrepreneurs can use to assist other items. This is particularly relevant in the Supreme Court, where new constitutional protections create precedents that various policy entrepreneurs hope can be adapted to their issues. Chapter 3, which shows the broader patterns of macrolevel change, supports these notions of policy windows and spillovers. These situations structure the nature of significant agenda change, alter existing dynamics, and introduce new dynamic forces.

At the next level, the connections are even more direct. Justices begin work in one subarea and spread their attention to related domains. For instance, decisions that create or abet the growth of one subarea on the agenda lead to the creation of new subareas or growth in related areas of law. The rise of specific issues tends to trigger other specific issues, reinforcing notions that there are elements of rationality to agenda change.[48] Decisions of the Court generate related cases, often more complex and requiring a drawing of finer lines. These relationships among subareas can be labeled "the dispersion of attention" and represent examples of spillovers.

Once a breakthrough occurs in a new issue area, it may well lead to a surge of activity in related areas. When an institution decides to consider an issue, it may, in effect, "commit itself to a whole chain of rationally related issues."[49] The dynamics of the dispersion of attention appear responsible for the Court's later agenda change. The Court cleared agenda space to resolve questions in the wake of previous landmarks and to shift attention to related issues. Thus, policy streams are recreated to open proximate policy windows.

The public policy literature explicitly accounts for the dynamic nature of the policy process. The agenda is affected by previous decisions in that specific issue area. The literature demonstrates that new policies evolve or expand their agenda space because of other issues that may be directly related or have only tangential connections to the new policy. This study of the Court's institutional agenda explicitly accounts for the nature of a dynamic policy process.

POLICYMAKING AND THE EVOLUTION
OF POLITICAL THEORY

The emergence of judicial policy and the evolution of the doctrine that will flesh out the various policies is certainly an important process in and of itself. If the premise is accepted that the collective judgment of the Court reflects a modern, evolving political theory, then the process of doctrinal construction becomes even more significant. The implications of this have been magnified in the last half-century because the Court has been adopting a new role. The changes in the Court's agenda necessitated the construction of theory and doctrine and were part of a broader institutional transformation.

Building and changing the institutional agenda are the first stage in the construction of doctrine and ultimately in the formulation of political theory. This is particularly true for the period of this analysis. The Court's previous inattention to issues concerned with individual rights has important consequences for the simultaneous construction of doctrine and the theory underpinning it. There was little existing theory for the Court to use in its early decisions. As a result, the Court had to construct this theory while it was dealing with these types of issues for the first time.

The construction of political theory should have important effects on the scope and pace of agenda change. Initially, the lack of experience with these issues should be expected to retard the growth of Civil Liberties issues at the broadest levels. Within the individual issue areas that compose the Civil Liberties domain, the nascent construction of political theory also had an impact. At the early stages of the growth of the Civil Liberties agenda, the lack of theoretical foundations for individual rights may be partially responsible for the slow emergence of new issues. The justices may not have made the connections between issues during the emergent periods of Civil Liberties growth.

As the Court became more comfortable with Civil Liberties issues, political theory was increasingly in place to guide the Court in the construction of doctrine. This situation was necessary to accelerate the growth of these issues on the Court's agenda. Once broader guiding principles had been established, the evolution of individual issue areas could proceed. These growth patterns in these individual issue areas, when summed, yield the overall growth in Civil Liberties that marks the Supreme Court in the last three decades.

The early emergence of political theory had important procedural consequences for the notions of agenda building and policymaking. Perhaps more importantly, the theoretical foundation had a substantive dimension. In notions of state building, the Court's attention to individual liberties and civil rights and changing attitudes toward economic concerns paved the way for the modern republic. A Court that was the last proponent of a decaying nineteenth-century liberalism needed to reformulate the theoretical foundation of its decisions. The process of agenda building and the nature of agenda change were important components of the Court's transformation of political theory. The cases provided the elements the Court could use to build doctrine and ultimately contribute to the development of theory.

The construction of the agenda is an important first step in the allocation of a fundamental, finite governmental resource: access to the Supreme Court. The decision of which groups or philosophies can achieve agenda status is a symbolic and practical signal of broader strands of political theory. Different groups, particularly those who are denied access elsewhere in the governmental structure, might be able to find a forum for their concerns. This notion of access is particularly critical in a pluralistic system. Giving access to different groups introduces new ideas, new issues, and different theoretical perspectives. The transformation of the Court's agenda was manifested in different patterns of access. The consequences of these macrolevel changes was reflected in fundamental revisions in the nature of American political theory and constitutional interpretation.

CONCLUSION

This chapter establishes a context for evaluating the nature of agenda building and agenda change. The propositions and properties identified in this chapter will be examined throughout the remainder of the book. The framework will be utilized to understand why some policy areas declined and how the Court implemented the demise of such areas. The same properties, perhaps in different balance, are also responsible for the surge in the agenda space granted other areas.

The major factor that establishes the context for agenda building and agenda change is the bifurcated nature of the Court's agenda. In a larger sense, this reflects the Court's need to attend to institutional rules and norms, which may inhibit the Court's ability to pursue its policy goals. The exigent and volitional portions of the agenda structure the scope and pace of change. The need to attend to the exigent agenda may reduce the amount of space on the volitional agenda and slow the pace of agenda change. Similarly, the desire to expand the volitional agenda means that some issues may have to be transferred to the exigent agenda or that the issues on the exigent agenda may be postponed for a while until sufficient resources are available.

These components of the Court's agenda suggest that agenda change, left alone, tends to be incremental in scope. The key in restructuring the pace of agenda change is to alter the dynamics or introduce some new elements to the agenda. Policy entrepreneurs, most notably the justices and organized litigants, are the agents of change. Case selection policies and decisions on the merits beget further cases. This stream of litigation, the essence of the "dynamics of the agenda," represents the processes that yield agenda change.

The primary means of initiating policy change that ultimately yields agenda change is the landmark decision. Such a decision can be one manifestation of a policy window that alters the policy stream. A landmark decision and a policy window may eventually create the conditions that yield changes in the patterns of agenda allocation. The form and structure of agenda change are apparently governed by the processes of issue initiation and evolution (the long-term cumulation of the dynamics of the agenda in each specific area) and spillovers. Issue emergence is important because of the overall novelty of some of the issues reaching the Court for the first time. The growth of the different areas is expected to occur through a process of spillovers. The initial opening of a policy window should create two forms of spillovers. The "expansion of concerns" represents a horizontal process of policy change: Policy fans out from one broad area to another. The "dispersion of attention" is a process of vertical integration, whereby policy changes in one subarea create the environment for policy emergence or change in a related area. Within the area of Substantive Rights, the rise of one specific issue should lead to concerns with other areas. In U.S. Regulation, the emergence of one specific area of regulation should spawn connections in the minds of legislators, administrators, justices, and litigants.

The analysis of the Court's agenda combines an examination of the overall agenda with attention to the major policy areas. The next chapter examines the overall pace of agenda change systematically. Tracing the macro-level patterns of change provides some insight into scope and nature of change and sets the context for examining the major policy areas that have competed for agenda space. These separate analyses present a variety of perspectives on the transformation of the Supreme Court's agenda, which is a function of changes in the institutional role and the transformation of American politics.

3

The Transformation of the Agenda and the Supreme Court

Before examining the agenda space allocated to the individual policy areas, we must view the institutional agenda as a whole. This perspective is necessary given the fact that agenda space is relatively limited and that the various policy areas are competing for that space. This holistic view of the agenda permits some inferences about the interrelationships between different policy areas and provides a more formal, systematic assessment of the nature and pace of agenda change. In addition, the scope of change can be assessed to reveal whether it is incremental and a function of previous agenda allocations or more rapid and generally not governed by past agenda policies. The analysis can help determine when large-scale agenda changes occur and whether they are purposive or are random and unrelated to an underlying dynamic.

Tracing the agenda's changes over time is important, but the nature of the changes cannot be divorced from the external events contributing to it. The Court's agenda must be placed in the proper historical context, particularly for those forces that set the agenda changes into motion. These forces were especially significant in the 1937 term and had an influence during decades to follow.

THE HISTORICAL CONTEXT FOR THE TRANSFORMATION OF AGENDA CHANGE

The year 1933, the initial year of this study, represents a watershed for the United States. Franklin D. Roosevelt assumed the mantle of power and ushered in a new era in American sociopolitical and economic history. To combat the Great Depression, Roosevelt presided over a dramatic transformation in the role of the U.S. government. He inaugurated the modern era for the presidency, the government, and the national economy.[1] The Roosevelt policy package, the New Deal, provided a new set of issues for the other branches of government to consider. These policies altered traditional mechanisms of separation of powers. The new power of the presidency also affected the internal procedures and authority of the legislative and judicial branches.

The election of 1932, which Roosevelt won, has frequently been described as a "critical election" leading to a partisan realignment.[2] The theoretical concept of a realignment refers specifically to the restructuring of the two major political parties, but if the notion of a realignment has any viability, then it certainly goes beyond the party structure: It is a fundamental reconstruction of the political universe. The realignment penetrates well below the party level and, in effect, changes the nature of political discourse for the next generation.[3]

Realignments have been dubbed the "peaceful American revolutions." The new party system that emerges from the ashes of the preceding party system after the realignment often removes many of the vestiges of the preceding generation. The government's institutional memory is temporarily purged. The era following a critical election is often characterized as the most propitious time, or situation, for true policy innovation.[4] Certainly this seemed to be the case in 1933 with the change in regime and the attendant changes in political philosophy.

Scholars have long debated whether the Supreme Court responds to changes of the magnitude that accompany a realignment. One school of thought suggests that the Court does indeed follow the election returns, particularly when they are emblazoned across the political terrain.[5] Other analysts, however, feel that the Court does not necessarily follow the political branches.[6] The partisan realignment of the 1928-1932 period brought the Democrats to primacy and a new Congress to Washington. The Constitution, however, provides the Court with some insulation from these political trends. The Supreme Court's membership was a carryover from the previous political structure. Many of the justices had been selected by Republican presidents whose policies were suddenly remnants of a bygone political era and a previous realignment.

The old agenda and the older Court were confronted with new problems and newer proposed solutions. President Roosevelt initiated his programs to cope with the Great Depression by creating agencies and policies that eventually presented the Supreme Court with a series of unprecedented constitutional questions. Such policies had the wide-ranging potential to alter relations between the levels of government (federal and subfederal) and among the branches of the central government. New Deal policies would enhance the power of the central government at the expense of the states and would strengthen both Congress and the president, but the latter would derive greater benefits. The New Deal would also require the construction of a large bureaucratic infrastructure.

The bitterly divided Court's initial response was resistance. The history of the Court is marked by occasional self-inflicted wounds, like the *Dred Scott* decision, that have threatened the Court's very legitimacy. The Court was on such a precipice in 1936. In the early period of the New Deal and the partisan realignment, the Court did not follow the election returns and defied the new political order.

In many of the early cases involving New Deal programs, four conservative ideologues--Justices George Sutherland, Willis Van Devanter, James McReynolds, and Pierce Butler--consistently opposed the new policies. These justices, often referred to as the "Four Horsemen," needed an additional vote for a majority and often got it from the newest member of the Court, Owen Roberts. To make the Court look more unified and stronger, Chief Justice Charles Evans Hughes, voting last as befits his position, joined the majority. Public opinion, newspapers, and the elected branches excoriated the Court, particularly focusing on the older conservatives.

President Roosevelt, with a resounding electoral mandate in his pocket, proposed his famous "Court-packing plan" ostensibly to help the beleaguered, overworked "nine old men." The thinly veiled plan to alter the Court's working majority failed to pass Senate scrutiny or attract public support, but when Justice Roberts and Chief Justice Hughes left the "Four Horsemen" and began upholding the building blocks of the New Deal (the so-called "switch in time that saved nine"), further crises were averted.[7] Thus, the Court finally moved into step with the reigning political order in economic matters.

The Court's ultimate decision to leave the foundation of the New Deal intact left the Court in a curious position. Having capitulated, the Court might have relegated itself to a subordinate, interstitial role rubber-stamping presidential and legislative prerogatives. The Court used its affirmation of executive and legislative initiatives as a point of departure for its own transformation and adopted a new role. In a manner vaguely reminiscent of the early Marshall Court, the Hughes Court had to establish its legitimacy and its proper niche in the governmental structure. Changing the nature of the agenda was an important stage in this institutional transformation. In a direct, if delayed, sense the partisan realignment percolated to the judiciary. The New Deal, which affected the presidency, Congress, and intergovernmental relations, now had an impact on the authority and role of the Supreme Court.

The revision of the Court's agenda and priorities can be traced to two cases with seemingly trivial fact situations that were announced on the same day: *Erie Railroad v. Tompkins* 304 U.S. 64 (1937 term) and *United States v. Carolene Products* 304 U.S. 144 (1937 term). The decision in *Erie*, which on its face was a simple tort question, applied state law to certain economic disputes and, in effect, created a barrier blocking access to the federal court to these types of cases. The Court refused to support the creation of a federal common law in such matters. In the long term, the *Erie* case effectively helped restrict access to the Supreme Court's agenda for those cases labeled "Ordinary Economic."[8] In issuing the *Erie* doctrine, the Court seemed poised to revolutionize its agenda by purging many venerable items that had been staples of the Court's agenda.

Certainly a series of emerging cases involving regulation of the economy would assume some of the vacated agenda space, but a footnote in the *Carolene Products* decision, itself an economic regulation case about filled milk products, appeared to articulate a new theory of jurisprudence, a new role for the Court, and a new set of issues that could occupy agenda space. Justice Harlan Fiske Stone's classic Footnote 4 essentially said that congressional statutes dealing with economic matters would be presumed constitutional unless actors challenging such regulations could demonstrate clear, inherent flaws. Concurrently, issues concerning individual rights and civil liberties would receive more exacting judicial scrutiny.[9] In such cases, the burden of proof would shift to the government to demonstrate the rational purposes achieved by laws that might limit individual rights. Stone argued that so-called "insular minorities," foreclosed from using the political branches, merit additional judicial protection for this very reason. The footnote represented the vanguard of the new order. The rationale moved from a footnote, to a dissent in *Jones v. Opelika* 316 U.S. 584 (1941 term), and ultimately to a majority opinion in *Murdoch v. Pennsylvania* 319 U.S. 103 (1942 term), like *Jones* a freedom-of-religion case involving municipal license taxes on the Jehovah's Witnesses. Civil liberties and individual rights would enjoy a preferred position. This change did not occur immediately, but the impetus had been set into motion. As Gerald T.

Dunne has noted: "If *Erie Railroad* came to destroy, *Carolene Products* remained to fulfill."[10]

From what we know about the Court's response to the events of the 1930s, the reasons for a shift in the agenda are clear. External forces and a new prevailing ideology forced the Court to rethink its economic orientations. Different external factors and internal forces on the Court brought a new series of concerns to the fore. The more interesting question is why the agenda shift occurred as slowly as it did. History hints at a 1937 turning point and yet the data seem to show that, in terms of agenda composition, the turning point occurred two decades later. This disparity is significant because it demonstrates the dynamics of agenda change.

THE TRANSFORMATION OF THE MEMBERSHIP

The external environment, in the form of a depression, a package of legislative and executive solutions, and a partisan realignment, forced the Court to reassess its position in the policymaking structure. Of course, the Court does not operate in a vacuum and a number of important social, political, and economic issues posed conditions that affected the Court's docket, agenda, and decisions. Following closely on the heels of the Great Depression and the New Deal, the storm clouds that would lead the United States into World War II were rapidly gathering. A Court struggling to reestablish its legitimacy and develop a new role in an evolving governmental order was now faced with a series of environmental constraints. Similarly, the end of the armed conflict brought an ideological and philosophical cold war that threatened the uneasy peace. The Court had to face economic and free-expression issues in this context.

Short-term economic fluctuations and international commitments were also part of the environment the Court faced, although their effects appeared to have less direct consequences for the judiciary. The domestic mood of the 1950s, in a nation recovering from economic and military crises, presented its own context for policymakers. The undeclared war in Vietnam raised a variety of issues that governmental agencies had to confront. On the domestic front in the sixties, the Vietnam conflict was one of a number of issues that ignited passions. The civil rights movement gained momentum, partially due to Supreme Court decisions and a series of social movements raised issues of equal protection and individual liberties. One structural difference between these issues and the economic and international concerns of previous periods centers on the fact that the Supreme Court is the dominant actor in the civil liberties and civil rights domains and a secondary, interstitial policymaker in other areas.

Just as the Court was responsible for abetting the civil rights movement, some of its decisions had negative consequences. Increasingly expansive civil liberties decisions provoked the ire of candidates running for elective offices at all levels. When those candidates were successful, they attempted to use a variety of the tools at their disposal to reverse or limit the effects of the Court's decisions. Through the appointment process, the enforcement authority, litigation strategies, legislative initiatives, and the amendment process, governmental actors placed constraints on the Court. The policies of the Nixon and Reagan presidencies were based in part on opposition to the social policies emerging from the judiciary. The appointment process afforded both presidents the opportunity to change the composition of the Court. Less important, but significant nonetheless, was the fact that elite and public opinion demonstrated diminished support for the more difficult policies emerging from the Court during a period of presumed economic scarcity.

The shifting political and social winds form a series of environmental constraints for policymakers. In a real sense, the Court is partially insulated from the effects of many external factors. Changes in the Court's doctrine and philosophies, and thus in its agenda and, decisions, are more directly attributable to changes in the composition of the Supreme Court. It is important to consider the transformation of the Court's membership as a context for evaluating changes in the Court's agenda and the changes in doctrine that are attendant to such changes.[11]

Although the "switch in time" predated any Court membership change, Roosevelt soon had the opportunity to reinforce these changes on the Hughes Court with a few appointments. The resignations of Sutherland and Butler brought Justices Hugo Black and Stanley Reed to the Court. When Justices Louis Brandeis and Benjamin Cardozo, more sympathetic to the New Deal and the Court's new role, left the Court, they were replaced by William Douglas and Felix Frankfurter, respectively. This provided the opportunity for Roosevelt to stamp his indelible mark on the judiciary. The effect of such changes was monumental. Not only did the president replace conservative opponents with justices attuned to his philosophies, he was able to replace older liberals with young supporters. Black and Douglas served into the 1970s, so Roosevelt's choices had an impact for decades.

Within a few terms, Roosevelt was able to replace the last two of the "Four Horsemen" and the leadership structure of the Court, replacing Hughes by promoting Stone to chief justice. The age of the former members and Roosevelt's style of office rotation meant a great deal of flux in the membership of the post-1937 Hughes and Stone courts. This instability may have interfered with the Court's ability to complete or continue the transformation of the institution. Coupled with the events surrounding World War II, the influence of the ideological changes may have been muted. The appointment process had profoundly altered the composition of the Court, but many of the appointments were made in an attempt to gain support on economic issues that were increasingly less central to the objectives of the Court. Many of the new justices were untested in issues involving civil liberties and civil rights.

The appointments to the Vinson Court, which emerged when Fred Vinson replaced Chief Justice Stone, have been roundly criticized as mediocre or worse. President Harry S Truman's nominees tended to be his cronies and they were unprepared for the increasingly difficult civil liberties issues that reached the docket during the cold war period. In ideological terms, the appointments made the Court somewhat more conservative by replacing liberal justices like Wiley Rutledge and Frank Murphy with Sherman Minton and Harold Burton.

In an ironic, indirect manner, President Dwight Eisenhower should arguably be remembered as the architect of the greatest advances in American civil liberties and civil rights. His selection of Chief Justice Earl Warren provided the effective leadership for a constitutional revolution. The later nomination of William Brennan provided Warren an important ally, who would remain on the Court through the 1980s and in a position to protect the advances of the Warren Court from the retreats of the Burger Court. Other Eisenhower appointments, like John Marshall Harlan and Potter Stewart, were moderate-conservatives, whose votes were available to the liberal wing in some cases. The early Warren Court, with Black, Douglas, and Brennan, had a liberal cadre of justices who could begin to change the nature of constitutional law.

President John Kennedy's selection of Byron White to replace Charles Whittaker made a marginal change in the ideological composition of the Court. The replacement of Frankfurter with Arthur Goldberg (and later Abe Fortas) was a harbinger of the later Warren Court. The Court now had the crucial, consistent, fifth liberal vote to push individual rights policies still further. The nomination of Thurgood Marshall reinforced the trend and made the later Warren Court the most liberal in history. More significantly, the nominations were increasingly being made with an eye to the impact on individual rights and liberties.

With the selection of Chief Justice Warren Burger, President Richard M. Nixon began to make good on his campaign pledge to alter the Supreme Court. The forced departure of Abe Fortas, coupled with the retirement of Earl Warren, removed two staunch liberals from the Court and replaced them with the "Minnesota Twins": Burger and Harry Blackmun, two conservatives. The selection of William Rehnquist, a strict conservative, to replace Harlan, a moderate-conservative, continued to tip the Court to the right. In absolute terms, the Burger Court may not have been overly conservative. In relative terms, it was considerably more restrictive than the Warren Court. President Gerald Ford's lone selection, John Paul Stevens, a moderate, is noteworthy because he replaced the most liberal justice, Douglas.

President Ronald Reagan left two legacies on the Supreme Court. On one level, he continued what Nixon had begun, tilting the Court to the right. Justices Sandra Day O'Connor, Antonin Scalia, and Anthony Kennedy have been arguably, if marginally, more conservative than the justices they replaced. More significantly, by replacing Stewart, Burger, and Lewis Powell, Reagan was able to solidify conservative seats on the Court by turning them over to younger individuals. Historians may regard Reagan like Roosevelt in that his imprint on the Supreme Court will last decades beyond the term of his presidency. What has restrained the move in the conservative direction is the behavior of Justices Blackmun, Stevens, and to a lesser degree, a few other justices, who have moved to the left in an attempt to balance the Court as the ideological composition of the membership changed.

As President George Bush assumed the mantle of leadership, the Supreme Court stood in a position that was somewhat similar to the early New Deal Court. The liberal wing of the Court--Brennan, Marshall, and Blackmun--was elderly and in declining health. The conservative wing had the votes to win many cases but not the strength to impose its will on the Court and completely rewrite constitutional doctrine and philosophy. The departure of Justice Brennan may provide the impetus for the ultimate demise of the precedents of the Warren Court. Not only does David Souter represent a more conservative philosophy than the man he replaced, but in Brennan the liberal wing has lost its most effective voice and coalition builder. Brennan was often able to sway a moderate or conservative vote. The selection of Souter moves the conservatives closer to a critical mass that can control the selection of cases, decisions on the merits, the tone of opinions, and the long-term construction of doctrine. This is analogous to the critical mass assembled in the later Warren Court, which had a profound impact on American constitutional law.

The changes in the ideological composition of the Supreme Court had the effect of altering the goals of the institution. This had some important consequences for the doctrinal development of individual areas of law. Theoretically, the influence of changes in the goals of the Court on the agenda is less clear. When the goals of the Court change, such changes may create the type of situation that will induce agenda and policy change. Alternatively, the ascendant ideological wing may accept the same types of cases as its predecessor to rewrite the decisions. If changes in the goals of the membership do not lead to changes in the Court's agenda, that may suggest the influence of institutional rules. With these changes in the composition of the Court as a backdrop, it is important to consider the scope and pace of change in the agenda as a whole.

THE AGENDA AND THE NATURE OF CHANGE

On the broadest level, the Supreme Court's agenda has undergone a fundamental transformation over the past half-century. Table 3.1 shows the number and percentage of cases in the major policy areas in the 1933-1987 period. The policy areas, described in Appendix 1, have significantly changed during that period. The economic concerns that dominated the agenda prior to the "switch in time," such as Internal Revenue, State Regulation, and Ordinary Economic cases, were gradually eliminated from the Court's agenda. Federalism questions, a result of the growth of the central government, flourished briefly. U.S. Regulation cases, a product of New Deal policies, gained the largest single share of agenda space but have declined more recently. Civil Liberties cases began haltingly but eventually supplanted Regulation cases as the most significant consumers of agenda space. Among the components of Civil Liberties, Due Process was the first to stake a claim to agenda space and holds the largest portion of the Civil Liberties agenda allocation. Substantive Rights was the second area within the Civil Liberties domain to reach the Court's agenda in significant

Table 3.1 Number of Cases and Percentage of Agenda Space Allocated to Major Policy Areas, 1933-1987 Terms

Policy Area	1933-1937	1938-1942	1943-1947	1948-1952	1953-1957	1958-1962	1963-1967	1968-1972	1973-1977	1978-1982	1983-1987	Total (n)
Due Process (n) (%)	41 5.2	54 7.1	66 10.0	73 14.4	84 17.1	124 20.9	165 25.0	222 31.0	233 27.8	213 26.8	222 29.6	1497
Substantive Rights	9 1.2	32 4.2	31 4.7	43 8.5	38 7.7	62 10.5	63 9.5	116 16.2	120 14.3	80 10.1	80 10.7	674
Equality	11 1.4	8 1.0	18 2.7	25 4.9	25 5.1	31 5.2	82 12.4	86 12.0	105 12.5	102 12.8	124 16.6	617
Criminal Law	12 1.5	20 2.6	17 2.6	20 3.9	24 4.9	19 3.2	16 2.4	22 3.1	17 2.0	14 1.8	13 1.7	194
Government as Provider	3 0.4	4 0.5	0 0.0	0 0.0	2 0.4	4 0.7	2 0.3	6 0.8	12 1.4	8 1.0	13 1.7	54
Foreign Affairs	12 1.5	15 2.0	41 6.2	21 4.1	12 2.4	2 0.3	5 0.8	1 0.1	5 0.6	4 0.5	2 0.3	120
Separation of Powers	6 0.4	2 0.3	2 0.3	4 0.8	5 1.0	3 0.5	2 0.3	8 1.1	11 1.3	14 1.8	9 1.2	66

												Total
Federalism	109 14.0	108 14.1	90 13.6	59 11.6	49 10.0	45 7.6	47 7.1	39 5.4	78 9.3	89 11.2	75 10.0	788
U.S. Regulation	220 27.8	258 33.8	232 35.7	166 33.9	162 33.0	202 34.1	202 30.6	139 19.4	165 19.7	168 21.2	133 17.8	2047
Internal Revenue	139 17.8	123 16.1	73 11.1	33 6.5	41 8.4	43 7.3	29 4.4	26 3.6	27 3.2	20 2.5	24 3.2	578
State Regulation	79 10.1	46 6.0	19 2.9	16 3.2	10 2.0	17 2.9	8 1.2	16 2.2	24 2.9	29 3.6	8 1.1	272
State as Litigant	14 1.8	4 0.5	7 1.1	2 0.4	6 1.2	3 0.5	8 1.2	11 1.5	11 1.3	19 2.4	5 0.7	90
United States as Litigant	11 1.4	29 3.8	24 3.6	15 3.0	6 1.2	14 2.4	6 0.9	5 0.7	6 0.7	11 1.4	19 2.5	146
Ordinary Economic	126 16.1	61 8.0	39 5.9	30 5.9	26 5.3	24 4.0	24 3.6	20 2.8	22 2.6	22 2.8	22 2.9	416
Total	792 10.5	764 10.1	659 8.7	507 6.7	490 6.5	593 7.8	661 8.7	717 9.5	837 11.1	796 10.5	749 9.8	7565

numbers. Equality cases have been the most recent additions and continue to grow throughout the period.

The influence of certain underlying factors and determinants of agenda change, such as changes in the membership of the Court, doctrinal revisions, and the existence of important landmark decisions will be examined systematically in subsequent chapters. The consideration of the individual policy areas is important, but it masks the interrelationships between the policy areas in their competition for agenda space.

Viewing these areas in isolation obscures the dynamics fundamental to a comprehensive study. A holistic analysis of the Court's agenda permits inferences about the nature and scope of agenda change. The method I have used to analyze the Court's 1933-1988 agenda is a factor analysis designed to measure the pace of agenda change. The annual agenda, defined as the proportion of space allocated to the various policy areas, is the unit of analysis.

Factor analysis is used to express a large number of variables (the fifty-six terms, 1933-1988) grouped as a smaller number of hypothetical underlying factors. The specific form of the factor analysis is a varimax rotation to yield orthogonal factors, which are uncorrelated with each other. An orthogonal rotation provides a clear separation that maximizes the differences between the factors.[12] The results yield two factors: a civil liberties agenda factor (Factor I) and an economic agenda factor (Factor II), which explain 92 percent of the variance. Substantively, Civil Liberties and Economics are unrelated to each other and are treated as opposite entities; this makes it relatively easy to trace the nature and pace of agenda change. The individual terms can be plotted relative to the two axes, which represent a purely Economic agenda and a purely Civil Liberties agenda. The changes, as the agenda moved from domination by Economic cases to control by Civil Liberties cases, can be mapped to determine how quickly change is manifested and what form it takes. Other methods, most notably time series analysis, confirm the results of the factor analysis, but the latter is used because of the ease of interpretation.[13]

The factor analysis provides formal evidence demonstrating a largely incremental change from an agenda decidedly economic to one dominated by individual liberties and rights. The trends reveal that agenda change occurred in two stages. The agenda changed slowly, but relatively steadily until the mid-1950s, then the pace increased. Figure 3.1 shows the flow quite vividly. The early terms load heavily on Factor

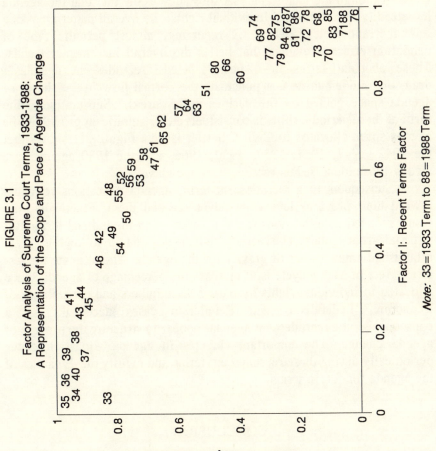

FIGURE 3.1

Factor Analysis of Supreme Court Terms, 1933-1988:
A Representation of the Scope and Pace of Agenda Change

Note: 33=1933 Term to 88=1988 Term

II, while the recent terms are related to Factor I. Some of the terms load relatively evenly on both factors, suggesting a transition from the early terms, with their focus on economic issues, to the more recent terms. Once the agenda passed the midpoint between economic and individual rights cases, the pace of agenda change accelerated. The terms after 1960 are increasingly crowded toward the Civil Liberties factor.

Although the factor analysis substantiates the fact that the agenda has steadily moved toward individual rights, the overall pattern masks a few aberrant judicial terms. A recurring, almost periodic type of pendulum effect is evident that belies the overall incremental trends. These aberrant terms have been labeled "recrudescent agendas": dramatic, sudden shifts that punctuate the normal flow in the shares of agenda space gained by the various policy areas.[14] Substantively, the form of these periodic shifts is consistent: clear, significant growth in the agenda space allocated to Civil Liberties issues. Figure 3.1 shows that the 1942, 1947, 1951, 1957, 1960, 1966, and the 1980 agendas are among those identified as recrudescent agendas.

Subsequent to a recrudescent term, agenda allocations retreated toward their previous levels but never reached them. Practically, the Court reduced its allocations to Civil Liberties in the judicial term after a recrudescent agenda. The recrudescent agenda and the following retreat established a new center of gravity for the agenda. The ultimate longer-term effect of such a cycle is to increase the percentage of agenda space allocated to individual rights by paring the numbers and percentages of Economic, Federalism, and Regulation cases accepted. As a consequence, the recrudescent agendas appear to structure the process of agenda change. The important changes in agenda allocation occur periodically during these recrudescent terms and modify the dynamics of the agenda for future terms.

CONCLUSION

The remainder of this study seeks to explain more thoroughly some of the broad trends in agenda change identified in this chapter. Such an explanation must account for a number of empirical trends. The factors that govern or influence agenda change must account for the significant decline in Economic cases, the long-term stability of Regulation cases, and the two-stage growth of Civil Liberties cases. Agenda change, while steady, was relatively incremental until the mid-1950s and explosive afterwards, particularly in Civil Liberties. Other empirical patterns to be explained include the recrudescent agendas. In addition, the nature of agenda change in the underlying areas that compose the summary areas is also considered. There are significantly greater fluctuations in many of the subareas that reveal important additional evidence about the dynamics of agenda change, the relationship of decisions to subsequent agenda priorities, and the relationships between issues that compete for agenda space.

The trends in the individual series and in the overall agenda suggest one preliminary conclusion. The empirical results appear to support the existence of an institutional agenda and the validity of a diachronic neoinstitutional perspective for research. The transition of the agenda appears to be orderly and relatively systematic and to reflect a conscious decision to pursue a new set of issues and continue to develop these patterns of change. Some of these patterns continue despite wholesale changes in the goals and composition of the Court.

At the same time, despite dramatic changes in the sociopolitical fabric of the nation, the economic infrastructure, the role of the federal government, and the Court's own intention to modify the types of issues it accepted, fundamental changes in the Supreme Court's allocation of agenda change did not materialize immediately. The remainder of the study seeks to explain why the scope and pace of agenda change took the form it did.

These interrelated changes reflect the transformation of American politics and the governmental system. The trends must be evaluated within the context of the changes in the sociopolitical environment. In addition, the changes in agenda priorities are a vivid record of an institutional transformation in the role and the nature of the U.S. Supreme Court.

4

The Waning of Economic Issues: Shifting Agenda Priorities

In 1925, Congress granted the Supreme Court discretionary review over the majority of the Court's business by creating the writ of certiorari. Before the Judiciary Act of 1925, the Court had to accept and decide every case properly brought to its docket. As a result, the Court's agenda reflected the cases and issues litigants considered significant. The Judiciary Act was an important change in the institutional rules and procedures of the Court. In turn, the act offered an opportunity for introducing significant change to the Court's agenda if the institutional goals were so disposed.

Prior to this procedural change, the Court's docket was dominated by cases that can be labeled "Ordinary Economic." The resolution of such cases often had few long-term consequences and little impact on similarly based litigants. Few of these decisions created any more than a limited ripple in U.S. constitutional law. Finally armed with the procedural authority to gain greater control over its agenda, the Court exercised some substantive discretion in its agenda building by issuing important landmark decisions that sought to condition the future behavior of litigants. In doing so, the Court began the long-term process of revising its agenda priorities.

The Court's docket (the cases brought to the justices) is some function of the current social, economic, and political concerns. The early decisions, most notably *Swift v. Tyson* 16 Peters 1 (1842), which allowed federal courts to substitute their judgments for state law in Ordinary Economic cases, helped buttress the U.S. economy. That decision and its progeny produced a uniformity in commercial law standards. In fact, according to Grant Gilmore, "the Supreme Court became a great commercial law Court."[1] The decision in *Erie Railroad v. Tompkins*, which overruled *Swift*, may have been a recognition that changes in the socioeconomic climate mandated a revised judicial approach. In the *Erie* case and concurrent and subsequent decisions, the Court began a process of bringing the political theory of its majority into line with decisions of the president and Congress. The policies of the elected branches were increasingly based on a twentieth-century view of liberalism, which permitted the intervention of the government into the corporate economic system.[2]

At different times, events or situations have conspired to change the role and the central policy focus of the Supreme Court. Before the Civil War the Court had been primarily concerned with the nation-state relationship. The temporary destruction of the union helped to change the nature of the issues attracting judicial attention.[3] Since Reconstruction, cases signifying changes in the structure of U.S. capitalism and the relationship between government and business have occupied the Court's docket.[4]

The concurrent decisions in the *Erie* case and Footnote 4 in the *United States v. Carolene Products* case (1937) suggested a dramatic recasting of the role of the Supreme Court. The new priorities of the Court involved governmental regulation (a burgeoning concern because of the New Deal), federalism (which increased in importance as the central government extended its tentacles at the expense of subnational governmental units), and individual rights. Each of these issues, particularly Regulation and Civil Liberties, had captured limited agenda space in preceding periods. Before those policy areas could attract additional agenda space, the issues that had staked long-term claims to agenda space had to be pushed aside to create room for the new volitional issues.

THE TRANSFORMATION OF THE ECONOMIC AGENDA, 1933-1988

A number of policy areas, such as Ordinary Economic, Internal Revenue, State Regulation, United States as Litigant, and State as Litigant, constitute an Economic dimension. One broad trend that can be readily identified is the decline of Economic cases over time. Although this is not surprising, the trends warrant closer examination. Figure 4.1 shows the precipitous decline in the agenda space allocated to Economic cases. In a more general systemic sense, the decline suggests that the Supreme Court made a conscious effort to reduce the agenda space

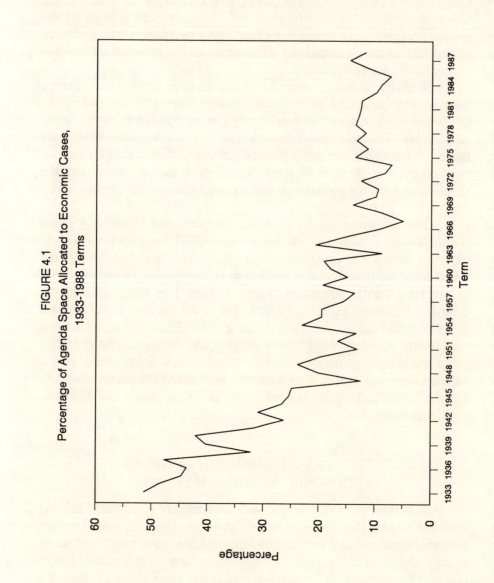

FIGURE 4.1
Percentage of Agenda Space Allocated to Economic Cases,
1933-1988 Terms

available to these types of issues. For a variety of reasons, to be examined below, the Court can rarely eliminate a policy area from its agenda altogether. Given these practical realities, the levels of Economic cases have reached their effective nadirs.

The Economic cases dominated the agenda prior to the 1938 term, capturing about 50 percent of the Court's agenda space as late as 1937. Their decline was sharp and sudden, but even as late as 1964, Economic cases earned 20 percent of agenda space. Since that time, their agenda space has continued to decline, stabilizing in recent Court terms at approximately 10 percent. The trends belie any changes in the ideological composition of the Supreme Court. Whether the Court was dominated by liberals, conservatives, or those in the middle, Economic cases were increasingly relegated to the Court's back burner.

The pattern of decline in the broader Economic dimension was reflected in specific ebbs in the major component areas: Ordinary Economic, State Regulation, State as Litigant, United States as Litigant, and Internal Revenue. Although they declined at slightly different times, the trends in each area were clear and decisive and can further reveal the dynamics of agenda decline and the conditions in the social, political, and economic environments that surround them.

Issues periodically change in status. Groups of concerns that have attracted the central attention of the Supreme Court may eventually lose their primacy. In terms of the agenda, this means the issue that had been part of the volitional agenda has been displaced and moved to the exigent agenda. From the perspective of judicial decisionmaking, situations and goals change and mandate alternative rules. As new issues emerge or existing issues reach later stages of development that demand more agenda resources, exigent issues must be culled to create space. The initial tool the Court can use institutionally is a landmark decision. The seminal decision changes the nature of law in that policy area and is a signal to litigants and to lower courts. Symbolically and practically, the landmark decision represents a commitment to change by the current Supreme Court. In the Economic issues, the most significant landmark ultimately revised the role of the Court and its priorities.

Landmark decisions are frequently used to open agenda space for new issue areas. In fact, in most instances, such decisions open the agenda to a flood of new litigation seeking to flesh out the new landmark and perhaps to extend it to other areas. In some areas, like the Economic issues, however, landmark decisions can have the opposite effect. Seminal decisions can be used to close agenda space to other areas of law. The Court may use a major pronouncement to begin preparing a path for an institutional retreat. If important decisions are used in such a manner, the Court may adapt a case by limiting the issue in order to send a clear signal and perhaps delegate future decisionmaking in that area to another agency.

These seminal landmark decisions represent an important vehicle for the justices of the Supreme Court and for organized litigants. Issuing such decisions is a conscious choice that reflects the priorities of the day and commits resources for the future. Virtually every important change in the Court's agenda can be traced to a landmark decision. In some instances, the litigant is responsible for carefully framing the issues and convincing a majority of the Court that a new or fundamentally revised policy initiative is necessary. More often, it seems that a purposive group of justices adapt a litigant's petition and expand the issue to create a new precedent and a landmark decision that will provide the foundation for new doctrinal development.[5]

ORDINARY ECONOMIC

Cases that involve injury compensation, insurance claims, personal economic disputes, and the allocation of goods or services between competing litigants compose the Ordinary Economic area. As noted, the *Erie Railroad* case was the major landmark decision that redefined the Ordinary Economic area and affected State Regulation as well. In this decision, the Court overturned *Swift v. Tyson* and applied state law to an injury case. The Court held that there was no federal common law for such cases and that state courts rather than federal courts should decide these issues.

The *Erie* decision was a powerful symbol of the Court's recognition of its institutional role. It represented the first and only time the Court went so far as to declare one of its own decisions unconstitutional.[6] It also endorsed federal judicial restraint in these Economic matters by redesigning the jurisdiction of federal courts.[7] The decision, reflecting institutional goals, modified the roles and norms of the Supreme Court and the lower federal courts. In this respect, the *Erie* decision encapsulated the Court's first support for the tenets announced the same day in Footnote 4 of the *Carolene Products* decision.

No landmark decision is immediately effective in fulfilling the goals of the members of the Supreme Court. A landmark decision that opens a new area of law requires extensive doctrinal construction. The initial decision only separates the new area from the existing area of law that spawned it and raises the core question that defines the new issue. For the foreseeable future, the Court must commit agenda resources to this new area.

A fundamental change in the nature of law in an existing area has similar practical effects, but for somewhat different reasons. When a venerable precedent like *Swift* is undermined, litigants and lower courts are left in a quandary. First, it is probably natural to wonder whether the new decision is an aberration that the Court will soon undermine. The forceful nature of Justice Louis Brandeis's opinion and his well-known opposition, joined by Justice Oliver Wendell Holmes, to the *Swift* doctrine[8] were probably clear indications that this was not an aberrant decision. These factors did little, however, to demonstrate just how far the Court would be willing to go to buttress this new doctrine. In other words, further elaborative cases would be necessary, particularly if the goal of the Court was to extricate itself from the policy area. In fact, a brief flourish of next-generation *Erie* cases found their way to the Court's docket and were accepted to clarify the meaning of the landmark decision. The tone and tenor of these later decisions were to push the decision of *Erie* even further.

The practical result of the *Erie* decision was to close the federal courts to the class of cases defined in this study as Ordinary Economic. Within a decade, the effects on the Supreme Court's agenda were pronounced. Figure 4.2 shows the dramatic reduction in the agenda space allocated to the broader Ordinary Economic policy area. In the Court's pre-*Erie* terms, 1933-1937, it allocated an average of 16 percent of its agenda space to Ordinary Economic issues. In the six terms after the *Erie* rule went into effect, that percentage was more than halved. Since that time, it has declined to less than 5 percent of the available agenda space. These sharp declines from over 20 percent of the agenda space in the 1933 and 1934 terms created vacancies that could be allocated to other areas rising in prominence as the Court's interest in Ordinary Economic cases waned. After 1937, the agenda space allocated to Ordinary Economic cases never reached 10 percent of the total agenda.

There is little reason to expect declines in the Ordinary Economic issues during the mid-twentieth century. Environmental factors suggest the rates of these areas of litigation should have climbed markedly. First, advances in technology have increased the numbers of injuries that have occurred in U.S. society.[9] In addition, social relationships have changed

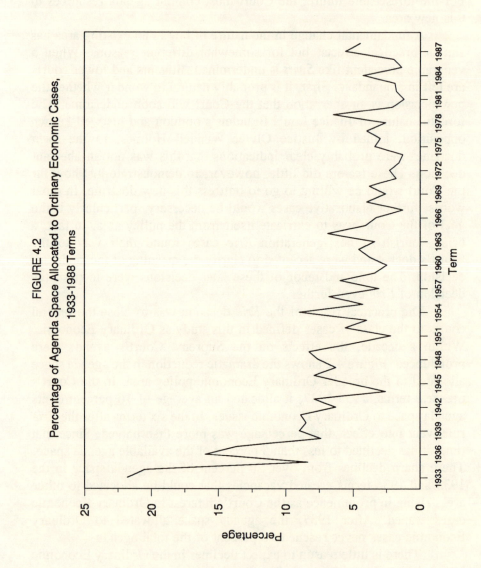

FIGURE 4.2
Percentage of Agenda Space Allocated to Ordinary Economic Cases,
1933-1988 Terms

over time. The increased complexity of society makes interpersonal relations more numerous and more distant. Analysts believe that these factors increase levels of litigation, because more formal means of dispute resolution are needed between parties who will have no future dealings. These expectations were certainly borne out at the lower court levels. The types of cases that comprise the Ordinary Economic domain have proliferated and flooded the lower courts.[10] Ultimately, the increase in such activities created the incentive for lower courts and litigants to settle these disputes out of court to avoid the delays and uncertainties of trials.

Despite the societal and judicial trends, the Supreme Court moved in the opposite direction. To be sure, one class of cases, individual claims against failed banks, was largely settled by the policies that pulled the country out of the Great Depression. The decline in the agenda space allocated to the remainder of the Ordinary Economic area (Table 4.1) appears to be a purposive choice of the Court. By 1940, the Court had reduced its overall attention to Ordinary Economic issues by three-fourths. The decline has continued and stabilized by the 1950s at levels of 2 or 3 percent of the total agenda, the functional equivalent of the complete absence of agenda space. The only subareas that attracted any significant agenda space since the 1950s involved personal injuries and property damage.

As noted, the *Erie* landmark decision appears to be responsible for a great deal of the decline. In essence, the *Erie* decision held that federal courts should not substitute federal authority for state prerogatives. The practical effect was to close the doors of the federal courts to such economic claims. In essence, the Supreme Court delegated the authority for these decisions to other courts. The *Erie* decision, cited as an example of issue suppression, was a conscious effort to deny access to these types of cases.

Under ordinary circumstances, the conditions present after *Erie*—the dramatic overturning of a precedent almost a century old, the difficulty of establishing new principles to clearly guide future behavior, and the level of underlying social activity in that area—would portend expanding agenda space. In fact, the opposite was true, suggesting the Court wished to rid itself of such issues, intervening only when truly important questions arose or when the lower courts were in disarray.

The Court's desire to transfer these issues to the exigent agenda and free its agenda space for other issues is particularly evident in the fact that *Erie* did not accomplish what Justice Brandeis had hoped.[11]

Table 4.1 Number of Cases and Percentage of Agenda Space Allocated to Selected Ordinary Economic Subareas, 1933-1987 Terms

Subareas		1933-1937	1938-1942	1943-1947	1948-1952	1953-1957	1958-1962	1963-1967	1968-1972	1973-1977	1978-1982	1983-1987	Total (n)
Contracts	(n)	13	8	3	0	1	0	3	4	1	1	6	40
	(%)	1.6	1.0	0.5	0.0	0.2	0.0	0.5	0.6	0.1	0.1	0.8	
Insurance		28	10	5	3	4	1	1	0	1	0	1	54
		3.5	1.3	0.8	0.6	0.8	0.2	0.2	0.0	0.1	0.0	0.1	
Banks		35	10	7	2	3	1	3	4	4	4	0	73
		4.4	1.3	1.1	0.4	0.6	0.2	0.5	0.6	0.5	0.5	0.0	
Veterans' Benefits		16	10	5	5	3	2	2	1	3	0	1	48
		2.0	1.3	0.8	1.0	0.6	0.3	0.3	0.1	0.4	0.0	0.1	
Torts Personal		11	3	4	4	2	2	7	0	2	1	13	49
		1.4	0.4	0.6	0.8	0.4	0.3	1.1	0.0	0.2	0.1	1.7	
Torts Property		15	7	5	8	10	11	2	4	3	3	2	70
		1.9	0.9	0.8	1.6	2.0	1.8	0.3	0.6	0.4	0.4	0.3	

Increased experience with the *Erie* rule led the Court to create exceptions when there was an overriding importance to the use of federal rather than state law. Critics on the Court and off complained that *Erie* had not succeeded in "articulating a workable doctrine governing the choice of law in diversity actions."[12] What was troubling about the *Erie* doctrine was the cognitive dissonance that accompanied it. The stated purpose of the *Erie* rule was to restore some of the balance between the states and the central government. This restoration was occurring precisely as the Supreme Court was removing virtually all state obstacles to the broad expansion of federal power under the New Deal. Control over the development of substantive law was not going to pass back to the states at the very time of the broadest expansion of the power of the central government.[13]

On the other hand, the Court's treatment of Ordinary Economic cases was a clear signal of institutional intent. Although the fact situations in such cases tended to raise issues of injuries to people and property, the Court tended to focus on important jurisdictional concerns. The decisions in Ordinary Economic cases focus on the authority of the Supreme Court or the relationships between the lower courts in the federal system and the state courts.

The only types of Ordinary Economic litigation that were decided on the merits of the fact situation stemmed from statutory provisions in the Jones Act and the Longshoremen and Harbor Workers Compensation Act. These statutes created the authority for compensating some classes of injured workers. Despite the novelty of these acts and the vagueness inherent in most statutes, these cases did not flood the Court's institutional agenda. Apparently, the Supreme Court chose to defer to lower courts in these types of cases.

STATE REGULATION

Economic conditions and political realities from 1933 to 1988 necessitated legislative and regulatory responses by governments at each level. State Regulation is composed of judicial responses to the regulatory and taxation policies of state and municipal governments. There are three large categories of cases within the State Regulation policy area: the scope of public service commissions, state taxation, and state licensing. The taxation and licensing cases are the most numerous. As with the Ordinary Economic issues, the environment should have created the grist for more litigation. The nature and scope of regulation grew dramatically, but the Supreme Court's allocation of agenda space to State Regulation cases declined precipitously. Figure 4.3 shows that State Regulation, which was an important staple of the Court's early agenda, declined significantly during the period and almost disappeared from the agenda in 1984.

Almost half (125 cases) the State Regulation cases accepted in the past half-century were granted in the first decade. The decline after 1942 was sharp, although in recent decades there has been a slight resurgence in the State Regulation cases reaching the Court's institutional agenda. The percentages are not striking but have clearly reversed a trend that lasted well over three decades. Moves by three Republican administrations to reduce the centralization of American government and the deregulation movement at the national level may have left a vacuum that state regulations have moved to occupy, to some degree.

The impact of the *Erie* decision spread to State Regulation cases as well and is partially responsible for the decline in State Regulation cases. In a number of these cases, the Court applied the *Erie* rule and held that state courts should determine the validity of the state regulations being challenged. In the 1933-1937 period, prior to the *Erie* decision, over 10 percent of the Court's agenda space was granted to State Regulation cases. This declined to just under 6 percent in the next five terms and has leveled at just over 2 percent since the early 1940s. In decisions that affected the area of State Regulation, "the Supreme Court held that the *Erie* rule required the enforcement of state procedural as well as substantive law."[14] In a number of cases, the Court ruled that *Erie* mandated that the federal courts not interfere with state court interpretations of their own regulations.

In recent Court terms, there has been an upturn in the numbers of State Regulation cases accepted. The levels are not great in any absolute sense, but relatively, they represent a growth in a once moribund area of law. Significantly, though, this recent trend does not appear to portend further levels of growth or any reactivation of this area of law.

Part of the decline and the recent, albeit slight, growth of State Regulation cases may be attributed to a form of issue transformation and its effects. Certainly, the numbers of State Regulation cases on the Court's agenda belie the volume of cases involving state regulatory schemes. Many of the post-1937 State Regulation cases were expanded to Federalism cases. Many of these cases raised objections to state regulations on the grounds that they violated the commerce clause and

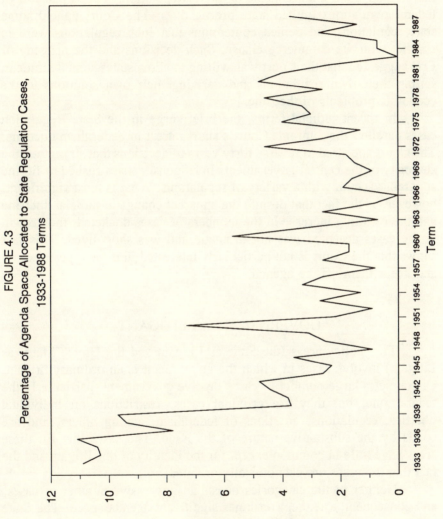

FIGURE 4.3
Percentage of Agenda Space Allocated to State Regulation Cases,
1933-1988 Terms

thus should be declared void as conflicting with federal prerogatives. In other cases, the Court focused on whether a state regulation was preempted by a similar federal law. The Court addressed these cases on constitutional grounds within the doctrinal framework of Federalism rather than within the context of State Regulation. The expansion of federal regulations limited state prerogatives. The Court upheld some state regulations and denied contentions that such regulations were in conflict with the commerce clause. Such decisions and the progeny of *Erie* suggested that the Court was willing to allow states some latitude in setting their own regulations and deriving their own solutions to the economic problems of the time.

In recent judicial terms, the brief surge in the State Regulation cases parallels the Supreme Court's short retreat in Federalism doctrine. The Court appeared to reverse forty years of decisions that strengthen the authority of the central government. In response, states rushed to fill the apparent vacuum with a variety of regulations. What is most significant, however, is the fact that despite the apparent change in judicial doctrine and the resulting increase in the numbers of cases docketed, the growth in the cases accepted was not dramatic and was short-lived. This fact shows that the Court is not particularly interested in these types of cases and keeps them off the agenda.

GOVERNMENT AS LITIGANT

Two policy areas (the State as Litigant and the United States as Litigant) involve cases in which the government is an ordinary litigant. Of course, a large number of cases involve government, particularly the federal one, but they are criminal cases, restrictions on individual liberties, regulations, questions of federalism, among others, and are coded by the substantive nature of the issue. The cases that fill these areas have little in common except for the identity of one litigant and the fact that the cases are economically oriented.

Neither of the categories boasts an impressive number of cases, and consequently neither consumes significant agenda space. The State as Litigant category has held a small but consistent level of agenda space, averaging one or two cases per term. Virtually all the State as Litigant cases involved border disputes and conflict between states over navigable waters. Many of these cases had acquired a life of their own. In other words, many of the disputes were recurrent, involving the same states and the same boundaries or waters. The conflicts were seldom settled permanently and the Court was periodically asked to arbitrate these cases.

The Court's reluctance to consider the State as Litigant cases was evident in its review and deposition of the cases. First, many of the cases arise under the Court's original jurisdiction. Thus, they are part of the exigent agenda, though in a different manner. Second, the Court's decisions are invariably brief, in order to avoid spending significant resources on them. In many instances, the Court further pares its work by appointing a special master to resolve the disputes and redraw the boundaries. The case reaches the Court when one or both states challenge the findings of the special master. In most cases, the Court defers to the expertise of the special master, thus refusing to expand the scope of the case.

The United States as Litigant area demonstrates some trends that are tied to legislative actions and judicial responses. The doctrine of sovereign immunity forbids a suit against government without its consent. Congress had to pass legislation that voluntarily gave up some of the government's immunity. This is necessary because the ability to sue government is a legislatively created right.[15] The Court, in turn, had to determine the extent to which the government was liable. In the government liability cases, important legislation like the Federal Tort Claims Act and the Miller Act created conditions for agenda growth. The surge of Government as Litigant cases, in fact, coincides with the period surrounding the passage of the Federal Tort Claims Act in 1946. The Court was charged with interpreting this new statutory authorization.

Given the normal ambiguity found in legislation, it is surprising that the allocation of Court agenda space, around 4 percent during the 1933-1988 period, did not reach greater levels.[16] The Court was responsible, at least in part, for the lack of agenda allocation. In a major decision, *Feres v. United States* 340 U.S. 135 (1949 term), the Court barred the use of the Federal Tort Claims Act in suits by members of the Armed Services for injuries incurred in the military. This closed judicial access to a large number of potential cases. Congressional silence in the wake of the *Feres* decision has left the decision intact. In *Bivens v. Six Unknown Named Federal Narcotics Agents* 403 U.S. 388 (1970 term), the Court appeared to expand federal tort actions by proposing an alternative to the exclusionary rule. Victims of illegal searches could sue the officer who participated in the search. But in *Chappell v. Wallace* 462 U.S. 296 (1981 term), the Court narrowed *Bivens* by refusing a racial discrimination suit against military superiors. In *United States v. Johnson*, the Court expanded the *Feres* doctrine by holding that the death of a pilot caused by a civilian air controller was still a military activity and therefore denied the claim.[17] Because military injuries would probably be the most significant portion of government tort cases, these decisions over almost four decades kept these cases off the Court's docket. The Court has averaged accepting only one or two United States as Litigant cases during the last twenty-five years.

Once again, such Court decisions have purposively limited the potential expansion of agenda space. The Court has virtually closed access to the judiciary for injuries that might be the result of governmental malfeasance. Perhaps as a result, Congress has created agencies and boards to address concerns with governmental liability. In addition, Congress itself has traditionally been a forum for private bills that provide compensation for those alleging wrongs by government. Most important, perhaps, has been the creation and expansion of an Article I or specialized court, the Court of Claims. Congress made this court a "regular" Article III court in 1953, but returned it to Article I in 1982 as the U.S. Claims Court. This recent change was coupled with the creation of the Court of Appeals for the Federal Circuit, which would receive appeals from the Claims Court.[18] Despite the changes in name and status, the Supreme Court apparently recognized these judges as experts and deferred to their judgment. In effect, the justices would seldom grant petitions to review the decisions of the Claims Court.

INTERNAL REVENUE

The Internal Revenue area of law did not have landmark decisions that even remotely approached the *Erie* decision in scope and magnitude. The Internal Revenue area is dominated not by judicial decisions, but by legislative pronouncements.[19] Internal Revenue cases involve interpretations of the tax codes and Internal Revenue Service policies. Two important Internal Revenue Codes in 1939 and 1954 would be expected to have a major impact on levels of litigation. The direction of the influence of these tax codes is uncertain, however. The tax codes could specify a number of conditions and answer a number of questions mitigating the need for judicial involvement. The normal course of statutory intervention should create more litigation. The congressional policy process is fraught with veto points and requires a great deal of compromise and vague language. Courts are often required to intervene and derive the legislative intent.

With the increase of tax revenues over time, the expectation is that levels of litigation in the lower court should expand. This should affect the Court's docket as well. The creation of specialized tax courts, however, could reduce the litigation coming to the Supreme Court by providing an alternative forum. This is particularly true if the Supreme Court delegates authority and autonomy to these specialized courts. In fact, the declines in the agenda space allocated to Internal Revenue cases paralleled the change that created the Tax Court of the United States out of the Board of Tax Appeals. Moreover, later changes in the Tax Court were advocated because the Supreme Court often refused to intervene unless there was direct lower court conflict and failed to deal with the ambiguities of the tax code.[20]

The Court's Internal Revenue agenda declined dramatically despite the perceived environmental trends. As Figure 4.4 shows, Internal Revenue cases held an important percentage of the Court's agenda space until the early 1940s and then declined significantly for a decade. In the 1933-1939 period, Internal Revenue cases held a steady share of the agenda space, averaging about 18 percent. The introduction of the 1939 tax code led to a brief surge in the allocation of agenda space. After 1942, however, the Court began to limit the agenda space granted to these tax cases. A brief surge of acceptances during the 1950s predated the second stage of decline, which was incremental. The Court apparently clarified the issues to its satisfaction and retreated from the area. By 1953, the annual allocation of agenda space was less than 6 percent, decreasing to 2 percent or less in a few terms. Congress restructured the tax code in 1954 and the Court allocated additional agenda space, reaching almost 10 percent in the 1954-1959 period. Since then, the available agenda space has declined to 3 to 4 percent per term.

From 1934 to about 1965, the area exhibited an "on-off cycle" of sorts. In two- to three-period cycles, the Court accepted a relatively large number of Internal Revenue cases one term, then sharply reduced its allocation of agenda space. In a subsequent term, this pattern repeated, with acceptance of a larger number of cases. The issue has reached its effective floor in the last two decades--less than 4 percent of the agenda space available. The decline in the agenda space allocated to Internal Revenue cases occurred a bit later than the declines in Ordinary Economic and State Regulation and was less sudden, but generally took the same form as the decline in the other two areas. This may be a

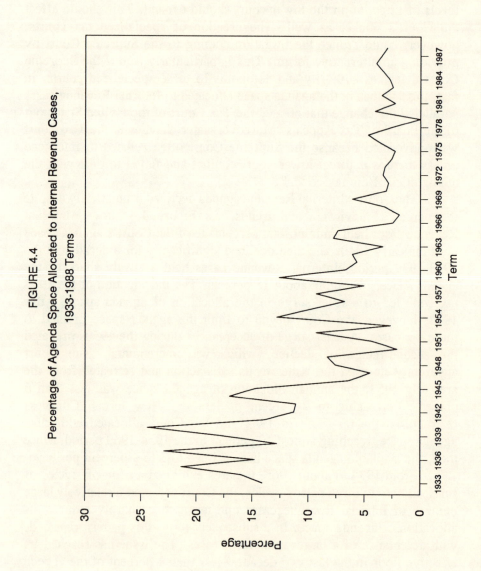

FIGURE 4.4

Percentage of Agenda Space Allocated to Internal Revenue Cases,
1933-1988 Terms

function of the involvement of the U.S. government and the fact that such issues are found at the intersection of the older Economic dimension and the rapidly emerging U.S. Regulation areas.

The brief surges in the agenda space that followed the introduction of new tax codes are expected given the fact that the language is vague and changes interrupt standard operating procedures. The uncertainty may find its way into the lower courts and then force the Supreme Court to intervene. As with the government tort cases, it is somewhat surprising given the dynamics of the agenda and the uncertainties inherent in the legislation that the Court would reduce its attention to these areas as quickly as it did and that the short-term expansion of agenda space was not more dramatic. It may suggest that the Court had other issues that were more important to its goals and limited agenda resources.

CONDITIONING BEHAVIOR:
THE EXIGENT AGENDA

In each of these areas of law the Court was quite purposive in its attempts to keep these issues on the exigent agenda and reduce the institutional resources expended on these areas. The surest path to institutional policy change is to change the ideological composition of the membership. From the 1937 term, when the *Erie* decision was announced, to the 1988 term there were over two dozen personnel changes in the Court's composition. The sum of the effects of these individual changes yielded significant broad-scale changes in the ideological balance of the Court. Those individual and institutional changes had important consequences for the doctrinal development in some areas of law, most notably, Civil Liberties. In the Ordinary Economic, Internal Revenue, State Regulation, and government litigation areas, these changes had virtually no effect.

Despite changes in the institutional goals, the Court adopted policies to deal with these types of issues and rigidly maintained them across a half-century. Institutional norms and rules that dictated a reduced concern for such issues and narrow consideration of those Economic cases that were accepted greeted new members of the Court. The Court had adopted a new role, restraint in regulatory matters and activism in individual rights, that instituted a new set of dynamics to govern the pace of agenda change and the nature of doctrinal development. This revised role permeated the institution despite significant changes in the membership.

It is the nature of the agenda that such a change in role and priorities is not self-executing. Although the reductions in agenda space for certain issues were significant, there was not an immediate cessation of Court attention. This suggests the Court's need to fulfill its institutional obligation to leave the Economic areas of law in a relatively coherent state so those agencies with future responsibilities in these areas would have a series of guiding principles available. It also speaks to the dynamics of the agenda. The Court must take dramatic steps to alter these dynamics, which represent a force of significant inertia. The fact that the Court had no discretion prior to 1925 placed these issues at the center of its docket. The discretion to control its agenda and the desire to do so were necessary elements in revising agenda priorities.

Even though the landmark decision is an important tool that the Court can use to alter the dynamics of the agenda, it alone is insufficient to achieve the long-term purposes and goals of the Court. The landmark decision is a signal that can set a new dynamic in motion, but it must be fleshed out. The Court has a variety of institutional tools at its disposal to continue the processes begun by the seminal decision. The empirical fact is that the Court reduced its attention to a number of Economic areas. This was not accomplished by pure judicial fiat. Rather, the Court had to marshal its institutional resources to create conditions that would transfer the Economic issues to the exigent agenda and reduce their consumption of agenda space. Only then could the Court proceed with its institutional transformation and the assumption of its role in the transformation of American politics.

The Court used an assortment of tactics to reduce consideration of these issues and signal that intent to litigants (the consumer population), bureaucrats (the implementing population), and the lower courts (the interpreting population).[21] The process began with the institutional desire to rid the agenda of certain issues, probably to convert the recently vacated agenda space to some emerging issues. As a result, the Court adopted policies to achieve that goal.

Ultimately, the Court would be interested in conditioning the behavior of litigants. In the long term, the Court would want to convince litigants that it is not sympathetic to such cases and bringing such petitions is a waste of their resources. The level of litigant demand did not decrease immediately, however. In other words, the same types of issues continue to reach the Court's docket. Litigants do not respond to these signals until they have reverberated through the system for a while. As a result, significant reductions are a function of the Court's priorities.

The shift in attention is not immediately evident due to the influence of the judicial role. The Supreme Court's institutional role mandates that its exit from a policy area cannot occur until it has resolved some of the outstanding questions to guide the lower courts. In addition, the Supreme Court must reserve some exigent agenda space, though limited and reduced, to settle disagreements that might paralyze lower courts and could affect the behavior of litigants uncertain of the standards in vogue. Having signaled its intent, the Court takes a few terms to manifest the changes in its review processes. Other changes that are less visible, however, begin almost immediately and their impacts become evident when the numbers of cases accepted in that issue area decline.

The philosophical justification for granting certiorari has changed over time as the nature of the issue was transformed. When the issue is an important part of the Court's agenda, the justices accept cases to fulfill their policy goals. In the Court's words, the cases are accepted because they raise "important or significant questions." When the members of the Court no longer regard the issue as critical to their policy interests, the cases are accepted for very different reasons. The rationale for the acceptance of such cases is based on different sets of principles. The Court will accept cases from this issue area strictly to guide lower courts. Certiorari is granted when there is a lower court disagreement. The Supreme Court accepts the cases not to break new ground but to settle a dispute between the courts that are now charged with deciding the issues the High Court has abandoned.

Internal Revenue and Ordinary Economic cases were among the first to be drastically reduced by the Court. Cases involving tort claims against the government join these two areas on a broader Economic dimension. Table 4.2 shows that the great preponderance of these cases, across time, are accepted for the sole purpose of resolving conflicts of interpretation between lower courts. Even this fact masks some of the influence of the exigent agenda. Many of the Ordinary Economic cases involve the jurisdiction of lower courts. Thus, when the Court states that it accepts such cases due to the "importance of the decision for the administration of the judicial system," the practical effect appears to be the functional equivalent of a lower court conflict. By contrast, the areas that compose Civil Liberties and U.S. Regulation have historically been important components of the volitional agenda. Less than 20 percent of

Table 4.2 Percentage of Cases Accepted to Resolve Circuit Court Conflict in Selected Policy Areas, 1938-1986 Terms

Policy Areas	1938-1952	Warren Court (1953-1969)	Burger Court (1969-1986)
Internal Revenue	84	65	77
Ordinary Economic	66	35	45
U.S. as Litigant	67	36	63
State Regulation	41	33*	44*
U.S. Regulation	19	19	22
Due Process	10	8	23
Substantive Rights	5	5	13
Equality	15	9	21

*Relatively small number of cases

these cases were accepted to resolve such disputes during the 1940-1969 period.

Over time, as agenda space has shrunk and demand has risen, the Court has modified even these policies. In the 1938-1952 period, the Court took Internal Revenue, Ordinary Economic, and government tort cases to resolve disputes between two circuits. During the Burger Court and the early stages of the Rehnquist Court, the dispute of only two circuits was normally not enough to attract the Court's attention. Instead, the Court allowed such limited inconsistencies to exist and waited for the conflicting interpretations to percolate and spread to a number of Courts of Appeals before expending exigent agenda space.[22]

The properties of case selection are an indication of the Court's treatment, but a clearer signal is sent to litigants and lower courts through the tone and tenor of the authoritative decisions of those cases accepted. Although there is a normative desire for justices to decide the issues before them on the narrowest grounds possible, in fact justices often expand the scope of the issue. The opposite process of narrowing the issues raised in the petition dominates the exigent agenda cases. Cases in issue areas the Court seeks to abandon or to reduce consideration of often contain explicit language that narrows the questions before the Court.

The Court must tread a fine line in deciding such cases. The goal is not to create new policy initiatives but to settle existing confusion. Deciding subsequent questions must be done with an eye to the implications of the current decision. As a result, the Court must decide the existing case narrowly to avoid reinstituting the issue as a viable policy concern and must modify the case on the docket or the issue as a whole, that is, suppress the issue.

Because the acceptance of the case is predicated on the desire to settle the issue that has caused lower courts to disagree, the Supreme Court normally couples its acceptance of the petition with specific language that indicates that the sole issue before the justices is the one that yielded the conflict. In this way, the Court does not raise additional issues that could confuse the lower courts. This process should gain momentum as issues move from the volitional portion of the agenda to the exigent agenda. This can take a number of forms. In most cases, the Court may simply dismiss a number of questions that accompany the petition and focus on one central concern.

In the 1938-1952 terms, the period of the sharpest reductions in the agenda space allocated to Economic issues, explicit limiting language accompanied almost 90 percent of the Internal Revenue decisions, and over 80 percent of the Ordinary Economic and federal tort cases. During the same period, only about 30 percent of the Civil Liberties and U.S. Regulation cases contained language that constrained the nature of the review. In recent terms, the limiting language continues to accompany the vast majority of the few Economic and Internal Revenue cases that survive the Court's rigorous exigent screening process.

The process of issue conversion goes beyond the manipulation of individual cases to Court-imposed structural changes in the issue itself. To initiate or continue a process of abandoning an issue area, the Court may need to narrow consideration of the issue. One form this process can take is the adaptation of an issue from constitutional to statutory interpretation. Such a conversion means the Court will address the issue on the narrowest possible grounds by interpreting statutory and regulatory language, rather than confronting the issue on the more expansive constitutional grounds. Litigants seeking Supreme Court review are encouraged to broaden the issue to attract attention to their petitions. For the justices, however, using constitutional provisions as the bases for evaluation runs the risk of expanding the issue, raising additional questions that will require review, and clogging the agenda for the foreseeable future.

Questions that raise constitutional issues are more likely to attract the Court's attention and more likely to be accepted than cases that raise questions of statutory construction.[23] A number of cases, even in areas like Internal Revenue, Ordinary Economic, State Regulation, and federal tort liability raise constitutional issues. In twenty-six of the thirty-one cases raising constitutional issues, the Court ignored the constitutional grounds and adopted the narrower avenue for the decision.[24] This process of narrowing the questions raised is consistent with the process of limiting review of the issues.

The abandonment of an issue means the Court must provide guidelines for lower court judges to help them deal with the issue. Most lower courts do not have discretionary review authority and must decide all cases properly before them. The Supreme Court must strive for a consistency in its decisions that will provide clear signals to the lower courts and perhaps to the litigants that might consider bringing additional petitions. The Court has two means of accomplishing this task. First, it can strive to impose a consistency on the trend of its decisions. Second, the language of the opinions should develop consistent themes that will send clear messages to the appropriate populations.

The decisions emanating from the Court in the areas losing agenda resources have high degrees of consistency both in absolute and in relative terms. Decisions are deemed consistent if one set of parties (such as individuals) is more successful than its opponents (businesses). Measuring consistency appears to be a simple task on one level. The percentage of decisions favoring the government in regulation cases or the accused in criminal procedure is but one measure of consistency and a relatively stringent one. The issue is a bit more problematic in the Ordinary Economic cases, where the concept of liberal and conservative has a less clear intuitive meaning.[25] Decisions that favor one class of litigants in two-thirds of the cases over time suggest a strong judicial commitment to achieving a clear consistency in decisions.

Table 4.3 shows impressive levels of consistency in the Economic cases. During the 1938-1952 period and the Warren Court, when there were significant numbers of these cases, each of the areas constituting the exigent agenda demonstrates greater levels of consistency than the levels for the volitional agenda issues. This consistency occurs across time and despite wholesale changes in the composition and goals of the Supreme

Table 4.3 Percentage of Decisions Favoring One Side in Selected Policy Areas, 1938-1986 Terms

Policy Areas	1938-1952	Warren Court (1953-1969)	Burger Court (1969-1986)
Internal Revenue	77	78	75
Ordinary Economic	62	73	72
U.S. as Litigant	71	72	56
State Regulation	79	60	56
U.S. Regulation	73	71	56
Federalism			
Central Gov't	82	62	60
State Authority	71	65	62
Due Process	54	52	72
Substantive Rights	57	55	60
Equality	58	75	56

Levels of consistency are measured as a function of pure consistency within a Court, regardless of whether that is manifested toward the liberal or conservative side.

Court. Such high levels of consistency send an important message to litigants and lower courts.

The pattern of the Court's decisions in an area can have important consequences for future decisions. Inconsistency will spawn repeated Court cases and induce further confusion in the lower courts. A consistent line of decisions can have the opposite effect: terminating litigation and clarifying policies so the lower courts have clearer standards to follow.

If the cases are accepted solely to resolve lower court conflicts, the stakes for policy-oriented justices are not particularly great. Achieving consistency in a line of decisions is more important than reaching specific ideological results. As a result, individual justices, regardless of ideology, may join the consensus to ensure intra-Court comity.

Because of the noncontroversial nature of the issue areas and the fact that judicial values and attitudes are not the determinants of the decision, many of the cases engender little or no opposition. The consensual and noncontroversial nature of the cases explains part of this, but there are other components as well. Dissenting and concurring opinions, particularly the latter, may create needless confusion among the lower courts. As a consequence, the percentage of unanimous decisions, relative to other policy areas, is significant in those areas that are being phased off the agenda. The number of concurring opinions is minimal in such cases.

Table 4.4 shows that the Economic cases are considerably more likely to be decided unanimously than Civil Liberties cases. This was particularly true in both the 1938-1952 period and during the Burger Court. This is especially noteworthy because the overall percentage of unanimous decisions in the universe of cases decided on the merits by the Supreme Court has declined markedly since 1938.

Most of the judicial decisionmaking literature uses nonunanimous decisions in analyzing the values and attitudes of the individual members. The underlying assumption is that unanimous decisions are guided by different determinants than the values of the members. Other determinants that may suppress the impact of values and attitudes include the dynamics and influence of the small collegial group of individual members and the judicial role. Issues that are less important to the policy goals of members of the Court can be decided on one or more of these alternate grounds.

Because individual justices are not making their decisions on the bases of their values and attitudes, the cases in these policy areas do not fit on a unidimensional scale. The preponderance of unanimous decisions reduces the number of cases available for scaling. Since the Stone Court, few cases can be placed on Economic scales due to the fact that most are unanimous. Among the nonunanimous decisions, the behavior of individual justices has been inconsistent and therefore does not yield clear and reliable scales. If the cases are not accepted on policy grounds, then the behavioral expectations for individual justices are clouded. The decisions of the justices do not fit the normal ideological continuum.

The unanimity in such decisions stems from the fact that the exigent agenda issues are decided more on the basis of the judicial role than the individual values and attitudes of the members of the Court and involve a narrower scope of review. The key issue in the petition that generated lower court conflict is the basis of the Supreme Court decision. The key focus for the justices is the settlement of the circuit conflict, rather than the substantive nature of the issue before the Court.

Table 4.4 Percentage of Unanimous Decisions in Selected Policy Areas, 1938-1986 Terms

Policy Areas	1938-1952	Warren Court (1953-1969)	Burger Court (1969-1986)
Internal Revenue	59	37	48
Ordinary Economic	55	41	67
U.S. as Litigant	65	25	37
State Regulation	52	50	72
U.S. Regulation	42	38	48
Federalism			
Central Government	44	57	42
State Authority	41	51	45
Due Process	22	30	29
Substantive Rights	26	25	24
Equality	31	38	39

Behind each of these factors is the conscious attempt of the Court to prune its agenda of certain issues. Each of the factors is designed to send a message to the litigants and groups who might bring subsequent cases and to the lower courts and administrative agencies, like the Internal Revenue Service, which have been delegated the responsibility for the preponderance of the policymaking in these Economic areas. Ultimately, the finite nature of the Court's decision agenda is a key determinant of the long-term process of agenda building. The way must be paved to provide the Court with the opportunity to attack a number of volitional agenda issues in a relatively systematic fashion.

THE TRANSFORMATION OF THE SUPREME COURT

In each of these areas and the minor policies composing the Economic area, the Court appeared to be quite purposive in its agenda-building processes. The desire to reduce the percentage of agenda space available to the Economic areas was never complete and was not perhaps accomplished as quickly as the Court might have desired. Nonetheless, the declines were significant and with the exception of a very few terms, agenda space of any consequence is not allocated to these areas. The reduction in areas that had once attracted half the available agenda space created a void the Court could fill with other issues.

The process by which the Court systematically limited agenda space is important procedurally and historically. It is a process that recurs in different policy areas during different periods of time. The means of closing the Court's doors underlines the nexus between the decisions the Court issues and future agendas. Historically, since 1938, Economic issues have been considered relatively unimportant by the Court regardless of its composition, underlying societal activities, or the litigants seeking judicial attention.

The reduction in agenda space granted one issue also has consequences for notions of pluralism. Pushing an issue off the agenda means that certain groups will be systematically denied access to an important policymaker. In a related vein, such issues will become the province of other actors and policymakers. Implicitly, such reductions are translated into available agenda space for other policy areas, thus creating access for other groups formerly excluded from the agenda. Diachronic changes in the agenda and agenda priorities have important consequences for the substance of policies emerging from the Court.

These changes, the concurrent revisions in U.S. Regulation issues, and the later growth of Civil Liberties had important implications for the way the Court transacted its business and the construction of a new political theory to buttress these changes. The Economic cases prior to *Erie* and a series of decisions that limited or overturned attempts to regulate the economy had the effects of helping the growth of big business. This was the essence of nineteenth-century liberalism: an attitude framed in laissez-faire capitalism. The members of the Hughes Court had been appointed during the previous party system, defined by the partisan realignment of the 1890s. The party cleavage issue during that realignment period involved the creation of an environment conducive to big business.[26]

Unfortunately for the members of the Court, a new realignment was taking shape and a new issue was at the center of the political universe. Such realignments tend to develop in the face of a crisis, in this case the Great Depression. Initially, the justices did not adapt to the changing mood of the political and economic environment. When the Court backed down in the face of Roosevelt's opposition, it was admitting the need to reevaluate its doctrines and, in essence, American political theory. The decision in *Erie* was a first step, removing precedents and doctrine that had helped business. Rather than a conscious effort to create a new doctrinal foundation, the Court essentially chose to exit from the Economic areas. The Court, which had been a commercial tribunal, was passing the mantle of leadership on these issues to others. The Supreme Court would allow other courts and policymakers to make future determinations concerning such issues. This created a vacuum that the Court filled with a series of other concerns. Doctrine would have to be built in other emerging areas of law. That would require the allocation of extensive agenda space over a long period of time.

In a sense, then *Erie* was a significant policy window that changed institutional rules and norms as a prelude to an emerging change in the Court's goals. This situation, provided by the Great Depression and the expansion of presidential power, permitted the Court to sound the death knell for nineteenth-century liberalism. In finally upholding the New Deal, the Court rewrote constitutional interpretation and political theory to allow governmental regulation of the economy. In closing access to the federal courts in these Economic issues and refusing to buttress a federal common law, the Supreme Court removed an ally of business and the chance for uniformity in this area of law. Allowing the states to make such determinations could potentially create a patchwork of policies that business would have to negotiate. To complete this multitiered revision, the Court began a process of constructing doctrine and theory to guide the nascent growth of the Civil Liberties agenda. Subsequent chapters show that this was a process that would take well over a generation to reach fruition.

The nature of the Court's role and its work would change in other fundamental ways as well. First, the nature of the issues the Court would consider would be increasingly broader. The percentage of constitutional questions would increase while narrower statutory questions would be delegated to other actors. The Ordinary Economic and Internal Revenue cases were largely statutory, had limited long-term effects, and did not affect large number of similarly based individuals and groups. In Federalism and Civil Liberties cases, the Court could address questions having significant implications and involving substantive interpretations of the Constitution and, for the first time, systematic attention to the Bill of Rights.

In addition, the Court was poised on the threshold of a different type of judicial activism. In the domain of Civil Liberties, the Court would be the central significant actor. Its decisions would set a context for lower courts and the other actors in the governmental structure. Attention to individual rights and liberties would become the reason for the existence of the modern Supreme Court. In its construction of political theory, the concern with Civil Liberties was manifested in emerging notions of a twentieth-century liberalism. The Court's restraint in Economic areas, particularly the Ordinary Economic and Government as Litigant areas, was designed to permeate the judicial hierarchy and, in effect, restructured the business of state and federal courts.

THE EFFECT OF THE COURT'S TRANSFORMATION

The exigent agenda represents those issues that have been on the Court's docket for many years. Economic cases have made up the largest portion of the exigent agenda across the 1938-1973 period. The behavioral expectations for justices confronted with these cases are relatively straightforward: avoidance whenever possible. Issues are part of the exigent agenda because they no longer fit the policy designs or goals of the Court's membership. The Court would be expected to grant petitions for certiorari in exigent cases if there is significant lower court conflict, an important issue, and the Court has available agenda resources. Before the number of petitions for Court attention grew, the Court would intercede to settle lower court conflicts even if limited. Since the explosive growth of its docket, however, the Supreme Court normally waits for the conflict to spread to a number of circuits and percolate before it expends agenda space to intervene. If each of these conditions is not present, the Court is likely to deny the petition unless the case is an important landmark.

For those exigent agenda cases the Court feels compelled to accept, on the basis of the judicial role, certain patterns should be evident. The most likely scenario is issue suppression. The Court uses this device to isolate questions that caused conflict between lower courts. The Court must decide existing cases narrowly to avoid creating confusion or additional questions in that issue area. Even landmark decisions in these areas are likely to be used to close the agenda to such issues.

Consignment to the exigent agenda poses a dilemma for litigants due to the Court's relative disinterest. The strategy for litigants must incorporate lower court conflict. Litigants are not above fabricating or exaggerating such conflicts to capture Court attention.[27] Economic cases may need to involve important jurisdictional questions that are central to the administration of the judicial system in order to capture the Supreme Court's attention. Analysts have posited the existence of cues to assist justices in culling important cases from the mass of petitions. More recently, signals and indices that prompt justices and clerks to examine some petitions more closely have been identified. The existence of lower court disagreement and dissensus within a panel and the presence of the United States government as litigant are among such factors. The Economic cases cannot survive the screening process without them. At the same time, the presence of such conflicts or the government as petitioner (in Internal Revenue and United States as Litigant cases) is no guarantee the Court will grant review. A significant cue is the nature of the issue. Civil Liberties issues are most likely to be granted closer scrutiny, while Economic cases are normally rejected with little consideration.[28]

CONCLUSION

The construction of doctrine is a long-term, continuous enterprise with new questions arising in the wake of Court decisions. As a result, the dynamics of the agenda work to expand or maintain the agenda space granted that area. When the Court decides to reduce the access to the agenda for an issue area, it must alter these dynamics. Using a variety of tools and institutional rules, the Court has effectively disenfranchised a number of Economic policy areas over the past half-century.

From the time of the Stone Court through the early tenure of the Rehnquist Court, Economic issues have been treated as part of the institutional rules and norms of the Supreme Court. As a result, the acceptance of these cases is designed solely to head off problems in the judicial hierarchy. Goals have little direct real or symbolic impact on Economic issues. To the extent that goals open new volitional areas, the exigent agenda must be pared even further. In recent Court terms, the growth of the volitional agenda has forced deeper cuts in exigent agenda space.

It is clear that the process of agenda change is protracted. It may take a while for lower court judges to adapt to major doctrinal changes or the Supreme Court's more subtle changes in intention. As a result, there may be some confusion in the lower courts that the Supreme Court feels that it must settle before paring its consideration of that issue. The process of reducing the available agenda space may be accomplished in stages. The major landmark sets the context, the Court continues to address similar cases to resolve differences between lower courts, and it continues to pare the agenda space available for such cases.

This process, referred to as the dynamics of the agenda, is the diachronic manifestation of doctrinal and policy construction. Decisions emanate from the Court and beget further rounds of litigation that fulfill the notions of issue evolution. This has consequences for exigent and volitional issue areas. First, it serves to keep an issue that is no longer part of the Court's collective goals on the agenda. Second, the process by which policy emerges and evolves means it will take a while before volitional issues stake a long-term claim to agenda space.

The transition of Economic issues to the exigent agenda is an important component of the transformation of the Court's agenda to concerns with Regulation and Civil Liberties. The Court's attempts to limit the agenda allocation to Economic issues were undertaken with the purpose of reorienting its role as a policy maker. In substantive terms, the Supreme Court reached a collective decision that issues thrust upon them when the Court had mandatory jurisdiction no longer required extensive Supreme Court attention. Having discretion in case screening allowed the Court this luxury.

The Court used landmark decisions to send the important initial signals to its most attentive publics and used its other institutional tools to flesh out its new priorities. First, the Court revised the queueing process of case selection. Levels of demand for Court attention did not change markedly, but the Court's case selection policies changed as a prelude to its broader agenda building processes. By denying increasingly larger percentages of Economic and Internal Revenue petitions for certiorari, the Court was sending a message: these cases were no longer significant enough to consume a precious finite resource, agenda space.

The acceptance of Economic, Government Liability, and Internal Revenue cases was largely the function of lower court conflicts. The narrowness and unanimity of these decisions continued the process initiated with the landmark decisions that began to close the door to the agenda. The effect was to alter the existing dynamics of the agenda. The Ordinary Economic and State Regulation cases were remnants of a bygone era and their continued appearance on the agenda was clogging the Court's docket.

Substantively and procedurally, the Court's retreat from the Economic issues had important consequences. Substantively, a majority of the Court decided that such issues were no longer central to its concerns or goals. In this sense, institutional rules also intervened to block their access to the agenda. The responsibility for dealing with these issues could be delegated to other governmental agencies and the lower courts. The Court transferred these issues to its exigent agenda and intervened only when other policymakers required some direction. In terms of the factors identified by Rohde and Spaeth, the acceptance of such cases was dependent on certain conditions and situations. In fact, a number of similar fact situations that were formerly found under the rubric of Economic issues were converted to Civil Liberties issues that might raise civil due process concerns, freedom of expression questions, or equal protection. In previous periods, the Court would have used issue suppression to eliminate the constitutional question or narrow the Civil Liberties issue. Since the 1940s, the Court has been likely to confront these issues on broader constitutional grounds and transfer them to a different policy area.

Procedurally, there are important elements of rationality found in the Court's treatment of the Economic cases. The signals the Court sent in its case selection policies and the consistency and narrowness of its decisions percolated through the system. Eventually, the levels of demand declined in response to the Court's indifference to Economic issues.

Coupled with the growth of U.S. Regulation and Civil Liberties cases, the systematic decline of Economic cases suggests the viability of notions of diachronic agenda building. The use of the procedural mechanisms support a conceptualization of an institutional agenda that is dependent on past decisions and creates the conditions for future agenda building. The growth and changes in the standards for evaluating Regulation policy and the two stage growth of Civil Liberties offer supplementary evidence that agenda building and policymaking have a rational structure.

5

Federalism and U.S. Regulation: The Transitional Agenda

The scope and pace of agenda change in the Federalism and U.S. Regulation areas are distinctively different from those of the Economic and Civil Liberties policy areas. As an issue, Federalism has been a part of the Court's agenda from the earliest days of the republic. Although not as venerable, U.S. Regulation cases were gaining agenda prominence well before the advent of the New Deal. Regulation of the economy began before the Great Depression and the New Deal, but these economic and political events certainly accelerated the growth of regulatory activities. In turn, that spurred the growth of the Regulation agenda. Regulation profited from the demise of the Economic areas, capturing most of the space left vacant as the older economic issues receded. The expansion of the central government also exacted a toll on the residual powers traditionally reserved for state governments. As a result, agenda space was needed to resolve these modern Federalism issues.

Regulation is more of an externally derived policy area than Economic and Civil Liberties. Congressional legislation and bureaucratic rule making are responsible for the questions that eventually materialize in the courts. The task for the Supreme Court in most of these cases is to determine legislative intent, fill in the interstices of the law, and determine whether proper procedures have been followed. In other areas, like Civil Liberties, the justices are normally asked to interpret the Constitution and the Bill of Rights. In the Economic areas, the Court often had to determine the scope of the judiciary's power and the administration of the system. Earlier economic questions involved constitutional issues, but the decision in *Erie* was an exercise in issue suppression. In the wake of this decision, the Court narrowed its consideration of economic issues to avoid the constitutional issue whenever possible.

Federalism questions are also derived from external sources. Congressional legislation establishes new boundaries between the authority of the states and the central government. In addition, state regulations have the potential to impinge on the prerogatives of the central government. Decisions concerning possible federal preemption of certain activities and the reach of congressional power under the commerce clause of the Constitution have important implications for Federalism.

The New Deal and Footnote 4 of the *United States v. Carolene* case set up the situation for the dramatic expansion of agenda space and the dominance of Regulation on the agenda until the mid-sixties. On the face, such factors should have done the same thing for Federalism. It is important to set up the historical context that faced the justices just before and after the Court's retreat in 1937. This is necessary in order to establish the doctrinal and philosophical foundation the justices faced on the eve of the growth of the Federalism and Regulation agendas. This had an impact on the early construction of the agenda, the formulation of new theory and doctrine, and the multidimensional building of policy. The agenda and the policy trends of Federalism and U.S. Regulation reflect the transformation of U.S. politics and government.

DOCTRINE AND THEORY BEFORE FOOTNOTE 4

Federalism

The Articles of Confederation (1781-1789) granted little authority to the central government. The states held the preponderance of power, but this form of government proved unworkable for the emerging nation. The Constitution was designed to rectify many of the shortcomings of the previous form of government. In theory, the power of the states and the central government derive from a common source: the people. The boundaries between the central government and the states, like many provisions in the Constitution, are vague and require the intervention of the Supreme Court to draw the lines. The Court has not been completely consistent over time in its decisions and interpretations. For the most part, the Marshall Court decided these disputes in favor of the central government, buttressing the authority of Congress at the nascent stages of the Republic. In *McCulloch v. Maryland* 4 Wheaton 316 (1819), Chief Justice Marshall wrote the decision that expanded the power of the central government. In a number of decisions, most notably *Gibbons v. Ogden* 9 Wheaton 1 (1824), the Court gave full effect to the interstate commerce clause. An expansive reading of the commerce clause (Article I Section 8 of the Constitution) provides additional authority for the central government.

The Taney Court (1836-1863) and its successors sought to establish a new balance between the states and the central government. In *New York v. Miln* 11 Peters 102 (1837), the Taney Court upheld state police power. This began doctrinal development that gathered momentum in *Cooley v. Board of Wardens* 12 Howard 299 (1852), which upheld state law in the face of a commerce clause challenge. The Court turned to a doctrine of "dual federalism," which held that the two levels of government were coequal sovereignties.[1] This was partially a function of the fact that the Court's decisions were inconsistent, upholding some state regulations while others were struck down as violations of the commerce clause. The effect was to respect the police powers of the state, thus limiting the prerogatives of the central government.

The laissez-faire economic philosophies dominating the Court in the 1890-1937 period increasingly necessitated an interpretation to shackle federal regulations of the economy. Thus, the notion of dual federalism was ascendant and helped thwart the provisions of the early New Deal. In fact, the philosophical struggles between the ideological wings on the Court in the mid-1930s were largely a battle between the philosophies found in the dual federalism of the Taney Court and those under a doctrine of national supremacy similar to that advocated by the Marshall Court.[2] In a series of decisions that defined the "switch in time," the Roosevelt Court opted for the latter interpretation. This situation and subsequent membership changes altered the institutional goals of the Court.

U.S. Regulation

Institutional rules and norms structure decisionmaking and agenda building. The most significant institutional norm in the Supreme Court is the judicial role. The strictures of this role orientation certainly influence the decisions of the Court. On the most general level, the Court seldom directly overturns previous decisions. The precedents that governed the U.S. Regulation area on the eve of the Great Depression were not conducive to the further development of a regulatory state. The Court had maneuvered itself into potentially hazardous straits through these decisions. At this juncture, another institutional norm concerned with the Court's legitimacy--its ultimate resource--had come into play. A brief analysis of the nascent stages of the Regulation agenda and policy prior to the "Court-packing plan" is necessary for an understanding of the ultimate changes in the agenda.

By the time of the Great Depression, regulatory activity was not facing a welcome environment, particularly in the Supreme Court. Two important early regulatory statutes, the Interstate Commerce Act and the Sherman Act, were emasculated by the Supreme Court in a pair of decisions.[3] The Court's desire to protect laissez-faire policies was determinative, and any national attempts to tamper with that were suspect. A majority of the Court was guided by an economic philosophy that was Lockean in principle: That government is best that governs least. On a practical level, that meant regulations, which interrupted or adversely affected the prerogatives of business, were viewed in a harsh light.[4]

The economic policies of the Court were increasingly at variance with the legislation emanating from state legislatures and Congress. Such a conflict, involving the interference of unelected policymakers with the decisions of elected officials, presents a dilemma for democratically based government. Normatively, the notion of judicial activism, manifested by the Supreme Court's occasional willingness to substitute its judgment for legislative initiatives, is troubling. To imbue these policy goals with the imprint of the Constitution is to expand the perceived legitimacy of the actions.

In jurisprudential terms, the Court's economic decisions bore the heavy stamp of judicial activism. The Court needed the constitutional authority to attack the regulations. The commerce clause was available, but it had limits. Eventually, a majority of the justices found support for this position in the Fourteenth Amendment. The Court's creation of the doctrine of substantive due process served as a powerful weapon to combat regulatory schemes. In *Smyth v. Ames* 169 U.S. 466 (1898), the Court declared itself the final arbiter of the reasonableness of regulations and rates.[5] Using the Constitution as a weapon, the Court could now attack the substance of law that a majority deemed arbitrary or unreasonable.

By the late nineteenth century, the notion of due process could be used as a bar to economic regulations. The Supreme Court used this doctrine to protect the sanctity of contract. The intent was to assist business and cut the power of government to intervene in economic matters. The controversial use of substantive due process is frequently cited as a classic example of "government by judiciary" and judicial activism. The doctrine was flexible enough to allow a majority of the justices the power to invalidate whatever measures they deemed "arbitrary" or "capricious." Substantive due process was abetted by a narrow view of the commerce clause and federal authority.

Congressional statutes were not the only regulations subject to attack and judicial scrutiny. In addition, substantive due process reached into the states, invalidating state legislation and regulations that might adversely affect business.[6] Many states were attempting to regulate businesses within their jurisdictions but having very limited success. The commerce clause and the Tenth Amendment (which reserved for the states the expressed and implied power not exercised by the central government) were used by the Court to narrow the authority of the central government. This expanded the potential scope of power available to the states. The problem, however, was that states were threats to laissez-faire and the freedom of business. The Court used substantive due process to control the ever-expanding amount of legislation designed to regulate the economy and ensure freedom of contract and liberty in the marketplace.[7]

One of the primary justifications for the modern federal system is the notion of the states as laboratories for experiments in government. Once a state has some success, it can diffuse to neighboring states and eventually the central government may adopt the principles and procedures.[8] Regulatory schemes follow this pattern rather well. In constructing the building blocks of the regulatory machinery, Congress had some state blueprints to use. The Court also had experience in evaluating state regulations that could be brought to bear on U.S. Regulation cases and vice versa.

The emergence of a new issue is considered to be an organic extension of an existing issue when the novel issue is structurally related to the issue from which it is derived.[9] This occurs when the Court creates the new issue from the precedents and rationale that govern the existing area. U.S. Regulation was an organic extension of State Regulation litigation, utilizing similar tests and standards. New issues can also emerge indirectly from policy areas that are not directly related. The new issue may have a logical nexus to the old issue but evolve from different sources and doctrinal bases. This less-prevalent pattern can be referred to as collateral development. The development of Federalism doctrine has, at times, lent momentum and occasionally undermined U.S. Regulation litigation.

In a large sense, U.S. Regulation as a separate and distinct area of law was dependent on favorable decisions in Federalism cases. The growth of the regulatory state was impossible without a grant of power to create the mechanisms for regulation, such as statutory authority and administrative agencies. Those mechanisms were impossible without a fundamental reconceptualization in the scope and authority of the central government, which required the Court to assent to a new constitutional order that redrew the boundaries between the national and subnational governmental units. If the Court decided to adhere to traditional Federalism doctrines, federal regulatory policies would be severely hampered. As a consequence, the Court's Federalism decisions had important implications for the direction and scope of regulatory policies.

The unique place of the Supreme Court in the U.S. polity has spawned a number of controversies. The most significant among these concern the making of public policy by judges. The most basic controversy, as noted, involves judicial activism and restraint and whether, in normative terms, the Court should be a proactive policymaker. Regardless of the ultimate answer, it is clear that on the eve of the depression and into the New Deal, the Court was an activist policymaker. Scholarly debate also focuses on the question of whether the Supreme Court "follows the election returns." In other words, does the Court march in step with the dominant majority coalition in the other branches?

Robert Dahl maintains that each Court soon aligns itself with the elected branches of government. If the Court finds itself out of touch with majority sentiment, its legitimacy could be threatened by the other branches.[10] Prior to the Great Depression, it appears evident that the Court was generally in step with the dominant ideological and philosophical thought of the time. The Progressive era, however, began to threaten the presumed nexus between the laissez-faire attitudes and nineteenth-century liberalism of the Court and the attitudes of presidents and members of Congress who began supporting some forms of regulation.

In general, the Supreme Court has often lent significant support to the dominant capitalist ideology. Many decisions from the Marshall Court through the Great Depression were designed to buttress the power of U.S. business, an important component of early nation building. In the early period, the Court built a foundation for a national economy. Later, business and corporativism flourished under the watchful eye of the Supreme Court. By the time of the New Deal, there was a serious question whether the Court was indeed part of the new coalition now headed by Franklin Roosevelt.

The supposed connection between the Court and the elected branches of government makes sense on a procedural level. The president and the Senate--the elected branches of government theoretically responsive to public opinion--select the members of the Court. Of course, the justices often remain on the Court well past the tenure of the president who selected them. Ultimately, however, the elected branches have the opportunity to replace justices from the old coalition with members sympathetic to the new majority. In this fashion, the Court is remolded in the image of the new coalition. That process of conversion may take a long time.

A test of this connection between the unelected Court and the elected branches was provided by the Great Depression and the subsequent election of Roosevelt and a Democratic Congress. A conservative Court, a majority selected by Republican presidents from a previous partisan period and wedded to older notions of laissez-faire capitalism, was now set to review a hastily prepared package of programs and agencies designed to combat the Great Depression and regulate the U.S. economy to an unprecedented degree. The election of Roosevelt was (depending upon interpretation) the result of or the triggering mechanism in a partisan realignment based on issues involving the governmental regulation of the economy. Those same issues were responsible for the restructuring of the role of the U.S. Supreme Court.

THE FINAL DAYS: THE ASCENSION OF THE REGULATORY STATE

This issue of governmental regulation was the basis of a partisan realignment that fundamentally restructured the nature of the two political parties and the American political universe.[11] That realignment had important implications for the Supreme Court as well. A Court majority, supportive of economic principles of laissez-faire that were in disrepute, resisted and provoked the ire of the president. This controversy eventually resulted in Footnote 4, the symbol of the ultimate change in the Court's role, the nature of its decisions, and eventually in the Court's institutional agenda. The *Erie* decision closed one avenue (Economic cases), but the Court opened others (Federalism, U.S. Regulation, and Civil Liberties).

President Roosevelt and Congress conducted a hundred-day campaign to combat the economic catastrophe with a number of administrative agencies and regulations. The Regulation cases were related to the evolution of the Federalism issue area. The Court's regulatory policies could not emerge until the Court settled Federalism issues. The interrelationship between these issues is evident in the fact that the earliest Regulation cases were decided under the framework of Federalism. Once the Federalism questions in these cases were resolved in favor of the central government, it opened the legislative floodgates to a variety of regulations. Once the hurdle of Federalism had been cleared, the substance and effect of the regulatory schemes could be addressed on their own terms.

In its first decisions concerning the New Deal, the "Four Horsemen"--conservatives weaned in an earlier economic era--gained the support of Justice Roberts and Chief Justice Hughes in favor of a variant of dual federalism and substantive due process. By declaring the various legislative schemes unconstitutional, the Court did not address the substance of the regulations. Thus, Regulation cases were often blocked from consideration because the Court imposed a barrier, the Federalism question. The restrictive nature of the Court's decisions was the impetus for Roosevelt's Court Reorganization Plan and the machinations that occurred in its wake.[12]

The "switch in time that saved nine" occurred when Justice Roberts changed his vote and helped lead the Court to a new interpretation of Federalism, a decline in substantive due process, and ultimately to a consideration of the substance of the regulations designed to extricate the United States from the Depression. In a number of landmark decisions, the Court began upholding key elements of the New Deal such as the Wagner Act, the Agricultural Adjustment Act, and the Fair Labor Standards Act. These decisions had different effects on the two areas of law. The less restrictive interpretations that led to national supremacy were an initial signal that the Federalism agenda was about to begin a long-term decline. The impact on the Regulation cases was the opposite and quite profound. Once the initial barrier had been razed by the Court, hundreds of questions concerning the specifics of regulatory policies could be addressed by the Court on their own terms.

Before systematically addressing the processes that created the explosive growth of Regulation cases on the agenda and the ebb in

Federalism, we must trace the empirical trends of each of these areas. The Court's dramatic changes in 1937 did not occur on an empty slate. They must be placed in the context of the preceding terms and the dynamics that the changes altered. The decisions in 1937 and the next few terms instituted a new set of dynamics and unleashed a different set of forces that affected the scope and pace of agenda change.

In a number of important ways, Federalism and U.S. Regulation represent transitional agendas. Federalism served as the transitional policy area for the U.S. Regulation cases. Federalism questions had to be resolved before the Regulation cases could emerge. Regulation cases represented a transition from Economic cases to the Civil Liberties agenda procedurally and substantively. First, the U.S. Regulation cases assumed the agenda space formerly given to Economic cases. In a sense, Regulation held the space until the Civil Liberties issues fully emerged. Second, Regulation cases involved economic considerations, but in the context of governmental power. The expansion of governmental authority created an environment that would ultimately involve restrictions on individual rights and liberties, which would mandate judicial attention. More directly, narrow Economic concerns led to new types of regulatory activities. Indeed, the nature of regulatory activity has changed systematically over time to involve broader ranges of social and economic behavior. In turn, economic regulations and activities occasionally restricted free expression or were used to discriminate against certain groups.

FEDERALISM

Federalism cases involve a variety of specific issues concerning the boundaries between the central government and the states. Among the types of questions that populate this area are those concerning the commerce clause, preemption of regulations by the central government, and land and fiscal disputes between the central government and the states. The legislation that came from the New Deal had a dramatic impact on the nature of relations between the central government and subnational units. Attempts to combat a national economic catastrophe led to a vast expansion of the power of Congress under the authority conferred by the interstate commerce clause. The increased exercise of congressional power encroached on the prerogatives of the state governments and shrunk the scope of the Tenth Amendment. The redefinition of the boundaries between the states and central government was perhaps the most significant since the interpretations of the Marshall and Taney courts set and readjusted the lines of demarcation.

In the 1933-1937 terms, the Hughes Court found that Congress had exceeded its constitutional limits in its prescriptions for the Great Depression. In decisions like *Schechter Poultry Corp. v. United States* 295 U.S. 495 (1934 term) and *Carter v. Carter Coal Co.* 298 U.S. 238 (1935 term), the Court tore huge practical and symbolic holes in the New Deal and congressional power under the commerce clause by striking down the National Recovery Act and the Bituminous Coal Conservation Act, respectively. The amount of agenda space allocated to Federalism cases averaged about 15 percent per term during this period. The "switch in time" and subsequent decisions removed the Court from jeopardy. An important set of landmark decisions, including *National Labor Relations Board v. Jones & Laughlin Steel Company* 301 U.S. 1 (1936 term) and *United States v. Darby Lumber* 312 U.S. 100 (1940 term), expanded the interpretation of the commerce clause of the Constitution. In these decisions, the Court upheld congressional authority to establish the National Labor Relations Act and the Fair Labor Standards Act. Yet, "it took several years of subsequent decisions to make clear the full sweep of the new constitutional order."[13]

The sudden reversal of precedents did not reduce the agenda space available to Federalism cases, as Figure 5.1 demonstrates. In fact, in the short term, it appears to have had the opposite effect. This is not surprising given the fact that this represented a broad-scale reversal of doctrine. Lower courts, states, and Congress would need to determine the long-term direction of Court policy.

In general, Federalism cases received a significant amount of the Court's attention through the 1940s, averaging about 12 percent of the total agenda. Although there were a number of exceptions, the trend line was a slight incremental decline that became pronounced in the mid-1950s, around the time of the ascension of the Warren Court. Over the period of a few terms, the available agenda space for Federalism cases was more than halved from levels of 12 to 15 percent to an average of about 5 to 7 percent of the agenda space per term.

By the 1970s, however, Federalism began an agenda resurgence, claiming 10 to 15 percent of the agenda space. With the exception of 1938, the current levels are virtually equivalent to the height of Federalism in the first decade of the period of analysis. A major landmark decision, *National League of Cities v. Usery* 426 U.S. 833

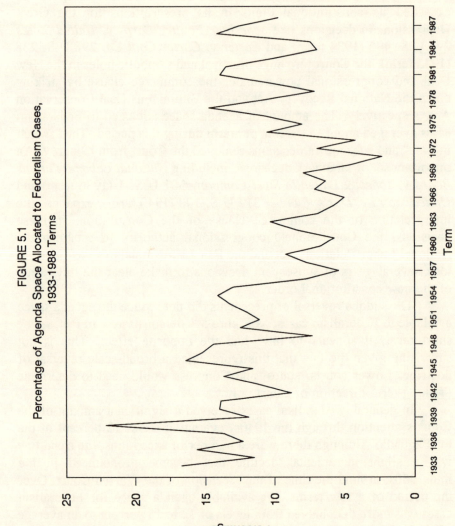

FIGURE 5.1
Percentage of Agenda Space Allocated to Federalism Cases,
1933-1988 Terms

(1975 term), appeared to reverse forty years of doctrinal consistency and seems to be responsible for this renaissance. In this case, the Court held that federal wage-and-hour requirements for state and municipal employees were unconstitutional violations of the commerce clause. There was an upturn that predated the *National League of Cities* decision, but it appeared to be the result of other disputes, most notably disagreements between the central government and the states over land.[14] Ultimately, the *National League of Cities* precedent turned out to be a temporary aberration rather than a full-blown reversal of doctrine. Justice Harry Blackmun, who was a member of the *National League of Cities* majority, switched his vote in subsequent cases to reestablish the previous status quo, although by a majority. The most noticeable effect of the Court's sudden inconsistency was an increase in the agenda space available to Federalism cases. In fact, as C. Herman Pritchett noted, "a substantial volume of litigation was also generated, some forty-two cases growing out of *Usery* being filed by 1978."[15]

The close division on the Court and the chance that the *National League of Cities* decision may have been a harbinger of future trends have apparently conspired to keep Federalism as a viable part of the Court's recent agenda. The Court retreated from the *National League of Cities* decision in a series of decisions in subsequent terms. Though the Court continued to state its adherence to the principles set out in *National League of Cities*, none of the subsequent decisions reached the same substantive conclusion.[16] This duality in the Court's decisions caused problems in application and in the interpretations of the confused lower courts. Ultimately, the Court expressly overruled *National League of Cities* in the *Garcia v. San Antonio Metropolitan Transit Authority* 469 U.S. 528 (1984 term) decision in allowing congressional regulation of the wages and hours of city transit workers. Thus, the Court took the unusual step of overruling a precedent within a decade and without extensive membership changes.

The *Garcia* case, which, like *National League of Cities*, involved the application of federal labor standards to municipal employees, appeared to settle the issue and suggested that the 1976 precedent was an aberration. A dissent in *Garcia* by then Associate Justice William Rehnquist, however, left open the possibility that the final word on the matter had not been said. Rehnquist predicted that the principles of federalism set out in *National League of Cities* would "in time again command the support of a majority of this Court."[17] Recent changes in the membership of the Court will determine whether Rehnquist was a prophet.

In general, the early landmark decision in *National League*, which was a function of an external situation (the Court-packing plan), began the process of restructuring the dynamics of agenda change. The Court proved its resolve over the next decade. The goals of the members consistently supported the authority of the central government and created a new set of institutional rules that aided the construction of doctrine and continued to pare the agenda. Changes in the goals of the members appeared to undermine the long-term consistency. A potential situation existed, in the form of Reagan's New Federalism and pressure from the states for a redress in the imbalance between these levels of government. *National League of Cities* appeared to be the landmark decision that might alter the existing dynamics. Institutional rules, however, provided a measure of restraint that convinced some of the justices to reinstitute existing doctrine.

Table 5.1, tracing the subareas across time, shows that the Federalism area is not composed of a monolithic set of cases. Questions concerning the commerce clause were involved in the most significant early set of cases, but they declined in the 1950s. Even though the Court seemed committed to the New Deal, a variety of other issues were raised in litigation. The most notable group of cases concerned the ability of the states to conduct their economic affairs in view of the encroachment on their powers that was sanctioned by the Supreme Court. Two sets of questions were involved in these cases and they have different life cycles. The first, involving the viability of state regulation and taxes, held agenda space until the early 1950s and have since declined significantly. The later cases, regulations of the federal government that might preempt state regulations, have reached their highest levels of agenda space since the late 1960s. This subarea was the only one to grow during this period as Federalism was reaching its lowest levels of Court attention.

While the Federalism cases declined in agenda space, there were some interesting shorter-term patterns. The long-term decline was part of the structural changes in Federalism. In the short term, there was a relationship between the Federalism and Civil Liberties cases. In the Court terms immediately preceding the expansion of the space allocated Civil Liberties, the agenda space allocated to Federalism grew. This suggests the existence of an on-off cycle and the use of paired cases. The Court apparently accepts and decides a number of Federalism cases concurrently. That procedure allows the Court the freedom to ignore

Table 5.1 Number of Cases and Percentage of Agenda Space Allocated to Selected Federalism Subareas, 1933-1987 Terms

Subareas		1933-1937	1938-1942	1943-1947	1948-1952	1953-1957	1958-1962	1963-1967	1968-1972	1973-1977	1978-1982	1983-1987	Total (n)
Interstate Commerce	(n)	33	32	27	19	8	12	16	4	17	25	15	208
	(%)	4.2	4.2	4.1	3.7	1.6	2.0	2.4	0.6	2.0	3.1	2.0	
State Taxation/ Licensing		31	24	14	14	4	7	5	7	15	7	7	135
		3.9	3.1	2.1	2.8	0.8	1.2	0.8	1.0	1.8	0.9	0.9	
Taxation U.S. v. State		7	10	5	4	7	2	3	0	2	4	2	46
		0.9	1.3	0.8	0.8	1.4	0.3	0.5	0.0	0.2	0.5	0.3	
Labor Relations		10	19	15	7	12	6	5	0	2	5	10	91
		1.3	2.5	2.3	1.4	2.4	1.0	0.8	0.0	0.2	0.6	1.3	
Full Faith & Credit		9	10	12	9	6	1	6	1	0	5	2	61
		1.1	1.3	1.8	1.8	1.2	0.2	0.9	0.1	0.0	0.6	0.3	
Regulation U.S. v. State		17	5	8	4	9	11	6	17	23	28	18	146
		2.1	0.7	1.2	0.8	1.8	1.9	0.9	2.4	2.7	3.5	2.4	
Navigable Water & Land Disputes		2	1	3	1	2	4	3	7	14	11	5	53
		0.3	0.1	0.5	0.2	0.4	0.7	0.5	1.0	1.7	1.4	0.7	

such cases during the next term while letting its recent decisions percolate through the system. In addition, it frees agenda space that can be used by the Court to attack another area in a more systematic fashion by concentrating its agenda resources.

FEDERALISM AND ISSUE TRANSFORMATION

The reduction in the agenda space allocated to Federalism is a consequence of two Court processes: the eventual consistency of the Court's decisions and issue transformation. The institutional goals of the Court clearly supported the expansion of the central government. The Federalism decisions were a prelude to the Regulation cases and the expansion of the regulatory state. The Court-packing plan and the Great Depression provided the situation or policy window for the change. Institutional rules and norms were stacked against this new interpretation of Federalism, but the confluence of the goals and situation created the wedge that interrupted the effects of the existing norms and rules.

The consistency of decisions has an impact on the future of the agenda. The more consistent a set of decisions, the clearer the messages that are sent to lower courts, states, legislators, and implementers. This reduces the Supreme Court's need to hear large numbers of future cases. During the later Hughes, Stone, and Vinson courts 82 percent of the Federalism cases were decided in favor of the central government. For decades, decisions concerning the commerce clause overwhelmingly supported the power of Congress and the central government. When the Court introduced elements of uncertainty in the *National League of Cities* decision, the agenda reopened. When the Court seemed to reverse four decades of decisions, a number of cases were docketed to determine whether this was an aberration or a new trend.

In the wake of the initial decision upholding the constitutionality of the National Labor Relations Board (NLRB), there were a number of cases searching for limits or loopholes in the new doctrine. When no loopholes were found, the agenda space was pared except for the occasional misinterpretation by a lower court. A similar process surrounded the Fair Labor Standards Act. In his opinion, Justice Stone asserted that there would be little need for extended discussion of the constitutional issue. A number of statutory issues remained, however, and captured Court attention for decades. In effect, though, these were not Federalism cases but substantive Regulation cases. This process of issue transformation spread across a number of domains.

The Federalism issue was a threshold that had to be navigated before U.S. Regulation could fully emerge as an independent issue in its own right. If the Court stuck to its doctrines of substantive due process and dual federalism, regulation policies would have been sharply limited. Once the federalism barrier was removed by the consistent interpretation that favored national supremacy, a plethora of Regulation issues could be addressed on their own merits. The landmark decisions in these areas were significant constitutional cases; the subsequent decisions in these areas were statutory. In this fashion, the Court limited the scope of its review and consideration of these issues. The effects were significant: the beginning of a long-term decline in Federalism and the explosive growth of agenda space granted to Regulation.

The decisions in the Federalism area had other significant indirect effects as well. Doctrine in this area had implications for each of the areas of Civil Liberties. In a sense, a body of decisions in the Due Process, Substantive Rights, and Equality policy domains occurred in the context of Federalism doctrine or at least were collateral development for individual rights doctrine. Once the Court upheld the prerogatives of the central government in economic and regulation cases, there was pressure to nationalize the protections of the Bill of Rights.[18] The Court did so with the religion clause of the First Amendment just after the New Deal Federalism decisions. The Warren Court continued to extend and maintain the authority of the central government in economic matters. Coincidentally, the Warren Court presided over the incorporation of significant portions of the procedural amendments of the Bill of Rights. The *Brown v. Board of Education* decision (1953 term) was the most significant of a number of Equality decisions that sanctioned the behavior of states in race relations. The power of government was also affected by decisions that expanded the scope of Civil Rights Act (Section 1983) litigation in allowing individuals to sue state officials in federal courts for depriving individuals of "any rights, privileges, and immunities secured by the Constitution and laws."[19]

Similar, more recent dynamics in doctrinal development are also evident. The Burger Court began to take steps to redress the imbalance between the levels of government in its economic decisions. In Civil Liberties, the Burger and Rehnquist courts have followed a similar pattern: The states are being afforded more discretion in individual rights. In most instances, this increased authority has allowed states to impose restrictions on the exercise of civil rights and liberties. In a few areas, however, states have been permitted to extend individual rights beyond the scope of the federal government's protection.

In a very real sense, the decisions that extended Due Process, Substantive Rights, and Equality protections and the recent decisions that have limited these advances are important Federalism decisions. In addition to delineating the boundaries between the liberties of individuals and the authority of the government, a number of the decisions affected Federalism in that they determined the power of subnational governments to regulate conduct. The cases are categorized as Civil Liberties due to the constitutional provisions and the nature of the rights. They are discussed in Chapter 6.

U.S. REGULATION

The U.S. Regulation policy area was a legislative and executive creation that flourished during the New Deal. Massive attempts to combat the depression created numerous programs, expanded the bureaucracy, and created the essence of big government. The area involves economic regulation of private business by the central government. Among the specific regulatory activities that make up this area are labor relations, commerce, securities, trade, antitrust, banking, environment, energy, and bankruptcy regulation.

The growth of the area was dependent on the Federalism decisions of the 1930s. Many of the nascent regulations were challenged as unconstitutional, alleged to be beyond the authority of Congress under the interstate commerce clause. As noted, the Court, led by the Four Horsemen, struck down a number of the early regulations. After the conflict with Roosevelt over the Court Reorganization Plan, the Court began to uphold similar regulations and congressional authority.

With the basic questions resolved in favor of the authority of the central government, the issues before the Court narrowed. As a consequence, the concern turned to statutory interpretation, the viability of specific rules and regulations, and the policies of administrative agencies. As Figure 5.2 shows, the U.S. Regulation area flourished on the agenda, becoming by the 1940s the largest consumer of agenda space. Regulation cases reached their peak in the 1944 term, occupying 43 percent of the agenda space.

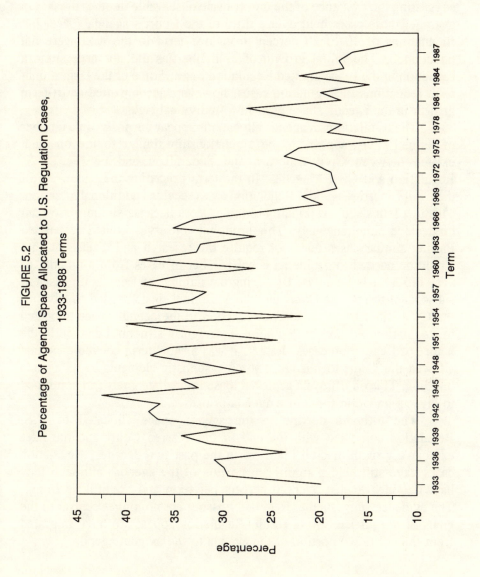

FIGURE 5.2

Percentage of Agenda Space Allocated to U.S. Regulation Cases,

1933-1988 Terms

Over the next two decades, there were significant year-to-year oscillations in the agenda space granted to Regulation cases, again suggesting the existence of the on-off cycle observable in other areas. On average, these cases held over a third of the Court's agenda space, but fluctuations of 10 to 20 percent from one term to the next were not uncommon. The initial growth of civil liberties did not necessitate a reduction in the space granted Regulation cases. Some of the largest one-term reductions in Regulation cases, however, accompanied short-term growth in the agenda space granted to individual rights.

The oscillations in agenda allocations appear purposive in a number of terms. There appears to be a relationship similar to the one that existed between Civil Liberties and Federalism and between U.S. Regulation and Civil Liberties. In the term preceding the expansion of the Civil Liberties agenda, Regulation cases received additional attention. This fact lends some rationality to the process because similar cases can be decided simultaneously. This grouping conserves limited resources: Pairing similar cases does not require the research and discussion that would be needed to decide an equal number of cases from a number of very different issue areas. By paring the number of Regulation cases in subsequent terms, the Court had the additional space needed to advance the Civil Liberties agenda. The reduction in the agenda space allocated to Regulation did not, at this point, represent a structural change in the nature of Regulation cases. Rather, it was a short-term convenience that allowed the Court to introduce some systematic elements to its agenda building. This on-off cycle achieved these immediate goals and continued to lay a foundation for future agenda priorities.

The ultimate decline in the agenda space allocated to U.S. Regulation coincided with the end of the Warren Court and the later explosive growth of civil liberties. In the past two decades, Regulation cases have still held a significant portion of the agenda, although they have declined to just over 20 percent per term and are still declining. The evidence suggests that Regulation issues are no longer central to the goals of the justices. As a result, Regulation appears to have migrated from the volitional portion of the agenda to the exigent agenda.

REGULATION AND ISSUE TRANSFORMATION

The U.S. Regulation area involved a number of transitions. First, there was the transition from constitutionally based Federalism issues to statutory Regulation concerns. Second, within the general Regulation domain, individual-level, traditional types of regulation issues were displaced by newer, broader-gauge regulations. In other words, narrower economic regulation was supplanted or broadened by regulatory schemes that encompassed social activity as well. Third, some Regulation cases and issues spawned Civil Liberties cases and areas. A large, active government that can regulate business can also regulate individual freedoms. The revamping of tenets of liberalism would be transferred from Regulation to individual rights. Finally, Regulation cases have migrated from the volitional to the exigent agenda. As a consequence, the nature of the cases and the Court's method of selecting and evaluating them have changed. Each of these transitions has important consequences for the process of agenda building and agenda change.

Perhaps more importantly, each of these transitions was related to the transformation of American politics, the Supreme Court's role, and the nature of the decisions. By consistently upholding the authority of the central government, the Court recognized the dominant political and economic needs and provided for the growth of the regulatory agenda and regulatory schemes. As regulations became more sweeping in their application, they crossed policy boundaries. Increasingly, the imposition of rules and regulations raised First Amendment, equal protection, or civil due process concerns, forcing the Court to construct doctrine and deal with those concerns. As these types of cases supplemented the Civil Liberties agenda and the Court's role as the appropriate forum for balancing the rights of individuals, the justices had to clear agenda space to continue this work. The only issue area with sufficient agenda resources that could be transplanted was Regulation.

Exit from Federalism

Landmark decisions were responsible for the process of issue transformation that triggered a growth in U.S. Regulation and the beginning of a decline in Federalism. The early U.S. Regulation cases came before the Court not as challenges to the substance of the specific regulation, but as challenges to the authority of Congress under the commerce clause to create the regulation. These early cases focused on the power of the central government in a federal system. In *National Labor Relations Board v. Jones & Laughlin Steel Co.* (1936 term), which also opened the agenda to labor relations cases, the Court began the process of converting Federalism cases into issues concerning the substance of the regulation. This process continued in a number of other areas. *United States v. Darby Lumber Co.* (1940 term) helped close Federalism while it opened a different issue of labor relations. Other important decisions had similar constricting effects on Federalism, while opening the agenda to other new areas.

These major landmark decisions served concurrent functions. They were responsible for the construction of nascent Federalism doctrine because past policies were being abandoned. At the same time, these cases had multidimensional components that led the Court to separate the issues and treat them on their own terms. In this regard, *Jones & Laughlin* also served as a labor relations case, helping to define the core issue of this area. With the core issue decided by these landmark decisions, which were based on constitutional grounds, later elaborative cases could be contested on statutory grounds.

This transition from constitutional to statutory grounds was manifested in another direction as well. Once the core issue had been settled, questions turned to the power of administrative agencies and the nature of the regulations. The Court turned its attention to the proper role of the nascent agencies created by the New Deal. A broad range of discretion was granted to these agencies in the charters that created them. The rise of a positive administrative state began the genesis of "government by expert." Congress and the Court reserved some authority to review the actions of administrative agencies. This placed the Court in a difficult position, balancing the prerogatives of Congress and the administrative agencies. In a sense, Congress served as the court of appeals between the administrative agency and the Supreme Court.[20]

The Expansion of Regulatory Concerns

The second transition involves the nature of regulations and supports the notion of policy emergence. In attacking the ills of the economic infrastructure, Congress and the president attempted to regulate major segments of the economy. When new issues arise in Congress, they tend to be broad and nonroutine and consume significant agenda space. To combat this problem, Congress divides the issue and parcels out components to specialists. This allows issues to be expedited, eliminates legislative bottlenecks, and expands the agenda space. This is what occurred during the New Deal as the president and Congress began the process of expanding regulation into a number of different areas. The problems that plagued the nation were seen as endemic to the economic order and involved the entire range of economic activity. Remedies would have to be broadly based and would need to involve the entire scope of business activity.

The successful opening of a policy window pushes a specific issue on to the decision agenda. Perhaps more significantly, it may serve as the impetus for other policy windows that will introduce related issues to the decision agenda. Empirically, such spillovers were found in Congress as it expanded its scope to involve a variety of related issues.[21] Congress grafted tested regulatory schemes and principles onto related issues. The evidence bears this out on two levels. On one level, "the expansion of concerns," the success in one subarea like labor relations could be transplanted to another subarea like antitrust or commerce. On the second level, "the dispersion of attention," the decisions in one narrow subarea within labor relations could be used in adjacent subareas.

The rise of an issue can create a recognition among members of Congress, interest groups, and regulatory agencies that other areas merit attention. Initial success causes the most powerful spillovers. Policy entrepreneurs are encouraged to rush to the next issue. New Deal legislation that spread across a variety of domains resembles the expansion of concerns and is a classic example of a powerful initial spillover.[22] Once a breakthrough occurred in a new issue area, it led to a surge of activity in related areas.

The evolution of congressional issues has continued to assume broadly based forms.[23] Recently, a noteworthy example of the dispersion of regulatory activities involves the amplification of safety legislation. The passage of auto safety legislation led to inspection of meat (1967), poultry (1968), and fish (1971); regulation of diet pills (1968); toy safety (1967); fire prevention (1968); coal mining safety (1969); and occupational safety (1974). A broad underlying consumer-protection dimension seems to fit these issues. The deregulation movement followed a similar pattern, an initial breakthrough and spillovers.[24] The success of entrepreneurs in aviation and airline deregulation created an impetus that led to deregulation in a number of other areas.

Similar processes also occurred in Civil Liberties. There was one notable difference between the existence of these processes in the Regulation sector and in Civil Liberties. In the latter, the Court determined the scope and pace of change. Using landmark decisions and issue transformation, the justices were able with the assistance of litigants to sequence change to a significant degree. In U.S. Regulation cases, however, the processes by which regulations expanded and dispersed to other areas were not Court dictated but were dictated by external actors. The president set the agenda for many of these regulations, Congress passed the programs, and administrative agencies and regulatory bodies implemented them. This placed the Court firmly in a reactive mode, but its decisions ensured that it would be a participant nonetheless.

The Supreme Court's activities involved two different but related directions. First, the Court had to reverse existing decisions limiting regulatory activities. In areas like antitrust and commerce, congressional legislation had been on the books almost a half-century. The problem was that previous Courts had emasculated statutes like the Sherman Antitrust Act.[25] The Court had to reinstitute the power and authority of these dormant statutes. Second, the Court had to legitimate the newer regulatory schemes developed under the New Deal. The Court's supportive decisions encouraged Congress and the president to continue to open new areas within each of the domains. The expansion was created by Congress and abetted by the Court.

The growth and decline of some of the subareas that make up the U.S. Regulation area seem related to broad trends in the environment. Table 5.2 shows the ebbs and flows in the most significant subareas within the broader U.S. Regulation policy area. The first two subareas to arise--bankruptcy and patents--had strong connections to the Economic issues that were about to decline in importance. These two subareas shared many of the structural elements and principles found in the Ordinary Economic cases. The types of litigants involved, the nature of the disputes, and the limited impact of decisions in bankruptcy and patent cases were more like the Ordinary Economic cases than the later Regulation cases.

Empirically, the agenda space allocated to these subareas had parallel declines to those in the Economic areas. Bankruptcy cases made up the largest portion of the Regulation area in the 1933-1942 decade. Clearly, this was related to the economic catastrophe of the Great Depression. In the first decade of the analysis (1933-1942), just under half the patent cases and almost two-thirds of the total number of bankruptcy cases were decided by the Court. By the early 1950s bankruptcy cases captured an average of less than one percent of the agenda space. Patents and copyright cases also were declining, with an average of less than one percent of the agenda space since the early fifties. As with the Economic cases, the Court found other fora, such as Bankruptcy Court and the Court of Patent Appeals, for these cases. The

Table 5.2 Number of Cases and Percentage of Agenda Space Allocated to Selected U.S. Regulation Subareas, 1933-1987 Terms

Subareas	1933-1937	1938-1942	1943-1947	1948-1952	1953-1957	1958-1962	1963-1967	1968-1972	1973-1977	1978-1982	1983-1987	Total (n)
Bankruptcy	47 / 5.9	32 / 4.2	23 / 3.5	8 / 1.6	3 / 0.6	5 / 0.8	10 / 1.4	4 / 0.5	6 / 0.7	5 / 0.6	4 / 0.5	167
Patents/ Copyrights	29 / 3.7	33 / 4.3	21 / 3.2	11 / 2.2	5 / 1.0	4 / 0.7	8 / 1.2	7 / 1.0	5 / 0.6	4 / 0.5	3 / 0.4	130
Commerce	25 / 3.2	33 / 4.3	30 / 4.5	19 / 3.7	21 / 4.3	21 / 3.5	26 / 3.9	10 / 1.4	7 / 0.8	6 / 0.6	3 / 0.4	201
Energy	12 / 1.5	10 / 1.3	6 / 0.9	10 / 2.0	7 / 1.4	10 / 1.7	12 / 1.8	5 / 0.7	10 / 1.2	11 / 1.4	8 / 1.1	101
Workers	29 / 3.7	28 / 3.7	24 / 3.6	35 / 6.9	38 / 7.7	40 / 6.7	20 / 3.0	11 / 1.5	10 / 1.2	20 / 2.5	12 / 1.6	267
Antitrust	13 / 1.6	19 / 2.5	24 / 3.6	17 / 3.3	18 / 3.7	23 / 3.9	41 / 6.2	26 / 3.6	26 / 3.1	16 / 2.0	20 / 2.7	243
Labor Relations	5 / 0.6	39 / 5.1	59 / 8.9	34 / 6.7	44 / 9.0	72 / 12.1	53 / 8.0	39 / 5.4	46 / 5.5	45 / 5.7	28 / 3.8	464
Securities	2 / 0.3	2 / 0.3	7 / 1.1	3 / 0.6	5 / 1.0	1 / 0.2	6 / 0.8	6 / 0.7	15 / 1.7	13 / 1.6	12 / 1.6	72
Environment	3 / 0.4	0 / 0.0	0 / 0.0	1 / 0.2	0 / 0.0	1 / 0.2	1 / 0.2	5 / 0.7	17 / 1.2	15 / 2.0	12 / 1.6	55

Supreme Court has delegated decisionmaking in these issue areas to other actors.

The Stone and Vinson courts presided over the growth of increasingly broader regulations, moving from more individual-level concerns like bankruptcy and patents to collective regulations involving labor relations, unions, energy, and antitrust. The Warren Court encouraged even more sweeping regulations that included social behavior. In this vein, securities regulation has been a recent addition to the agenda. Though the percentage of agenda space is relatively small, environmental regulation cases, also broadly based, have gained greater agenda space in the last fifteen terms. Both of these subareas grew despite the overall declines in U.S. Regulation in the past decade.

Three sets of these Regulation cases (antitrust, commerce, and labor relations) merit particular attention. These are the three largest subareas within the Regulation area. The pattern of commerce cases has also been a consistent allocation of agenda space and a sharp decline in the last two decades that once again reflects the overall decline in Regulation. After an initial period of growth, antitrust has retained a consistent portion of agenda space, except for one period in the early 1960s, when the number of cases accepted rose dramatically. In fact, the most significant growth in antitrust occurred during the Warren Court. This was probably a result of the policies of the Warren Court, which was suspicious of the growth of business and tendencies toward monopolization. In the last decade, the percentage of antitrust cases has declined significantly, paralleling the decline of the entire Regulation area.

Labor relations litigation includes a variety of individual issues involving unions, the Wagner Act, and the Fair Labor Standards Act, among others. In totality, labor relations is the largest single area of Regulation litigation. After a very modest beginning, the sharp growth of labor cases was, in large measure, responsible for the overall expansion of the Regulation agenda. As with antitrust, the peak was reached during the tenure of the sympathetic Warren Court. Similarly, by the late sixties, labor relations began to attract decreasing agenda space and that translated to the overall decline of Regulation, especially during the Burger Court. This is not surprising in view of the fact that the Burger Court was less supportive of labor.

During the Warren and Burger courts, a different type of transition was occurring. The types of regulatory policies emerging from Congress and the administrative agencies had changed significantly. The New Deal regulations tended to be economic in scope, focusing on markets, rates, and the obligation to serve. At their inception, these economic regulations were controversial. The partisan realignment of the 1930s was based, in part, on these types of issues. Soon such policies became widely accepted, even by the Republican party, which had initially opposed such ventures.

The policies of the Warren Court and the programs of the Great Society were responsible for introducing other elements into regulatory schemes. The Warren Court was willing to go well beyond the simple economic effects of regulations to the social consequences. Congressional and executive policies also sought a variety of means of combating poverty. As a result, a new series of regulatory agencies, like the Occupational Safety and Health Administration (OSHA) and the Environmental Protection Agency (EPA), were created and some existing agencies, like the NLRB and the Food and Drug Administration (FDA), were given different, broader charges. Regulations emanating from these and other agencies were social in scope, involving the conditions under which goods and services were produced.[26] Such regulations cut across industries and traditional boundaries and evoked considerable controversy both on and off the Supreme Court.[27]

The transition from the volitional portion of the agenda to the exigent agenda, to be examined below, occurred a few years before the deregulation movement reached its policy window. The normal expectation of an external shock to the system, like widespread deregulation policies, is that the Court's agenda would be reopened. Regulation as an issue might be expected to move back to the volitional agenda. That transition has not occurred to date. In one sense, that is not surprising. It takes a while for issues to percolate in external fora and in the lower courts before the Supreme Court gets directly involved. The Court may be allowing deregulation to evolve and let other actors stake policy positions before intervening.

In fact, there is some evidence the Court may be moving toward a reconceptualization of such issues that may eventually restore this issue to the center of the Court's concerns. Justice Scalia, an expert on regulation and a proponent of deregulation, may be instrumental in altering the goals of the Court. He may be able to serve as a policy entrepreneur, the key type of actor who can work toward breaking the inertia of existing institutional rules that keep U.S. Regulation issues on the exigent agenda. Further changes in the Court's membership may create a policy stream that facilitates the movement of Regulation cases.

Such a movement may be underway, but will probably take a number of terms to manifest itself fully.

Transition: Economic to Regulation to Civil Liberties

The early Regulation cases resemble the Economic cases, particularly the Ordinary Economic and Internal Revenue cases, in the individual nature of many of the disputes. Changes in society and the nature of business relationships were certainly partially responsible for this transition. A different conception of the role of the Court, the judicial view of liberalism, and changing ideas about governmental-business relations also contributed to the different form of economic issues. The intervention of the governmental component was responsible for a transition from the Economic issue and the emergence of a broadly based U.S. Regulation area that eventually led to the evolution of a number of specific substantive areas of U.S. Regulation, like labor relations, commerce, energy, communications, and securities regulation.

As noted, new issues seldom emerge full blown. Rather, the emergence of a new issue is tied inexorably to the development of another issue at a later stage of the evolutionary process. Many of these new issues are found when there is a series of structurally different issues involved in a single case. Before a new issue can emerge, be evaluated on its own terms, and doctrine can be constructed for that area, the multiple issues must be separated.

Each of the three areas that constitute the broader Civil Liberties domain was affected by cases involving U.S. Regulation. Labor relations cases, often involving strikes, were transformed into First Amendment freedom-of-expression cases. In fact, such cases spurred the early growth of the Substantive Rights agenda. Cases like *Hague v. C.I.O.* 307 U.S. 496 (1938 term), which overturned a prohibition against assemblies on public streets, and *Thornhill v. Alabama* 310 U.S. 88 (1939 term), involving picketing, helped define freedom-of-expression doctrine between the world wars. The additional freedoms granted workers in the course of Regulation litigation led unions and workers to more drastic action and led states to restrictions involving the First Amendment. Cases concerning the Federal Communications Commission (FCC) might also implicate First Amendment concerns.

Due Process decisions also arose from Regulation cases. Questions and procedures concerning wiretapping fell under the Federal Communications Act, a broadly based regulatory statute. The Court began a process of converting them to questions more closely tied to the standards used to evaluate search-and-seizure issues. Some early civil due process cases, involving the right to an attorney in such cases and general procedural issues, were also raised in the context of a Regulation case. The ultimate emergence of civil due process, an issue at the intersection of Due Process and Regulation, occurred a few decades later.

Although the Court's decisions in Due Process and Substantive Rights during this period were not overly protective of individual rights, the justices of the Stone and Vinson courts were beginning to protect the rights of minorities. Some Equality issues arose from cases that ostensibly involved Regulation questions. The preponderance of these cases were labor relations issues involving alleged discrimination against blacks. Although the Court often limited the scope of its relief, it did recognize that some practices were discriminatory. Relatedly, cases from the Equal Employment Opportunity Commission involved regulations against discrimination.

It should not be surprising that Regulation cases were responsible for spawning some individual rights issues and cases. The growth of the regulatory state and the power and influence of government could not easily be confined to the economic sector. As the authority of government grew, it spilled over into individual rights and liberties. The government might well flex its new muscles and restrict the rights of unpopular groups and individuals. In turn, the Court had to implement the designs of Footnote 4--restraint in economic and regulation matters and more proactive concern for possible abuses of individual liberties and civil rights.

Transition from the Volitional Agenda to the Exigent Agenda

The landmark decisions that reconstructed the nature of Federalism and allowed the positive regulatory state to emerge narrowed the scope of Regulation review. The Supreme Court has increasingly become a forum for constitutional issues, but Regulation cases have bucked the trends and been decided on statutory grounds.[28] Such processes of issue narrowing normally accompany Court efforts to leave a policy area. In fact, the opposite occurred--the agenda opened up dramatically. Part of this is due to the fact that the issue of Regulation was being fought on a number of fronts simultaneously. Decisions in one area were having effects on other areas that already existed and led to the creation of new, related areas.

Legislative expansion processes were largely responsible for the growth of the Regulation agenda. Many regulatory issues came out of Congress quickly and filled the Court's dockets; the goals of the members were relatively clear and consistent; and a strong majority supported the regulation of the economy. In fact, many of the new justices were chosen by President Roosevelt primarily because of their views on the regulation issues. On a philosophical level, the justices followed judicial restraint and increasingly deferred to administrative agencies. A new set of institutional rules would govern such cases for the foreseeable future.

The emergence and growth of these issues was abetted by the activities of two groups of litigants. First, business groups apparently did not understand the process or properly read the clear signs.[29] These groups continued to litigate and bring cases to the Court. These actions were detrimental because a number of the regulations they challenged were legitimated by the Court. Strategically, these groups erred in raising new issues they could not win. On the other side, the solicitor general and the administrative agencies had or were learning the skills that translated to successful litigation. With the assistance of the policy entrepreneurs on the Court, these government litigants were able to sequence cases and build policy and doctrine. The result was burgeoning agenda space for Regulation cases and the growth of the positive (social welfare) state.

Through the Stone, Vinson, and Warren terms, the stated reason for accepting 20 percent of the Regulation petitions granted was conflict in the lower courts, the core of the exigent agenda. Most of the Regulation cases were taken to settle the question or because the issue was important. As a result, the preponderance of these cases were accepted to fulfill the goals of the members of the Court and therefore were part of the Court's volitional agenda. On the individual level, the Regulation cases during the 1938-1968 period fit on the B and E scales, involving justices' attitudes toward business and economic issues.[30] Rohde and Spaeth refer to these cases as part of the "New Dealism" dimension, involving economic issues in a context of governmental authority.[31] The ideological goals of the members of the Court appeared to explain the preponderance of the nonunanimous economic decisions during the Stone, Vinson, and Warren courts. Deference to the decisions of administrative agencies was also an important component of the

Regulation cases. Furthermore, individual levels of consistency seemed to hold across time. These behavioral patterns continued through the early Burger Court, though harbingers of change were developing.

The Hughes Court ultimately legitimated the positive state and the authority of the central government to regulate the economy. This opened or triggered the growth of the individual areas of regulation policy. The Court narrowed the consideration of the cases to statutory grounds. In subsequent terms, the Court had a number of precise questions to address. During the tenure of the Stone Court, the justices largely deferred to the administrative agencies. The Court decided over 70 percent of the cases in favor of the government. The Vinson Court retreated a bit, deciding 62 percent of the cases in favor of governmental authority. This favoritism is attributable to two factors: changes in the goals of the Court and the process of policy evolution. An influx of new members who were somewhat less supportive of Regulation changed decision patterns marginally. Complicating the process was the fact that the cases reaching the Vinson Court were more likely to raise more borderline questions and required the balancing that was the trademark of the Vinson Court.

The decisions of the Warren Court in U.S. Regulation reflected the tone and tenor of its policies in Civil Liberties. The Warren Court used egalitarian principles to govern its decisions concerning the influence of various regulatory schemes. During the 1953-1968 period, the Court increasingly supported the underdogs, whether they were involved in disputes concerning individual rights or economic matters. The Warren Court pursued a liberal, populist ideology in deciding Regulation cases. In contrast to the Burger and Rehnquist courts, the Court under Earl Warren was concerned with the qualitative rather than the quantitative aspects of regulatory policies.

During its tenure, the Warren Court decided 72 percent of the cases in favor of the government. Table 5.3 shows that levels of support varied significantly among the various areas of Regulation. Except for bankruptcy cases, the Warren Court was largely supportive of regulations and deferred to the various administrative agencies in its decisions. This level of support masked some ideological traits. The Warren Court was more likely to support agency decisions when the agency was anti-business or prolabor.[32] In its decisions, the Court did not weigh solely the economic evidence that was raised in the cases. The goals and values of the individual members and the institution tended to reflect a distrust of business. The Warren Court incorporated social values as well as

Table 5.3　Percentage of Proregulation Decisions in Selected U.S. Regulation Subareas, 1953-1986 Terms

Subareas	Warren Court (1953-1969)	Burger Court (1969-1986)
Antitrust	70	50
Bankruptcy	39	42
Securities Regulation	94	34
Environment	85	41
Commerce	59	90
Energy	77	68
Telecommunications	57*	61*
Labor Relations	63	52
Copyright	83	40

*Relatively small number

economic concerns in its calculations. In general, the Court treated the claims of the solicitor general, the administrative agencies, and the Justice Department's Antitrust Division as presumptively valid, and this treatment placed the burden of truth on defendants and those challenging the rules and regulations of the various agencies.[33]

The Court consistently upheld just over 70 percent of the regulations across the 1938-1968 period. Such levels of consistency are normally a first sign of agenda decline, but no decline was evident. Again, this lack can be attributed to the vast array of regulatory schemes that continued to emerge. The positive response of the Court to the early regulations after 1938 encouraged the expansion of concerns, spreading regulations to other areas (the process of moving questions across individual domains).

The Burger Court retreated from the decisions of its predecessors. The real percentages do not reveal the scope of the changes. First, the early Burger Court was only marginally different from the Warren Court. Second, while aggregate levels showed a moderate reduction, the important landmark decisions emerging from the Burger Court signaled significant departures from the doctrine and ideology of the Warren Court. Third, support for the agencies was partially a function of the substance of those decisions. The Burger Court upheld almost 90 percent of the decisions that were probusiness or antilabor, but just over half the decisions that favored labor or were antibusiness.[34] Finally, the later Burger Court began to push Regulation cases off the volitional agenda and on to the exigent agenda. The numbers of cases accepted by the Court declined as a consequence. In addition, once the cases moved to the exigent agenda, the patterns of decisions did not have a coherent ideological foundation.

The early Burger Court had only a few personnel changes from its predecessors. Those changes did not translate to important aggregate-level changes in the early Burger Court. With the majority still intact, the retreats from the levels of support for administrative agencies declined only marginally. In view of normal notions of policy evolution, it is likely that these cases raised somewhat more problematic questions than the cases decided by the Warren Court, and the declines in support in the early Burger Court were effectively nonexistent.

Beneath the aggregate levels, significant changes were beginning to unfold, however. As justices left and were replaced, the Burger Court assumed a personality distinct from that of the Warren Court. Lost in the overall numbers was the fact that the Burger Court was issuing important decisions that signaled a change in priorities in regulation policy. The Burger Court changed the basis of evaluation for labor relations and antitrust decisions. Organized labor and other workers suffered under the hand of this Court, which overhauled long-settled labor policies. The effect was to undermine workers' rights and union democracy.[35] The values that appeared to dominate the Burger Court in labor relations cases were the sanctity of private property and entrepreneurial freedom.[36] In antitrust policy, the hostility of the Warren Court toward horizontal mergers was replaced by less suspicious attitudes. The Burger Court insisted that antitrust laws contain economic tests of legality and it rejected the Warren Court's assumptions about functions and the competitive impact of various types of business conduct.[37]

There were two results of the changes in labor relations and antitrust policies. Even if the decisions did not change dramatically, the effect had important manifestations. The nature of the briefs and arguments used in these types of cases changed. The early decisions altered the nature of the debate on these issues. Regulations in these two areas increasingly took on important social aspects, which engendered more controversy and ideological divisions than economic regulations.[38] These changes, in turn, affected the development of these issues, leading to more difficult, complex cases in the labor relations and antitrust areas. The changing nature of the cases kept these issues on the volitional agenda. The ideological changes in the membership of the Court appear to be responsible for the changing nature of the decisions in these areas.[39]

While labor relations and antitrust decisions remained on the fringes of the volitional agenda, most of the rest of the Regulation cases were moved to the exigent agenda. There were significant reductions in the number of business regulation cases accepted. The newly created agenda space was transferred to Civil Liberties issues. The rationale for acceptance of cases was increasingly to settle lower court conflict. Furthermore, the Supreme Court often confined its acceptance of such cases to lower court conflicts that pervaded multiple circuits. Also on the institutional level, the percentages of unanimous decisions in Regulation cases climbed to close to half the cases decided.

The increase of unanimous decisions had individual-level consequences as well. First, the normal ideological patterns that had defined individual-level decisionmaking virtually from the time of the New Deal were no longer useful in explaining or predicting judicial behavior. The significant growth of unanimous decisions meant that normal ideological antagonists frequently voted together. Even among nonunanimous decisions, normal blocs and cliques did not materialize. Through the early Burger Court, the traditional E scale identified decades earlier seemed to explain the nonunanimous Regulation decisions. A second dimension, reflecting deference to administrative agencies, was also evident.[40]

In a sense, a form of issue suppression dominated many of the Regulation cases. The rise of unanimous decisions and the atomization of existing blocs suggest that the justices were using other standards to decide cases that had situations and actors that had placed similar cases under the rubric of Regulation. Many of the Regulation cases, except labor relations and antitrust, appeared to move to the exigent portion of the Court's agenda. The direction of the decisions, the institutional move to consensus in the individual cases, and the changing rationale for case selection in these areas suggest that the judicial role was suppressing the normal ideological values that tended to govern these decisions. The substance of the decisions was less important than the fact that disagreements between lower courts were being addressed and resolved.

THE REHNQUIST COURT: A RETURN TO
THE RECENT PAST?

The Regulation decisions of the Supreme Court after 1940 were at the center of judicial concerns for three decades. The cases received the greatest proportion of agenda space until the late 1960s. While situations, the vast expansion of the federal government, and the initiatives of the president and Congress fueled the growth of the agenda, the appointment process played a major role by altering institutional goals. A number of the selections, particularly those of Franklin Roosevelt, were often predicated on the president's desire to get justices amenable to his programs and sympathetic to his notions of regulation on the Court.[41] As a consequence, such issues were at the core of the concerns of the new members, whose influence on Regulation introduced new dynamics that kept such issues on the Court's agenda.

Later nominations, particularly those by Presidents Nixon and Reagan, were based on other grounds and issues. Reflecting the growth of individual rights on the agenda and the decisions of the Warren Court, these presidents were more concerned with civil liberties and broader philosophies of constitutional interpretation than regulatory issues.[42] The decisions of these justices have increasingly reflected the fact that concerns with Regulation were not a central focus of their individual decisionmaking values.

There are harbingers of change in the Rehnquist Court, however. This is partially a function of the continued attention to labor relations and antitrust cases, which never moved to the exigent agenda. The deregulation policies of previous administrators have filtered through the political branches, the regulatory agencies, and the lower courts. Furthermore, in the normal course of events, it would take the Court about a decade to get fully involved in such issues. In addition, the significant decisions of the later Burger Court that changed the nature of law served as signals that could be interpreted as invitations for subsequent litigation.

The evidence suggests that systematic change is taking place and may affect the agenda for the foreseeable future. Situations and goals once again appear to be responsible for the changes that may be occurring. The influx of members, most notably Justice Scalia, who are concerned with regulation issues means there are advocates for change on the Court. Whether these changes are temporary aberrations or the beginning of another reconceptualization of Regulation policy remains to be seen.

FEDERALISM AND REGULATION:
A REFLECTION ON THE COURT'S TRANSFORMATION

The trends in the growth and decline of Federalism and U.S. Regulation cases in agenda prominence provide further evidence of the dynamics of the Court's institutional agenda. Each of the areas was a central facet of the Court's volitional agenda for significant portions of history. Over time, each of these policy areas was deemed settled or less important by the Court and received reduced agenda space.

During the 1933-1988 period, the issues were a fundamental part of the transformation of American politics. Upholding the authority of the central government over the prerogatives of the states and regulating the economy were significant components of the partisan realignment of 1928-1932. After a period of bitter resistance the Court capitulated. This removed the last important obstacle to the introduction of new policies and the initiation of a political revolution. When the justices joined the newly emerging political majority, the action also institutionalized a new role for the Supreme Court, which would eventually trickle down through the judicial hierarchy.

The decisions and trends in Federalism and Regulation were the first stages in the conversion of the Court's role. In each of these areas, the justices had to reverse the initiatives of their predecessors. Previous Federalism doctrine was an impediment to the emergence of the Regulation cases. Once it was removed, Regulation issues could be addressed on their own terms. This permitted the Court to make good on the first part of Justice Stone's pledge in Footnote 4: The Court would not interfere with economic issues unless there was a compelling reason.

In an important sense, the Federalism and Regulation issues were transitional parts of the Court's agenda. The initial growth of these issues was constrained by the agenda space that had to be allocated to continue the process of settling remaining questions in the Ordinary Economic, State Regulation, Government as Litigant, and Internal Revenue policy areas. The Court had made a conscious institutional decision to reduce consideration of these issues, but its retreat was tempered by institutional norms that required attention to some of these cases to resolve lower court disputes or provide for the administration of the judicial hierarchy.

Sufficient agenda space to resolve important matters of federal-state relations and regulatory policies was increasingly available as the Economic issues faded or became the province of other actors and before the full-scale emergence of Civil Liberties as the most prominent consumer of agenda space. Doctrinally, important questions of Federalism and Regulation needed to be settled to abet the development of individual rights and liberties. Once the Court had buttressed the authority of the central government and provided the impetus for increasing uniformity in economic laws, concerns for the uniformity of Due Process, Substantive Rights, and particularly Equality policy across the nation gained the Court's attention. The incorporation cases and the civil rights decisions were responsible for the nationalization of Civil Liberties, a process that would have been impossible without the Federalism decisions of the previous two decades.

The patterns of growth in Federalism and Regulation gained momentum due to the Court's early inconsistency that required subsequent litigation to determine the ultimate path of doctrine. Important landmarks opened the agenda space. The explosive growth and sustained levels of Regulation were a function of the entire range of activities that could ultimately fall under the authority of the positive regulatory state. Policy entrepreneurs, particularly interested justices and administrative agencies, helped sustain the growth of agenda space. The dynamics of the agenda (the process by which cases come to the Court, are decided, have various impacts, and spawn subsequent litigation) kept Regulation cases on the volitional agenda. The novelty of the issues, the changes in doctrine, the normal patterns of issue evolution, and the expansion of governmental activities helped keep these issues viable and at the center of the Court's concerns.

The Court's agenda was a reflection of the transformation of American government. The recent reductions in agenda space have coincided with the deregulation movement and attempts to downsize the central government. The changes in the national mood and the policies of deregulation may eventually find full expression in the Court's decisions. Institutional and individual goals may lead to a reevaluation of Regulation issues and their return to the volitional agenda.

The decisions and the doctrinal trends have provided the situation or opportunity for the full-scale introduction of Civil Liberties issues to the Court's agenda. The increase in the power and authority of government could be brought to bear on economic problems. That power might not be confined to benign economic policies, however. It could also be used to restrict individual rights and liberties. This duality poses a dilemma for democratic theorists. Modern liberalism could justify the intervention of big government in economic matters but support a much more limited governmental role in individual rights and liberties. The Court might be able to legitimate freedom from economic oppression, but its capacity to limit or control other types of oppression is still uncertain. It is up to the Court, as the republican schoolmaster, to devise theoretical and doctrinal principles that would achieve both goals concurrently. The Court's ability to tread this path would vindicate the second tenet of Footnote 4--the protection of insular minorities. The core of the "manifesto in a footnote" has been reflected in a twentieth-century liberalism that permits governmental latitude in regulating economic affairs but limits the reach of government into the domain of civil liberties.

GOVERNMENTAL POWER IN OTHER POLICY AREAS

There are four additional policy areas that consume small percentages of agenda space and do not align with other issues into a summary area: Separation of Powers, Foreign Affairs, Government as Provider, and Criminal Law. The allocation of agenda space and the substantive nature of the policy in three of these areas (all except Criminal Law) were related to the agenda allocations and the nature of decisions in the Federalism and Regulation domains. Given the impact of the government on each of these areas, the connections are not surprising. There are no patterns evident in the analysis of substantive criminal statutes. The area attracted an average of 2 to 3 percent of the agenda space.

None of the remaining three areas (Separation of Powers, Foreign Affairs, and Government as Provider) attracted an average of 2 percent of the agenda space over the 1933-1988 period. Foreign Affairs received some measure of attention in a few terms, mostly due to war-related concerns. Within a decade of the cessation of hostilities, these cases largely disappeared from the agenda. In general, the selection of these cases follows no general pattern of growth or decline. Separation of Powers cases involve the boundaries between the branches, normally between the executive and legislature and do not arise systematically.

In a sense, these cases are thrust upon the Court by circumstances or, in the case of Foreign Affairs, environmental factors. In the

Separation of Powers and Foreign Affairs areas, the decisions are much more important than the sheer numbers of the cases might suggest. Some of these issues require extensive decisions by the Court and may require considerably more time and work than the average case that is on the agenda annually. As a result, the appearance of these issues may force the Court to trim its allocations to other areas.

The decisions in the U.S. Regulation and Federalism areas had spillover effects that had an impact on a number of these minor issues. In terms of the framework of policy evolution, the effects of the two dominant areas on the Separation of Powers, Foreign Affairs, and Government as Provider can be labeled collateral development. As such, doctrine being developed to underpin Regulation and Federalism decisions did not directly lead to changes in the nature of the other areas but had indirect effects. In general, the policy that was emerging in Regulation and Federalism was conducive to the expansion of the power of the central government. The Court needed to bring its doctrine involving other areas of governmental authority into line with its other policies.

In the Government as Provider area, the Court upheld the authority of the central government to establish and maintain the Social Security Administration. This was the logical extension of the positive state emerging from the Regulation decisions. Supreme Court support for U.S. Regulation created the notion of a positive governmental authority that could intervene for the protection of the citizen and could affirm its responsibility for the economic well-being of the nation. Having established the general principle of the positive duty of government, the Court's support of social security programs is an example of collateral development. The Regulation programs lent psychological and doctrinal support to Government as Provider. Social security programs would provide insurance for the victims of business cycles, the disabled, and the elderly.

As the power of government to take an active, positive role became accepted, these cases went into a long period of dormancy. In the 1950s, cases involving government-subsidized housing projects made up the Government as Provider questions on the agenda. Most of the Government as Provider cases have reached the agenda in the past decade and a half. These cases typically involved questions about specific programs such as Food Stamps and Aid to Families with Dependent Children as well as amendments to the Social Security Act.

The Great Depression provided the impetus for the advent of Regulation, changes in the authority of the central government in the Federalism cases, and an increasing recognition that government needs the unencumbered authority to conduct international affairs. Global conditions reinforced notions that the economy needed national remedies and international concerns. The advent of World War II, which was already on the horizon as the Court began to support Regulation, further strengthened the momentum for increased national power and authority. It has long been an axiom of American politics that times of war and international crises create an environment for the expansion of executive power at the expense of the legislature and for national power at the expense of subnational prerogatives. Memories of the depression and the rise of the cold war kept Foreign Affairs on the agenda.

In total numbers, Foreign Affairs cases averaged less than 2 percent of the agenda space over the 1933-1988 period. The space allocated to Foreign Affairs cases varied significantly across time. Over half the Foreign Affairs cases accepted were decided in the 1943-1952 decade. In two terms, the Court allocated 10 percent to these areas. World War II was the impetus and most of the cases dealt with war claims issues, primarily dealing with the Trading with the Enemy Act. These issues resembled the cases arising concurrently in the Regulation cases. Occasional Korean and Vietnam War questions reached the agenda, but the numbers were insignificant.

The most dramatic effects, practically if not in terms of the agenda, occurred in the Separation of Powers area. The Constitution provides that Congress passes the laws and regulations and formulates a budget. In practical terms, however, the Great Depression, the New Deal, and the growth of the regulatory state created a dramatic shift in the relationship between the executive and legislative branches. The need for a planned set of economic policies to attack the depression had two consequences. Power and authority had to be shifted to centralizing agents and away from centrifugal instruments of government. This meant an increase in the authority of the central government, which was under way in the Federalism decisions, and an increase in the power of the president, which slowly began to unfold in the Separation of Powers decisions. The president has increasingly set the congressional agenda and wrested the power to control the nature of debate from the legislature.

In real terms, Separation of Powers cases did not expand their share of agenda space. Rather, the substance of the decisions changed as a result of the doctrine in regulation cases after 1937. The largest growth in the agenda space allocated to Separation of Powers occurred in the wake of the Watergate crisis and the effects it had on executive-legislative relations. Later surges have resulted from civil service cases and questions involving the use of the legislative veto. Decisions like *Immigration and Naturalization Service v. Chadha* 462 U.S. 919 (1982 term), in which the Court invalidated a number of legislative veto provisions, and *Bowsher v. Synar* 478 U.S. 714 (1985 term), striking down portions of the Gramm-Rudman-Hollings Budget Act, made a small impact on the aggregate agenda but have enormous consequences for the doctrine in the area of Separation of Powers.

The small percentages of agenda space allocated to these three areas (Separation of Powers, Government as Provider, and Foreign Affairs) artificially depress the number of cases involving them. Many of the cases that arose from these domains were multidimensional issues affecting other areas as well, in particular, Government as Provider and Foreign Affairs cases.

Cases within the area of Government as Provider went through the most different permutations. Initially, these cases, like early New Deal Regulation cases, were decided on the grounds of Federalism. Having established the constitutionality of the Social Security Act and the authority of the central government to establish the program, the Court changed the nature of the issues. Ultimately, many of the cases raised issues that fell under the rubric of Due Process and Equality. Reductions or eliminations of such benefits were contested on the grounds that the changes were made without due process, such as proper notification, or on the grounds that such changes were based on discriminatory grounds.

Cases that raised Foreign Affairs concerns often contained other issues as well. Some, for instance, involved the suspension of an individual's rights as part of the restraints a government considers necessary during crises. These cases were classified as part of the Substantive Rights policy area. Free expression and cases involving conscientious objection were the most numerous of these claims. The right to travel and the rights of naturalized citizens were also raised in the context of Foreign Affairs but represented Substantive Rights concerns. Crises and wartime restrictions also involved important immigration questions that fit within the context of Equality policy.

In these four areas, minor in numbers of cases only, there are few patterns or trends. In a sense, the appearance of such cases is more closely tied to exigent agenda than the volitional agenda. Vague language in criminal statutes requires judicial attention because such legislation must be applied across a vast network of courts. Major cases that involve the constitutional boundaries between the branches of government or the authority of judges must be settled by the highest court. Some Foreign Affairs questions have similar implications.

Because of their occasional status and the wide variety of the questions posed, the normal patterns of issue evolution whereby one case spawns other related issues do not explain the dynamics of these issue areas. In one important way, however, cases in these areas (Foreign Affairs and Separation of Powers in particular) differ from exigent agenda cases. Many of these issues are significant interpretations of constitutional law, as opposed to the Economic cases that merely settle lower court disputes.

Because of the significance of the individual cases in Foreign Affairs and Separation of Powers, such cases may require more institutional resources than individual cases in other areas of law. Such cases are relatively rare, so long-term decisional cues and perceptual shorthands are not available as in issue areas that are hardy perennials. Justices are more likely to write separate opinions in these cases. The implications of these decisions are often far reaching and affect other institutional actors who have the power to harm the Court. Ultimately, the Court's legitimacy may be at stake, causing justices to pause and consider the implications more carefully. The result may be that such cases may keep some volitional issue cases off the Court's agenda for that term.

6

The Growth of Civil Liberties: The Modern Agenda

The Supreme Court is widely seen as the appropriate, if not the sole, forum for balancing the rights of individuals with the demands of society. It is taken as an axiom that the Court is a protector of individual rights and a bulwark against tyranny of the majority. Yet the Court's acceptance of this role has been a relatively modern phenomenon.[1] Indeed, it is only over the last half-century that the Supreme Court has become a court emphasizing civil liberties and civil rights. The transformation of the Court and American politics has been tied to events that generated such changes.

Although the Court acceded to the pressure to change its notions of economic liberalism, in a sense it finally adopted a traditional liberal view of individual rights and liberties. Lockean liberalism supported limited governmental intervention in economic matters and individual rights. The Great Depression proved that the tenets of nineteenth-century economic liberalism had become unworkable in the new corporate state.[2] A new strain of political theory was the result. In the economic realm, the Court eventually came to support systematic governmental regulation of the economy. In terms of judicial policymaking, the Court adopted judicial restraint in economic matters. In other words, if the regulation was reasonable--a standard that was not hard to meet--the Court would defer to Congress, the president, and the bureaucracy.

The early liberalism that underpinned the Constitution and the formulation of the nation did not carry specific formulas for the protection of civil liberties and civil rights. By implication, Lockean notions of limited government seemed to apply to individual rights as well as the economy. The Court did not have many occasions to develop case law and doctrine that would create a viable political theory to serve as the foundation for individual rights policy. The Court's response to changes in the political and economic environments was to adopt policies of selective activism. In the area of individual rights and liberties, the Court placed limits on the authority of the government to constrict the rights of individuals. A new strain of American political theory, incorporating this selective activism, emerged from the New Deal.[3] The process of theory building accompanied the changes in the agenda and the making of judicial policy. This multitiered process appears to be responsible for the early patterns of change.

An important set of questions relates to the manner in which the wholesale agenda change from Economic issues to Civil Liberties has occurred. This chapter examines the growth of civil liberties cases on the Supreme Court's agenda. The goal of this analysis is not to confirm the obvious but to understand the dynamics by which Civil Liberties cases displaced the other dominant policy areas that had consumed the preponderance of the agenda space in preceding periods.

Analysts have identified the major events that transformed the Court into an actor primarily concerned with matters pertaining to civil liberties,[4] but there has been little systematic attention to the dynamics that underlie this transformation. Studies of judicial policies typically focus on seminal decisions and important constitutional doctrines without reference to the piecework that occurs between landmark decisions. Concentration on major pronouncements obscures the vast majority of decisions the Court issues and ignores the significant process of constructing policy and filling in the voids left in the wake of the more celebrated doctrinal shifts and landmark decisions.

In selecting cases for review and issuing decisions on the merits, the Court, through the collective and individual work of the justices, makes basic decisions concerning the authoritative allocation of values. Judicial decisionmaking is important for notions of pluralism and access to the agencies of government. Decisions to emphasize one set of cases to the possible exclusion of others have important political implications. The rights of insular minorities, mentioned in Footnote 4 of the *Carolene Products* decision (1937 term), had long been neglected. Although there was no guarantee that civil liberties and civil rights would receive a broad level of protection at the outset, it was clear that these issues would have a forum in which they would systematically receive a hearing for the first time.

The decision in *Erie Railroad* (1937 term) appeared to be responsible for moving Economic issues to the exigent agenda. Footnote

4 created the impetus for the issues that would assume a predominant place on the volitional agenda and fill some of the increasingly vacated space. Concurrently, the Court wrote important decisions in two areas of Civil Liberties: Due Process and Substantive Rights. In *Palko v. Connecticut* 302 U.S. 319 (1937 term), a case involving double jeopardy, the Court tried to refine its approach to the incorporation issue. In a First Amendment case--the core of Substantive Rights--a majority overturned a state conviction on explicit clear and present grounds for the first time. Although neither of these cases broke new constitutional ground, they did prepare the way for the construction of theory and doctrine, helped open the agenda to Due Process and Substantive Rights cases, and sustained the early growth of Civil Liberties.[5]

The growth of Civil Liberties had to be tempered by the need to put the Economic issues in order. Extensive volitional agenda space was not available until the exigent agenda had been pared. The Court was in the process of accomplishing that as Civil Liberties issues made their first sustained impact on the agenda. The early surge in Regulation and Civil Liberties cases came at the expense of the Ordinary Economic, Internal Revenue, and State Regulation cases. The later explosive growth of Civil Liberties was a result of the reduced agenda space granted to U.S. Regulation, which appears to have migrated to the exigent agenda in the past fifteen terms. A brief analysis of these trends provides a background for understanding the systematic patterns of change.

TRENDS IN CIVIL LIBERTIES

Because agenda construction is related to policymaking and the diachronic process of agenda building is a function of the goals, rules of the Court, and the situation or environment surrounding the Court, it is necessary to trace the agenda trends through the tenure of the various chief justices. This places the changes in a historical context and helps identify key decisions that spawned agenda change. The dynamics of the agenda introduce some continuity to the patterns of agenda change, but different Courts may alter those dynamics by accelerating or slowing the pace of such change.

The steady linear growth of Civil Liberties is the story of the modern Supreme Court. Such cases consumed less than 10 percent of the agenda space until 1941, as Figure 6.1 shows. For the next two decades, the trend of agenda growth was clear: The pace of change was

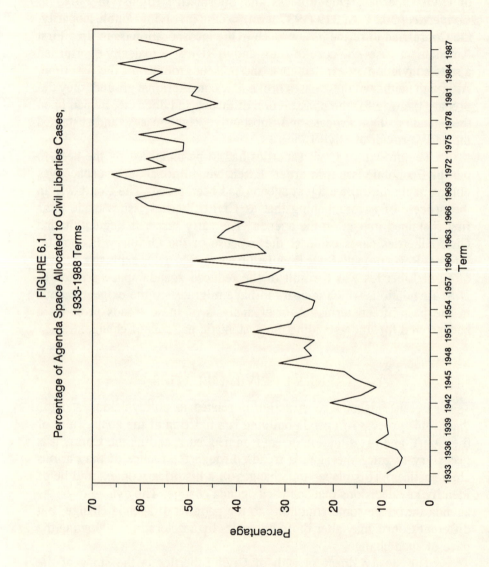

FIGURE 6.1

Percentage of Agenda Space Allocated to Civil Liberties Cases,
1933-1988 Terms

incremental except for some periodic bursts of activity that seemed to belie the normal pace of agenda change. This constrained level of growth seems somewhat surprising in view of the fact that members of the Court continued to commit to the ideals of Footnote 4. Despite the fact that the Court was increasingly supportive of a preferred position for individual rights, the agenda grew incrementally until the late 1950s.

After 1957, the pace of the growth of Civil Liberties on the Court's agenda hastened dramatically. The Court took two decades to increase the agenda space granted Civil Liberties by 20 percent, but an equal rate of change took only a half-dozen more terms. This pace points out the existence of two trends. First, the initial rate of growth is constrained by existing dynamics. Once an area establishes its threshold claim to agenda space, the dynamics ensure that growth will continue. The Civil Liberties agenda declined slightly since 1970 and then stabilized around 60 percent of the total agenda; in the past few terms, the percentage has once again increased. Given the necessity for the Court to hear some other cases, Civil Liberties has reached its effective ceiling of agenda space.

The growth of Civil Liberties is a function of the process labeled the "expansion of concerns." Judicial attention moved from one summary area to other broad areas. The initial growth of Civil Liberties began in the Due Process area and spread to Substantive Rights. Ultimately, the pattern of growth included issues that fall under the rubric of Equality. In a sense, this process is broadly reflective of issue evolution. Criminal procedure issues created an environment for more difficult concerns with the First Amendment, most notably freedom of expression cases. The remedy sought in Due Process and Substantive Rights was largely negative: The government should refrain from certain activities that infringe upon an individual's rights. It was another step to equal protection issues that might require positive steps from government.

THE HISTORY OF THE
CIVIL LIBERTIES AGENDA

Reviewing the Civil Liberties agenda of the Hughes Court (1930-1940) does not require extensive effort. Caught in the middle of the transition from the decaying economic infrastructure and the modern regulatory state, the agenda of the Hughes Court was dominated by the Economic cases, which were about to decline, and Federalism and U.S.

Regulation, which were about to flourish. This left little available agenda space for the few individual rights cases that made it to the Supreme Court. There were few discernible patterns to the limited number of Due Process, Substantive Rights, and Equality cases that were decided by the Court between the 1933 and 1938 terms.

In retrospect, the contribution of the Hughes Court to individual rights was very indirect. In issuing its decisions, this Court began the long process of putting the Economic issues in order so that agenda attention to those areas could be reduced. Ultimately, other issues, still to emerge, could occupy the vacated agenda space. The important early decisions were merely the opening salvos in the long-term battle over the proper role of individual rights and liberties in a majoritarian government. These cases were agenda setters in every sense of the word. The Court's early decisions were unclear and required subsequent cases to develop consistency in the nascent doctrine. Furthermore, increasingly difficult cases would arise in the wake of these early landmark decisions.

There were good reasons to believe the Stone Court (1941-1945) could be the vehicle for a fuller consideration of individual rights and liberties. As the author of the famous Footnote 4 and the sole dissenter in the first flag-salute case, *Minersville v. Gobitis* 310 U.S. 586 (1939 term), Harlan Fiske Stone was the source of the preferred position doctrine. That doctrine held that civil liberties and rights should be given more exacting scrutiny by the Court. For a variety of reasons, however, the Stone Court did not become a beacon for individual rights protections. A number of factors tied to goals, rules, and situations appear to explain why Civil Liberties did not flourish during this period. First, changes in membership brought in justices who were less supportive of individual rights. Thus, the collective goals of the Court were not conducive to an expansion of individual rights. Second, rules mandated attention to the exigent agenda and other items on the volitional agenda, notably the emergent U.S. Regulation cases. This crowded Civil Liberties off the agenda. Finally, and perhaps most important, World War II affected the types of issues on the Civil Liberties agenda. The war brought a variety of Due Process, First Amendment, and Equality issues to the docket during a period of heightened suspicion. The Supreme Court's track record on individual rights issues during times of war, most notably the Civil War and World War I, was far from impressive. During World War II and in the Red Scare hysteria that followed, the Court deferred to the government in restricting liberties and rights.

Historical analyses of the Supreme Court's doctrines in civil liberties and civil rights almost invariably criticize the decisions of the Vinson Court (1946-1952). Compared to the Warren Court and even the more recent Burger and Rehnquist courts, the Vinson-led tribunal pales. There are mitigating circumstances, however, that support a somewhat gentler assessment of the Vinson Court. Membership changes continued to bring in justices who were less protective of individual rights. The Red Scare was not conducive to the expansion of civil liberties, particularly freedom of expression.

In decisions like *Dennis v. United States* 339 U.S. 162 (1950 term), which upheld the Smith Act, the Court created an unfavorable judicial environment that would chill litigants interested in civil liberties for over a decade. In terms of policy evolution, the problem stemmed from the fact that complex and difficult cases were coming to a Court facing decidedly hostile external forces.

The only major personnel difference between the early Warren Court and the Vinson Court was the name and identity of the chief justice. The change of one vote, in and of itself, would not be sufficient to usher in a new period of constitutional law. The skills of Chief Justice Warren, in contrast to his two immediate predecessors, appeared to alter the dynamics of the Court. The result was a change in the institutional goals of the Court. The early Warren Court did not profoundly change the Civil Liberties agenda, but it set into motion the forces that would ultimately affect the growth of individual rights.

The growth of Due Process had been well under way before the appointment process advanced the liberal wing of the Supreme Court. The surges in Substantive Rights and Equality were responsible for the major growth of Civil Liberties. The later Warren Court presided over a constitutional revolution marked by consistent liberal decisions in each of the areas of Civil Liberties. What separated the Warren Court from its predecessors was its liberal decisions in Substantive Rights and Due Process, particularly the former. The climate for free expression was more propitious given the waning of the Red Scare.

Within a few years of the ascension of Warren Burger, President Nixon was able to stem the liberal tide and begin to reshape the Court in a conservative direction. Changing the goals of the Court, while the rules were less of a problem due to the waning of the exigent agenda, provided the agenda space for the Court to pursue its goals and the volitional agenda. The increasingly conservative goals of the Burger Court did not, however, lead to a decrease in the amount of agenda space allocated to Civil Liberties. Quite to the contrary, Civil Liberties and its component areas reached unprecedented levels of attention. This growth appears to be a function of agenda context left by the Warren Court, the opening of additional rights by the Burger Court, and its retreats from some of its predecessor's work.

Although the Burger Court has been labeled as conservative, more systematic analysis demonstrates that this assessment is not completely accurate. Certainly, the Burger Court was less liberal than its predecessor. In some areas, the Burger Court was quite conservative, but in other policy domains, this Court expanded rights beyond the advances of the Warren Court. In a sense the Burger Court, like the Vinson Court, was a victim of its predecessors' policies. For the Burger Court, this was manifested in three ways. First, the vast expansion of rights implemented by the Warren Court left unresolved questions that the Burger Court would have to face. The notion of issue evolution was important. The Burger Court confronted more complex cases, like gender discrimination, abortion, and affirmative action, which were the natural progression of cases in issue areas opened by the Warren Court.[6] In addition, a number of organized groups had become accustomed to using the judiciary to address their concerns and would continue to do so. Finally, the perceived conservative nature of the Burger Court encouraged new litigants to use the courts and introduced some inconsistencies to doctrine.[7] This, in turn, created confusion in the lower courts and among implementers and required Supreme Court intervention. The result was increased and sustained levels of agenda space for Civil Liberties and its component areas.

When President Reagan promoted William Rehnquist to the *primus inter pares* (first among equals) and selected Antonin Scalia, the collective goals of the Court were not changed in any significant fashion. The selection of Scalia, a conservative, balanced the resignation of Burger, another conservative. There was a parallel to the Warren nomination in that the new chief justice was widely perceived to be a more effective leader than his predecessor. The ability to marshall a closely divided Court could prove advantageous in the selection of cases and in votes on the merits of cases. The resignation of Justice Powell, a perceived voice of moderation on the Burger and Rehnquist courts, held the potential to tip the balance and create a true Reagan Court. The nomination of Robert Bork seemed to be a forceful step in that direction. The eventual selection of Anthony Kennedy and, recently, David Souter by President Bush appear to have created a Reagan Court even though

Reagan is now a private citizen. The ultimate impact of this tribunal is yet to unfold, but the agenda of the early Rehnquist Court is beginning to take a definable shape. Some recent developments in agenda construction may be temporary or may portend structural changes in case selection and agenda building. This will be examined in Chapter 7. Within the three areas of Civil Liberties, the Rehnquist Court has not significantly diverted from the course of the later Burger Court. In general, Civil Liberties continues to consume the preponderance of volitional agenda space, although underlying changes in its component areas and their subareas are increasingly evident.

DUE PROCESS

The growth of the Civil Liberties area has been relatively consistent over time, but its components have had somewhat different patterns of development. Criminal procedure cases make up the largest percentage of the Due Process area. Civil due process issues in administrative proceedings are also included in this area. Due Process, as the largest area within Civil Liberties, has a growth trend resembling the summary area. Figure 6.2 demonstrates the growth in Due Process across the 1933-1988 period. To be sure, there are more numerous fluctuations than in the broader Civil Liberties area and these interrupt the overall trend. The growth occurred in two stages, moderate before the 1960s and dramatic since that time. Due Process was the first of the Civil Liberties areas to flourish and establish a significant claim to agenda space.

The trends of growth in Due Process are linear and relatively steady, but there was a great deal of fluctuation in the subareas that constitute the general domain. Table 6.1 shows the percentage of agenda space allocated to the important subareas of criminal procedure. There is evidence of the dispersion of attention. Search-and-seizure and right-to-counsel cases created the impetus for the emergence of the *Miranda* rights in *Miranda v. Arizona* 384 U.S. 436 (1965 term). Jury procedures and concerns with double jeopardy were the next areas to emerge. Ultimately, attention has shifted to issues involving cruel and unusual punishment. The dispersion of attention is also evident in the nature of the issues that make up Due Process. The Court has always been concerned with criminal procedure but increasingly has extended protections to prisoners and to civil and administrative procedure cases.

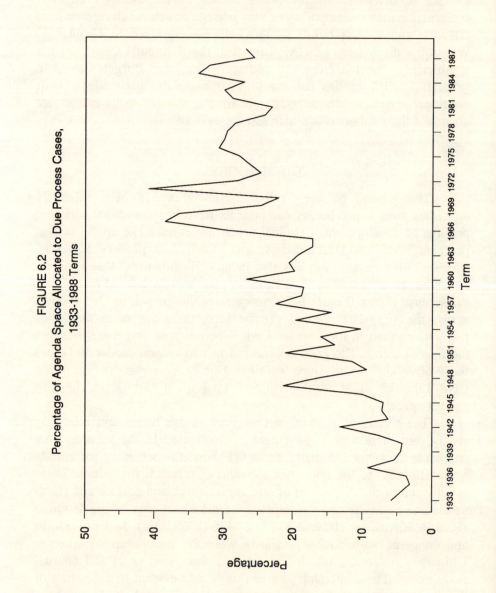

FIGURE 6.2
Percentage of Agenda Space Allocated to Due Process Cases,
1933-1988 Terms

Table 6.1 Number of Cases and Percentage of Agenda Space Allocated to Selected Due Process Subareas: Criminal Law, 1933-1987 Terms

Subareas	1933-1937	1938-1942	1943-1947	1948-1952	1953-1957	1958-1962	1963-1967	1968-1972	1973-1977	1978-1982	1983-1987	Total (n)
Evidence (n) (%)	2 0.3	10 1.3	5 0.8	6 1.2	6 1.2	9 1.5	12 1.7	13 1.8	12 1.4	11 1.4	15 2.0	101
Witnesses	2 0.3	1 0.1	1 0.2	3 0.6	3 0.6	6 1.0	13 1.8	12 1.7	5 0.6	5 0.6	13 1.7	64
Confessions	1 0.1	6 0.8	6 0.9	6 1.2	7 1.4	12 2.0	10 1.4	9 1.3	2 0.2	1 0.1	0 0.0	60
Self-Incrimination	0 0.0	2 0.3	1 0.2	5 1.0	6 1.2	0 0.0	16 2.2	11 1.5	7 0.8	10 1.1	9 1.3	67
Search & Seizure	1 0.1	1 0.1	8 1.2	8 1.6	10 2.0	14 2.4	27 3.8	27 3.8	22 2.6	36 4.5	38 5.1	192
Right to Counsel	1 0.1	6 0.8	14 2.1	7 1.4	14 2.9	20 3.4	21 2.9	21 2.9	12 1.4	17 2.1	25 3.4	158
Jury	5 0.6	8 1.0	14 2.1	7 1.4	10 2.0	4 0.7	11 1.5	16 2.2	14 1.7	20 2.5	26 3.5	135
Double Jeopardy	1 0.1	1 0.1	2 0.3	2 0.4	5 1.0	11 1.9	2 0.3	16 2.2	26 3.1	11 1.4	12 1.6	89
Miranda Rights	0 0.0	0 0.0	0 0.0	0 0.0	1 0.2	0 0.0	3 0.4	4 0.6	10 1.2	6 0.8	10 1.3	34
Cruel & Unusual Punishment	0 0.0	0 0.0	0 0.0	2 0.4	1 0.2	1 0.2	2 0.3	2 0.3	12 1.4	12 1.5	24 3.2	56

Table 6.2 shows the steady but declining agenda space for criminal procedure and the more recent growth in prisoner rights and civil due process.

An analysis of the long-term patterns of growth in Due Process and its constituent areas must trace the decisions and trends in each of the Courts in the 1933-1988 period. The levels of agenda space granted to Due Process during the Hughes Court were modest. Interestingly, the preponderance of the Due Process cases involved the rights of minorities in jury composition, right to an attorney, grand juries, and confessions. At the end of the Hughes Court, the portent of future change was evident. The numbers of cases did not rise appreciably, but some of these cases were significant. Perhaps the most important Due Process case was *Palko v. Connecticut* (1937 term), which raised the issue of incorporation of a criminal procedure amendment.

The process of incorporation was also raised in Due Process cases during the Stone Court, but a majority of the justices steadfastly refused to extend these policies in *Adamson v. California* 332 U.S. 146 (1947 term), a self-incrimination case. In this decision, Justices Black and Frankfurter, the standard bearers for conflicting constitutional principles, disagreed sharply on the question of incorporation. The influence of this judicial debate had a long-term impact on the Court's agenda. Over the next three decades, a number of cases on specific criminal process provisions from the Bill of Rights came to the Court; they concerned questions of incorporation. In criminal procedure cases, more generally, the agenda was affected by the Court's inability to specify clear, coherent standards for the evaluation of procedural irregularities. The Court used a "fair trial" standard to determine whether arrest and trial procedures ensured or interfered with the defendant's right to a fair trial. The lack of clarity in this standard provided little guidance for lower courts and ensured that future cases would reach the Supreme Court.

Due Process reached new levels of agenda space, over 20 percent in two terms of the Vinson Court. The "fair trial" standard continued to create problems through the judicial hierarchy, particularly in search-and-seizure cases. Like its predecessor, the Vinson Court wrestled with right-to-counsel cases. Since *Powell v. Alabama* 287 U.S. 45 (1932), the Court required counsel for indigents only if "special circumstances" were present. In a series of cases, the Court was forced to decide what constituted such circumstances and whether they were present. The Court continued to involve itself in criminal procedure cases that involved discrimination against blacks.

Table 6.2 Number of Cases and Percentage of Agenda Space Allocated to Selected Due Process Subareas, 1933-1987 Terms

Subareas	1933-1937	1938-1942	1943-1947	1948-1952	1953-1957	1958-1962	1963-1967	1968-1972	1973-1977	1978-1982	1983-1987	Total (n)
Criminal (n) Procedure (%)	27 3.4	47 6.2	60 9.1	61 12.0	81 16.5	111 18.7	149 22.6	173 24.1	172 20.5	150 18.9	199 26.7	1230
Prisoner Rights	7 0.9	2 0.3	4 0.6	6 1.2	1 0.1	6 1.0	9 1.4	16 2.2	29 3.5	33 4.1	8 1.1	121
Civil Due Process	7 0.9	5 0.6	2 0.3	6 1.2	2 0.4	7 1.2	7 1.1	33 4.6	32 3.8	30 3.8	20 2.7	151

As late as 1954, less than 10 percent of the agenda space was allocated to Due Process cases. The dramatic growth of Due Process coincided with the later Warren Court. This is not particularly surprising in view of the important landmark decisions that supported the rights of the accused. The early Warren Court decisions set the stage for the ultimate growth of the criminal procedure agenda. While the vague "fair trial" rule was still in effect, the Court increasingly found police and trial procedures violated the rights of the accused. In the period from the early to the later Warren Court, the justices undermined the "fair trial" rule and set off the eventual explosion in the Due Process and Civil Liberties agendas. The later surge in the agenda space granted to Due Process appeared to result from the favorable decisions of the Warren Court and the creation of additional rights. The key Due Process decision during the early Warren Court was *Mapp v. Ohio* (1960 term), which incorporated the exclusionary rule to the states. The addition of Justice Goldberg (and Justice Fortas to replace him) created a critical mass for the liberals on the Court. By altering the ideological leanings (goals) of the Court, appointments created the situation for further policy advances. These appointments galvanized the liberal wing of the Court that presided over the great expansion of civil liberties into the 1960s. Thus, there was a cadre of entrepreneurs armed with solutions and looking for problems. Nationalization of the criminal procedure provisions of the Bill of Rights was orchestrated by a coalition of justices in a short span of eight years.[8]

The dispersion of attention explains the process by which the advances in one area of Due Process spilled over to other protections. Major landmark decisions like *Miranda v. Arizona* and *Gideon v. Wainwright* highlighted this process. By the end of Earl Warren's service as chief justice, Due Process cases consumed almost 40 percent of the total agenda. Perhaps more importantly for the dynamics of the agenda, the decisions of the Warren Court left his successor with an agenda dominated by such cases. The Burger Court had to deal with the unresolved issues left by the Warren Court.

In 1971, Due Process cases filled over 40 percent of the Court's agenda. Due Process has retained a significant portion of agenda space despite the advent of the Burger and Rehnquist courts, which were often hostile to the rights of the accused. In the Due Process cases, the Burger Court earned its conservative reputation. In its later, more difficult criminal procedure cases, the Warren Court began a partial retreat that was continued and hastened by the Burger Court. Even though the justices embarked on this increasingly conservative path, the Due Process agenda continued to grow. Under normal expectations, this pace might be expected to chill litigant behavior. In fact, the percentage of agenda space allocated to criminal procedure cases did decline to levels matching the early Warren Court. The retreat from the substantive decisions of the Warren Court sent confusing signals through lower courts and police stations and would keep cases coming to the Supreme Court. More to the point, the criminal cases that came to the Warren Court were largely brought by defendants who had been unsuccessful in the lower courts. Roles reversed under the Burger Court as the moving party in criminal procedure cases tended to be the government.

Not all of the influence was negative or the result of inconsistencies. The Burger Court initially restricted the imposition of the death penalty and considered a number of similar cases during a period of agenda retrenchment in search and seizure, self-incrimination, and right to counsel. Double jeopardy cases also flourished during the Burger Court. The reason for the expansion of the Due Process agenda can be attributed to other issues in this realm. Prisoner rights and civil due process cases are responsible for this growth. Prisoner rights is an area resulting from a number of other rights, including criminal procedure and First Amendment considerations. Civil or administrative due process cases were multidimensional; they involved economic aspects that emerged from the search-and-seizure area and created a separate area of law. Decisions involving the procedures of noncriminal, administrative searches, like *See v. Seattle* 387 U.S. 541 (1966 term) and *Camara v. Municipal Court* (1967 term), opened the agenda to civil due process cases and kept the broader Due Process cases at their previous agenda levels.

In the area of criminal procedure, the Rehnquist Court has continued to limit the rights of the accused. The justices have limited the ability of the accused to challenge improper searches and the procedures occurring in trial courts. The Court has not taken the extraordinary step of overturning the precedents that incorporated key provisions of the Bill of Rights, but the practical effects have not been significantly different. The Supreme Court is increasingly allowing state and local police officers and judges some flexibility in balancing the rights of the accused with the power of the state to maintain order.

Criminal procedure cases have always dominated Due Process, but cases involving prisoner rights and civil due process have grabbed larger percentages of agenda space in the past fifteen terms. The criminal cases have declined from their peaks. Cases in the specific subareas of search-

and-seizure, self-incrimination, and right-to-counsel (the subject of the major landmark decisions *Mapp v. Ohio*, *Miranda v. Arizona*, and *Gideon v. Wainwright*) have been regular staples of the agenda. Other issues, such as the death penalty and jury procedures, would emerge and assume an important percentage of agenda space for a decade before declining in significance and numbers.

SUBSTANTIVE RIGHTS

Substantive Rights primarily involve First Amendment issues such as freedom of expression, religion, association, and the press. The right to privacy, which was created from such First Amendment rights as well as from a variety of other amendments, is included in this category, as is the issue of abortion, which is based on the right to privacy. Chronologically, Substantive Rights was the second of the individual areas of Civil Liberties to grow in agenda prominence.

Figure 6.3 shows the pattern of growth and recent decline for Substantive Rights. Prior to 1940, Substantive Rights only once captured more than 2 percent of the agenda. As late as the 1955 term, the Court accepted no Substantive Rights cases. In general, though, after the mid-1940s, the growth of Substantive Rights on the agenda was linear. Though the overall trend was steady, there were some large-scale fluctuations that punctuated the overall trends. In recent Court terms, the percentage of the agenda space granted to Substantive Rights has declined.

Although the overall area demonstrated a relatively linear trend of growth until recently, the underlying areas that compose Substantive Rights varied greatly over time. Table 6.3 shows that core issues like freedom of expression and freedom of religion were normally present on the agenda, even though the shares of agenda space were relatively small. The dispersion of attention is particularly noticeable in Substantive Rights. Early expression cases created the environment that led to libel, obscenity, symbolic speech, and commercial speech issues. Cases involving conscientious objection had peaks tied to wartime, and issues concerning alleged Communists were also tied to the external environment, peaking during and just after the height of the Red Scare and McCarthyism. A number of First Amendment freedom-of-expression cases were tied to other issues: One early group of cases came from restraints placed on individuals during World War II. Another source of

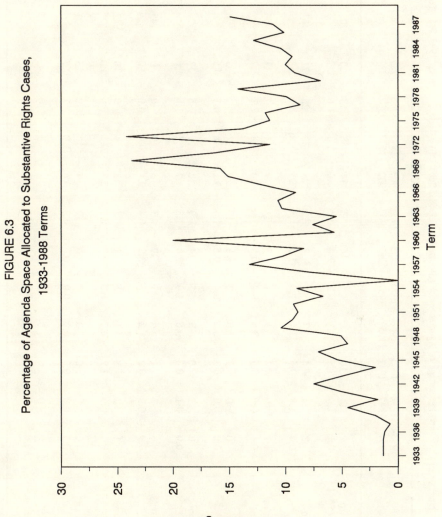

FIGURE 6.3

Percentage of Agenda Space Allocated to Substantive Rights Cases,
1933-1988 Terms

Table 6.3 Number of Cases and Percentage of Agenda Space Allocated to Selected Substantive Rights Subareas, 1933-1987 Terms

Subareas	1933-1937	1938-1942	1943-1947	1948-1952	1953-1957	1958-1962	1963-1967	1968-1972	1973-1977	1978-1982	1983-1987	Total (n)
Religion (n)	1	11	10	6	1	14	3	14	8	13	20	101
(%)	0.1	1.4	1.5	1.1	0.2	2.4	0.4	2.0	1.0	1.6	2.7	
Expression	3	14	4	17	5	8	13	25	32	25	21	167
	0.4	1.8	0.6	3.4	1.0	1.3	1.8	3.5	3.8	3.1	2.8	
Libel/Slander	1	0	3	3	1	3	11	7	15	9	13	66
	0.1	0.0	0.5	0.6	0.2	0.5	1.6	1.0	1.8	1.1	1.7	
Obscenity	0	0	1	0	2	3	10	22	32	2	3	76
	0.0	0.0	0.2	0.0	0.4	0.5	1.4	3.1	3.8	0.3	0.5	
Association/ Assembly	0	1	0	3	5	14	9	12	10	8	12	74
	0.0	0.1	0.0	0.6	1.0	2.4	1.3	1.7	1.2	1.0	1.6	
Communists	0	2	1	6	11	19	3	3	0	0	0	45
	0.0	0.3	0.2	1.2	2.2	3.2	0.4	0.4	0.0	0.0	0.0	
Conscientious Objection	1	2	8	1	5	1	2	18	4	0	0	42
	0.1	0.3	1.2	0.2	1.0	0.2	0.3	2.5	0.5	0.0	0.0	
Abortion/ Privacy	0	0	0	0	0	0	2	4	10	10	5	31
	0.0	0.0	0.0	0.0	0.0	0.0	0.3	0.6	1.2	1.3	0.7	
Freedom of Information Act	0	0	0	0	0	1	0	1	3	10	2	17
	0.0	0.0	0.0	0.0	0.0	0.2	0.0	0.1	0.4	1.3	0.3	

First Amendment cases during the 1940s involved unions and labor protests. Labor relations issues from the U.S. Regulation area imposed new rules on labor-management relations. The increased power and voice of labor and unions gave rise to protests and strikes. As a consequence, some of these issues migrated from the Regulation area to Substantive Rights.

The agenda trends of Substantive Rights were also tied to internal determinants on the Court. The Hughes Court was not overly supportive of individual rights in the few Substantive Rights cases that survived the screening processes. The First Amendment cases during this time were relatively minor and unrelated to each other. In terms of policy, some of these issues evolved in their own right for the first time. Labor disputes and political protests spawned a number of early free-expression cases.

There were a few important constitutional law cases decided by the Hughes Court. Such cases were landmark decisions that were important in and of themselves and, more significantly, signaled future directions for litigants and the Court. Among the important cases were *Cantwell v. Connecticut* 310 U.S. 296 (1939 term) (the free-expression and free-exercise-of-religion rights of a Jehovah's Witness) and *Minersville v. Gobitis* (flag salute).

The Stone Court was perceived as more liberal than its predecessor and more protective of individual rights; however, its decisions in Substantive Rights did not always reflect more tolerance. On freedom-of-expression issues, the Court appeared to abandon the postulates of the preferred position doctrine in the face of the perceived threat of Communism. The Court permitted Congress to use its broad range of power to limit the expression and advocacy of unpopular ideas. The use of the commerce clause, so effective in buttressing the regulatory authority of the central government, was extended to limit freedom of expression. The Stone Court did make some strides on First Amendment issues, notably freedom-of-religion cases, where the Court incorporated the Establishment and Exercise clauses to the states.

The Vinson Court has not been regarded as a protector of individual rights and liberties. Support for the preferred position doctrine waned and more moderate balancing tests were increasingly advocated by a majority of that Court. The clear-and-present-danger standard was weakened by a variety of provisions that were less protective of individual rights. The agenda space granted to Substantive Rights climbed over 10 percent, fueled by previous decisions and the external environment.

The Vinson Court appeared to be a victim of full-scale policy evolution. The Stone Court had opened what Pritchett referred to as "a Pandora's box" and the Vinson Court was left to face the consequences. The free-expression cases, which had involved harmless nonconformity in previous terms, now involved perceived subversion during the hottest period of the cold war. The relatively easy free-exercise cases of previous periods generated the more difficult Establishment questions that reached the Vinson docket.[9] The situation dictated the responses of the Court. The decisions left litigants in an uncertain position and meant that the agenda would grow slowly.

The sociopolitical environment was responsible for some of the growth of the Substantive Rights agenda that occurred during the early Warren Court. Cases involving alleged Communists were partially responsible for the trend of the Substantive Rights agenda during this period, although the decisions were far from uniformly protective of individual rights and liberties. A surge in religion cases (including the Sunday-closing-law cases) in the middle of Warren's tenure drove Substantive Rights to a level it had never achieved and would not again reach until the early Burger Court.

The general sympathy of the Warren Court for the First Amendment appeared to have an impact on the growth of Substantive Rights issues on the agenda. There were obvious specific effects of the decisions of the Warren Court as well. Though there were many landmark decisions, two merit particular attention. In *Roth v. United States* 354 U.S. 476 (1956 term), the Court dealt with obscenity, an issue that had typically been a part of substantive criminal law, and moved the standards of evaluation to the First Amendment. The impact on the agenda was pronounced for over a decade. Part of the overall decline in Substantive Rights can be attributed to another important decision, *Miller v. California* 413 U.S. 15 (1972 term), which in effect closed the agenda to obscenity cases.

The second landmark, *New York Times v. Sullivan* (1963 term), was remarkably similar in origin and effect. In this case, the Court took the issue of libel, which had traditionally been a part of tort law, and placed it under the rubric of the First Amendment. By the mid-1960s, the addition of libel cases helped expand the Substantive Rights agenda as the Court determined the standards of evaluation for different classes of individuals. The decision also appeared to help the growth of other areas involving freedom of the press. Litigants, perceiving a favorable environment toward the press, sought to expand those protections.

The Warren Court created additional rights in the Substantive Rights area as well. The Court readopted the preferred position standards that favored individual rights and liberties. More significantly, the substance of a number of decisions, such as libel and obscenity law, laid a foundation for later agenda growth. In *Griswold v. Connecticut* 381 U.S. 479 (1964 term), involving the Connecticut contraception laws, the Court created the right to privacy from a number of other areas of law and paved a path that would eventually lead to the creation of abortion law. While Substantive Rights issues were reaching increasingly complex and difficult stages of development, the later Warren Court's support for them did not flag.

Substantive Rights grew to unprecedented levels across the board under the Burger Court. In freedom-of-expression cases, the Court reverted to moderate balancing tests. A majority of the Court expanded use of time, place, and manner restrictions and ad hoc balancing tests. These decisions, however, provided little guidance for implementing and interpreting populations and litigants. The effect is to increase the number of cases the Supreme Court must address to flesh out doctrine. Similarly, in establishment-of-religion cases, the vague tenets of the test laid out in the *Lemon v. Kurtzman* 403 U.S. 602 (1971 term) decision (a case involving salary supplements for parochial school teachers) governed the Court's interpretation.

While freedom-of-expression and religion cases retained their previous levels, other more developed cases expanded the Court's agenda. Some of the growth was tied to external activities like the conscientious objection cases that arose from the Vietnam War. The growth of obscenity cases led the Burger Court to issue the *Miller v. California* decision, which ultimately turned responsibility to lower courts and local community standards. As a result, this decision virtually closed the agenda to such cases. The creation of new rights, most notably abortion in *Roe v. Wade*, expanded other areas of the Substantive Rights agenda.

The Rehnquist Court, abetted by shifts in the membership, has altered the goals of the institution. Important decisions have continued retreats begun under the auspices of Chief Justice Burger. The Court has adopted a more accommodationist stance in church-state relations cases. In a free-exercise case involving the use of peyote in religious services, *Employment Division Department of Human Resources of Oregon v. Smith* 110 S.Ct. 1595 (1989 term), the Court has recently adopted a new standard that may allow the government to limit religious practices. The federal government and a number of states have experimented with regulations to restrict abortions. A number of abortion cases have provided the increasingly conservative Court with the chance to narrow the scope of the *Roe* precedent and perhaps plant the seeds for its ultimate demise. The general pattern of retreat in religion, expression, and abortion cases is punctuated by some major exceptions, like *Texas v. Johnson* 109 S.Ct. 2533 (1988 term), protecting the right to burn the flag.

The agenda space allocated to Substantive Rights cases declined from its peak levels during the Burger and Rehnquist courts. Part of this decline can be attributed to the changing goals of the Court. In general, the decline of the Substantive Rights area has coincided with the rise of the Burger Court. Although the Burger Court was not outwardly hostile to Substantive Rights (after all, abortion rights were created during its tenure), it was not as favorably disposed to the rights of individuals as its predecessor.

As the Court has gotten more conservative, litigants interested in protecting individual rights have been reluctant to use the Supreme Court. There is evidence of retreat by some groups[10] and an increasing reliance on the state courts and state constitutional grounds to protect issues that fall under the rubric of Substantive Rights.[11] In addition, notions of policy evolution have affected levels of Court support for civil liberties. The issues, notably commercial speech, abortion rights, and affirmative action have raised more complex, often multidimensional concerns. Many of these emerging issues changed the nature of the civil liberties conflict. Traditionally, individual rights have been balanced against the authority of society to maintain order. Increasingly, such emergent issues pit the individual rights and liberties of one group against the rights of other groups. The difficulty of such cases has prompted the Court to draw increasingly fine lines and has created declines in the Burger and Rehnquist courts' support for civil liberties and civil rights.

EQUALITY

The final individual area of Civil Liberties is Equality. This area is composed of equal protection claims largely emerging from the Fourteenth Amendment. Among the claims and types of discrimination housed in this area are violations of equal protection on the basis of race, national origin, gender, age, and the like. This is the Civil Liberties issue area that has been most affected by group litigation. Within this broader Civil Liberties domain, Equality was the last of the three areas to capture agenda space. Figure 6.4 shows the pattern of development of the Equality agenda over the 1933-1988 period.

The growth of Equality litigation was different from that of the other two areas, Due Process and Substantive Rights, in a number of respects. The long-term process of gain and the shorter-term fluctuations are significantly different. The long-term trend was marked not by a steady growth, but by three stages of growth. In the first decade, Equality gained 2 to 3 percent of the agenda space. This was doubled for the next decade and ultimately grew to its present levels. In addition, Equality has not been subjected to the same levels of recent decline present in the other areas of Civil Liberties. In the short term, the fluctuations have been dramatic, suggesting the existence of an on-off cycle in agenda allocation. For over two decades since the early 1960s, the normal pattern has been increased attention to Equality one term and a sharp reduction in the following term.

The growth in the agenda space allocated to Equality appears to have important systematic elements and reflects the dispersion of attention in two ways. First, concern for equal protection issues spread from one group to a variety of other groups. Table 6.4 shows the patterns of attention given various groups seeking equal protection under the Fourteenth Amendment. Immigration cases involving the rights of aliens made up the first wave of Equality cases. The ebb of these cases corresponded to the initial surge of racial discrimination cases. Race cases have declined slightly in the past fifteen terms, coincidental with the rise of gender cases and the recent extension of agenda space to a variety of other groups, including discrimination on the basis of age, illegitimacy, or disability. There are also elements of rationality present in the activity involved in race discrimination disputes. Once some activities had been legitimated by achieving the agenda, justices and litigants sought to extend concern to other types of activity. The patterns of growth and decay among the substantive policy subareas are shown in Table 6.5. Early race cases involved election rights, moved to education in the next period, and ultimately led to concerns with employment.

Historically, a few patterns emerge. The levels of agenda space granted to Equality areas were never particularly impressive during the Hughes Court, but there were a few important cases that had future implications. The early Equality cases, for the most part, involved

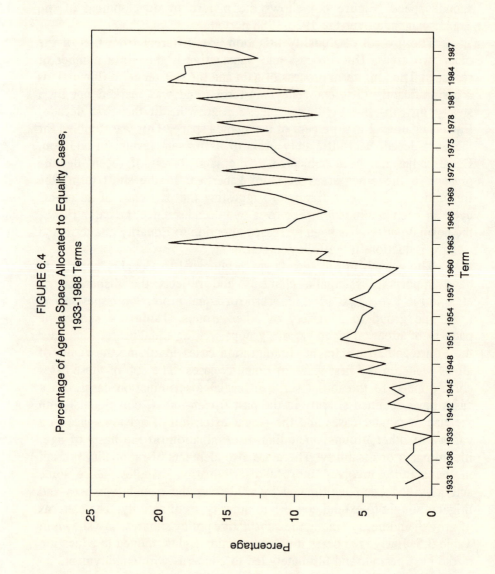

FIGURE 6.4

Percentage of Agenda Space Allocated to Equality Cases,
1933-1988 Terms

Table 6.4 Number of Cases and Percentage of Agenda Space Allocated to Selected Groups in Equality Litigation, 1933-1987 Terms

Group	1933-1937	1938-1942	1943-1947	1948-1952	1953-1957	1958-1963	1963-1967	1968-1972	1973-1977	1978-1982	1983-1987	Total (n)
Aliens (n)	5	1	8	10	18	2	11	5	7	3	12	82
(%)	0.6	0.1	1.2	2.0	3.7	0.2	1.5	0.7	0.8	0.4	1.6	
Race	2	6	6	10	8	25	40	47	44	40	31	259
	0.3	0.8	0.9	2.0	1.6	4.2	5.6	6.6	5.3	5.0	4.2	
Gender	3	0	0	2	0	0	0	6	24	22	14	71
	0.4	0.0	0.0	0.4	0.0	0.0	0.0	0.8	2.9	2.8	1.9	
Illegitimacy	0	0	0	0	0	0	2	3	7	6	2	20
	0.0	0.0	0.0	0.0	0.0	0.0	0.3	0.4	0.8	0.8	0.2	
Age	0	0	0	0	0	0	0	0	2	3	3	8
	0.0	0.0	0.0	0.0	0.0	0.0	0.0	0.0	0.2	0.4	0.4	
Handicapped	0	0	0	0	0	0	0	0	0	1	11	12
	0.0	0.0	0.0	0.0	0.0	0.0	0.0	0.0	0.0	0.1	1.5	
Others	1	1	0	0	0	0	3	0	8	10	7	30
	0.1	0.1	0.0	0.0	0.0	0.0	0.4	0.0	1.0	1.3	0.9	

Table 6.5 Number of Cases and Percentage of Agenda Space Allocated to Selected Equality Subareas, 1933-1987 Terms

Subareas	1933-1937	1938-1942	1943-1947	1948-1952	1953-1957	1958-1962	1963-1967	1968-1972	1973-1977	1978-1982	1983-1987	Total (n)
Immigration (n)	5	0	7	10	17	1	10	4	5	3	10	72
(%)	0.6	0.0	1.1	2.0	3.5	0.2	1.4	0.6	0.6	0.4	1.3	
Elections/ Reapportionment	2	2	4	4	0	10	41	36	20	21	4	144
	0.3	0.3	0.6	0.8	0.0	1.7	5.7	5.0	2.4	2.6	0.5	
Schools/ Colleges	0	1	1	4	6	3	7	17	14	8	12	73
	0.0	0.1	0.2	0.8	1.2	0.5	1.0	2.4	1.7	1.0	1.6	
Accommodations/ Housing	0	3	2	1	0	8	14	8	4	2	4	46
	0.0	0.4	0.3	0.2	0.0	1.3	2.0	1.1	0.5	0.3	0.5	
Employment	3	1	2	4	1	0	0	8	35	35	29	118
	0.4	0.1	0.3	0.8	0.2	0.0	0.0	1.1	4.1	4.4	3.9	
Family	0	0	0	0	0	0	2	4	5	8	4	23
	0.0	0.0	0.0	0.0	0.0	0.0	0.3	0.6	0.6	1.0	0.5	
Social Security	0	0	0	0	0	0	0	0	9	1	7	17
	0.0	0.0	0.0	0.0	0.0	0.0	0.0	0.0	1.1	0.1	0.9	

questions concerning aliens. More importantly, for constitutional law and agenda trends, the first systematic Supreme Court attention to racial discrimination was beginning. The most significant case, *Missouri ex rel Gaines v. Canada* 305 U.S. 337 (1938 term), was decided on narrow grounds allowing a black student to attend an all-white law school. It provided a victory for the NAACP and the first part of the doctrinal foundation that would eventually culminate in the school desegregation decisions. Interestingly, in support of the notion of the expansion of concerns, the preponderance of the Due Process cases decided by the Hughes Court involved the rights of minorities in jury composition, right to an attorney, grand juries, and confessions.

In the area of equal protection, the Stone Court did not pull in the reins as readily as in freedom-of-expression cases. The lessons of World War II, the oppression by the Nazis in particular, forced the United States to face its own race problem. In the wake of the *Gaines* case, the Court demonstrated its commitment to the rights of minorities when the rights involved education and voting (abandoning the white primary). In a decision that would forecast future trends, *Screws v. United States* 325 U.S. 91 (1944 term), the Court sanctioned the use of federal laws to punish state officials who violated the constitutional rights of individuals in the capacity of their duty. The full agenda effects of this decision would not be felt for almost two decades.

The Vinson Court made few major strides in Equality litigation during its tenure. Part of this was a function of the "all deliberate speed" strategy that the NAACP used. The Court continued the incremental pattern of allowing individual graduate students into all-white universities and protecting the students' rights once they were admitted. In *Shelley v. Kraemer* 334 U.S. 1 (1947 term), the Court terminated judicial recognition of restrictive covenants in housing contracts. In general, the record of the Vinson Court in Equality cases stands in marked contrast to the tone of the conservative cases in the other areas of Civil Liberties. The sympathy for these causes encouraged the NAACP and the Legal Defense Fund to continue to probe the Court. The general effects were to expand the Equality agenda. The case that threw open the doors of the Court to Equality issues, *Brown v. Board of Education*, was docketed during the Vinson Court, but was not heard and decided until the Warren Court during the 1953 term.

Any discussion of the early Warren Court must begin with *Brown v. Board of Education*. The decision encouraged the NAACP to continue to attack segregation. The significant growth in Equality litigation postdated the *Brown* landmark, though clearly that decision was an important impetus for agenda growth. More significantly, the broad, unprecedented use of equity by the Court ushered in a type of judicial activism that could be adapted to other areas.[12] In this regard, it is an example of the expansion of concerns. The success of the NAACP provided a blueprint for organized litigants interested in systematically attacking problems through the courts. Although the substantive importance of *Brown* cannot be overestimated, the growth of the Equality agenda did not occur until the later Warren Court. *Brown* laid the necessary groundwork for this later agenda growth.

Equal protection litigation also flourished under the auspices of the later Warren Court. The issue of segregation in education still reached the Supreme Court and was abetted by litigation concerning accommodations as part of the dispersion of attention. Race litigation, which was supported by earlier Courts, was joined on the Equality agenda by other issues, most notably reapportionment. *Baker v. Carr* 369 U.S. 186 (1961 term), the landmark reapportionment case, and decisions refining its broad holdings were responsible for pushing Equality to unprecedented levels of agenda attention. The levels of agenda space were relatively important, but the real significance of the Warren Court decisions lies in the expanse of its doctrine. The reapportionment and race discrimination decisions are among the most consequential in American constitutional law. The importance of these decisions was far greater than the numbers of cases accepted might suggest.

The sustained growth of the Equality area occurred in the Burger Court, which is typically viewed as antithetical to civil rights. In truth, though, a number of the important advances in Equality doctrine such as affirmative action and the recognition of some forms of gender equality occurred during the tenure of the Burger Court. The growth of Equality has belied the declines of Substantive Rights and Due Process. In the aggregate, Equality has largely offset the decline of the other areas, keeping Civil Liberties at similar levels of agenda allocation.

The Burger Court's Equality decisions opened up some new avenues and expanded agenda space. In the wake of *Brown*, the Burger Court pushed the boundaries of education even further in expanding the remedies for southern school segregation. The Court balked at efforts, however, to extend such remedies to northern patterns of segregation. Under the process labeled the "dispersion of attention," concerns with equal employment grew out of earlier concerns with education, voting, and equal accommodations. More significantly for the expansion of the

Equality agenda, the dispersion of attention took another form: spreading equal protection to other groups. The primary beneficiary was gender issues, first addressed by the Burger Court. The success of groups dealing with race litigation provided the impetus and patterns that groups concerned with gender equality could follow.

The Burger Court had other issues to deal with in the Equality area. First, a number of other groups, such as the elderly and the handicapped, sought agenda space with varying amounts of success. The Warren Court bequeathed standards of strict scrutiny for racial discrimination. The Burger Court was forced to determine whether similar standards would apply to other groups claiming discrimination. More difficult and complex cases involving issues like affirmative action also received initial consideration by the Burger Court.

In Equality, the Rehnquist Court has not been sympathetic to claims of race discrimination and has sharply limited affirmative action programs to aid blacks. Concurrently, the Court has not been as likely to limit claims of gender discrimination and, in fact, has allowed affirmative action programs that assist women. The changing goals of the Rehnquist Court have had important symbolic effects and portend practical limitations that may be in the offing. The Court accepted a case that would allow justices to reconsider an important civil rights decision involving privately based discrimination against blacks--*Runyon v. McCrary* 427 U.S. 160 (1975 term). Public and congressional opinion opposing such a retreat was swift and decisive. Ultimately, the Court narrowly upheld the original decision. Increasingly, though, members of the Rehnquist Court support limiting the protections of the Fourteenth Amendment to visible *de jure* discrimination.

DOCTRINAL AND ROLE DEVELOPMENT

This concern with the trends of agenda change and the nature of the substantive decisions over time begs an analysis of the standards of evaluation and the Court's underlying rationale for its decisions. This analysis is particularly important if the Court is assumed to be the "schoolmaster of the republic" and the justices are seen as the modern American political theorists. The decisions of the Marshall and Taney courts drawing the lines between the authority of the states and the central government were the result of a majority of the Court's conceptions of the proper balance between national and subnational governmental authority. Those decisions, however, essentially rewrote or reinterpreted the constitutional provisions that dealt with federalism. Similarly, the impact of the decisions of later Supreme Courts on the economic infrastructure of the United States created a theoretical and philosophical justification for capitalism and its relationship to the American republic.

After 1937, the nine political theorists began to turn their attention to the relationship between the individual and the state. In their decisions over the next half-century, they reconceptualized the Bill of Rights and the Fourteenth Amendment. In those decisions, the justices offered their views of the constitutional polity and the rights of minorities in a majoritarian democracy. Discussions of the role of precedent and the Court's relative adherence to the doctrine of *stare decisis* (allowing previous decisions to stand) are often too narrowly construed. The written opinion is another document in the evolving political theory that emerges from the Supreme Court. Whether it is followed, distinguished, or reversed, a precedent must be addressed and reconciled on some grounds. It creates an American variant of the thesis-antithesis-synthesis dialectic. The continually evolving result is a constitutional political theory that is to guide litigants, lower courts, and other public officials.

The philosophical grounds guiding notions of individual rights were more closely tied to John Stuart Mill than John Locke. Mill's philosophy influenced American constitutional law, but did not attract Court attention until the twentieth century and the transformation in American society. The use of this philosophy was no guarantee of immediate protections for individual rights. Prior to the 1950s, the Court held to a narrow reliance on Mill: protecting political and religious speech. In the Court's early decisions, there were no significant innovations in the Court's rationale and the theory underlying the doctrine.[13] Eventually, in the scheme of policy evolution, more difficult and refined issues reach the docket. That process forced the Court to recognize the future consequences of its current decisions and to provide some guiding principles for future litigants and lower courts.

In this vein, the 1937 watershed and the ideals that emerged from it can be conceived of as the birth of a new paradigm. The fundamental shift in emphasis was a move away from economic issues and in the direction of concerns for individual liberties and rights as enunciated in Justice Stone's Footnote 4. This shift in emphasis can be likened to a change in a paradigm. A paradigm is a set of ideas or theories that direct thoughts and provide puzzles to solve. It represents a reformulation or novel approach to certain problems. A revised paradigm is slowly fleshed out. In the wake of the nascent paradigm, work is slow, fitful, and less than coherent.[14] The change in the agenda possessed many of the properties found in these phenomena. As the other factors will demonstrate, there was an irrevocable, albeit initially slow change in the nature of the agenda and in the means of dealing with the issues on the agenda. The new paradigm was to be built around concerns with individual and minority rights and liberties.

Although it appears that the Court made a conscious effort to change its agenda designs, the changes came incrementally at the outset. The transformation of any paradigm, by definition, takes a great deal of time to materialize. No one theory of individual rights dominated the Court in this period. Rather, a dialectic struggle for a majority of the Court ensued, with one side assuming an extreme position while the other side retained a more traditional stance. Such an intellectual chasm is expected in the wake of an emerging paradigm. In addition, the battle lines drawn in the Court reflected those that arise when the vanguard of the old order confronts those armed with a new paradigm. In a sense, a good analogue is the notion of partisan realignment: a fundamental reordering of the political universe. A new issue arises and shatters the existing lines of cleavage. The result is that one side seeks to cling to the methods, policies, or issues that were the foundation of the declining order. Those groups that were disadvantaged under the existing political structure use the new paradigm as their rallying point.

These competing positions seem to represent those assumed by Hugo Black and Felix Frankfurter. Black came to support absolutism in First Amendment cases and the total absorption of the Bill of Rights to the states. Black refused to accept the balancing and fair trial tests because he felt they too closely resembled the "natural law" perspective the Court had used to control economic issues, which moved the Court into perilous straits during the early New Deal.[15] Frankfurter, however, favored the judicial restraint in economic and civil liberties cases advocated by Oliver Wendell Holmes. Frankfurter took exception to the preferred-position double standard of Footnote 4 because he feared judicial imperialism in civil liberties cases that would resemble the imperialism in economic cases prior to the "switch in time."[16] The doctrines of the Stone and Vinson courts fluctuated between these poles, depending upon the ideological composition of the Court's extant majority. As a result, the precedents provided little guidance for lower courts and litigants. The Supreme Court was operating on a case-by-case basis in confronting subsequent related litigation.

The Court's initial foray into the realm of civil liberties and civil rights brought relatively straightforward issues involving substantial violations of individual liberties that could be corrected rather easily. These decisions reverberated through the system and spawned a second generation of issues that presented the Court with more difficult issues and required the drawing of finer lines. Many members of the Court were reluctant to push civil liberties too quickly. To a Court in flux and uncomfortable with its new role as the defender of individual liberties, these cases caused more angst, less consistency in the decisions, and more time considering the consequences of these more highly evolved questions.

In a sense, the Court magnified the normal problems that exist with individual-issue policy evolution. When an individual issue moves from the core issues to more elaborative and complex stages of development, by definition the cases and the questions raised become more difficult. This is evident in the decline of Court and individual-level support. What compounded the problem in the 1940s and 1950s was the fact that a number of newly emerging issues were entering the policy stream at the same time. As a result, the Court was forced to grapple with a large number of issues that were entering more difficult and complex stages simultaneously. The justices lacked experience in dealing with these issues and were increasingly aware of the interrelationships between the individual areas. Thus, decisions in one area were bound to have ripple effects that would have an impact on separate areas of law.

The Court adopted a new role, but the process of doctrinal construction was painfully slow. Analyses of the period often described the Court's work as "deeds without doctrine."[17] The emergence of new issues, the evolution of cases from relatively clear-cut cases to increasingly grayer areas of law, and the flux in the Court's membership combined to give the Court a more limited perspective. In other words, the Court's decisions reflected a case-by-case determination rather than a systematic process of doctrinal construction guided by broader theoretical principles. Furthermore, the expansion of concerns, the process by which decisions in one area opened up unrelated areas of law, also undermined attempts to build any coherent doctrine or create a philosophical paradigm that would guide decisions across a number of issues. There was little historical philosophy to guide the justices; the early attempts to introduce some principles were interrupted by World

War II and the cold war.[18] The Court had to balance national security considerations with individual freedoms in a potentially volatile and dangerous environment.

The discussion of some of the important substantive decisions and the doctrinal development of each of the Courts since the 1930s demonstrates the long-term trend that led to Civil Liberties agenda prominence. This historical description also demonstrates periods of surges and declines that belie the overall trends. Implicitly, it reveals some of the dynamics that were responsible for the scope and pace of agenda change.

Despite dramatic changes in the sociopolitical fabric of the nation, the economic infrastructure, the role of American government, and the Court's own intentions to modify the cases it accepted, wholesale changes in the Supreme Court's agenda allocation patterns did not materialize immediately. The remainder of this chapter examines the factors that influenced agenda change in the Civil Liberties areas. More specifically, which factors account for the form and pace of agenda conversion to Civil Liberties? The causes must account for patterns of agenda change that gathered momentum over time.

FACTORS LIMITING THE EARLY GROWTH OF CIVIL LIBERTIES

As a result of the goals of litigants and justices, there should be important elements of rationality present in the judicial policymaking process. At the same time, there are a number of countervailing factors that can constrain rapid agenda and policy change. Similar types of constraints exist in any institutional setting, but they may be especially relevant in the judiciary. Civil Liberties issues faced a number of significant barriers on the eve of their first significant appearance on the agenda. First, these issues had historically attracted little court attention. This fact had a number of consequences. Under the rubric of the factors identified by Rohde and Spaeth in their theory of judicial decisionmaking, the goals of the members are constrained by rules and situations. The institutional rules mandated the Court's attention to issues in order to settle lower court conflicts and stabilize the law. Other issues, most notably the economic cases, had claims to the agenda space that militated against the sudden expansion of a new issue. The lack of existing theory to guide individual rights doctrine and the factors that constrain the emergence of new issues serve as situational influences that affect agenda building and policymaking. Because the justices were not attuned to these issues, the processes of screening and decisionmaking these new issues would be protracted.

More specifically, three sets of factors conspired to limit the early surge in Civil Liberties issues. First, the judicial role constrained the Court's ability to clear the agenda of the older issues crowding the docket. Second, the dynamics of the agenda are an inertial force. Once issues establish a claim, these dynamics keep them a central focus of the agenda. On the other hand, the fact that these issues are not established parts of the agenda means the dynamics can keep cases from initially expanding their agenda space. Finally, the process of the emergence and evolution of issues works to slow the early development of issues. Once these barriers were supplanted, the pace of agenda change accelerated. Compounding the problem was the fact that these processes were occurring as a new paradigm was unfolding.

LIMITING THE PACE OF AGENDA CHANGE

The Judicial Role

The judicial role is perhaps the most significant factor limiting the scope of agenda change. With a new set of issues seeking attention, the need to stabilize the exigent policy areas became even more imperative. Filling the agenda with the new individual rights cases meant that attention to some items, most notably Economic cases, had to be reduced to create the necessary space. The move to an individual rights agenda, however, had to be tempered by a need to put Economic issues in order. The Court needed to stay with these issues in order to secure doctrinal consistency and to close some remaining gaps in policy. As a result, Economic cases, no longer in vogue, were able to attract a significant but diminishing proportion of agenda space for a number of terms.

The Court's role induces it to expend precious agenda space that policy designs might reserve for other issues. In short, the role of the Court appears to set an omnipresent context for its agenda building. The irony, perhaps, is that a Court poised to change policy and willing to do so may be constrained: That is, it has to prepare the agenda by taking the very cases it may wish to avoid in order to resolve remaining questions and thus to clear space for other issues. The Court can begin to redirect its priorities as it fulfills institutional obligations to the area it seeks to vacate. Only at that point can the Court expend enough agenda space to consummate the intended changes.

The volitional agenda may have been dominated by individual rights cases, but for a decade after the *Erie* decision and Footnote 4, the Court had to reserve exigent agenda space to put Economic issues in order. This action limited the size of the volitional agenda over that period. While the stated reason for granting certiorari in 80 percent of the accepted Economic cases was to settle lower court disputes or because the resolution of the case was important to judicial administration, less than 20 percent of the granted Civil Liberties or U.S. Regulation petitions were accepted to resolve conflicting interpretations of lower courts. The growth of the two latter areas was a consequence of the decline of the Economic areas.

The Court's current agenda also has a strong bifurcated component. As noted, U.S. Regulation cases appeared to move from the volitional portion of the agenda to the exigent agenda. The later growth of Civil Liberties appears to be related to the changing nature of the Regulation cases, which were reduced in number to create agenda space for the burgeoning Civil Liberties cases.

The Dynamics of the Agenda

The "dynamics of the agenda" refers to the protracted process by which cases come to the Court, are accepted or denied, are decided on the merits, have various impacts, and create waves of subsequent cases. The dynamics of the agenda take this form and pace as a consequence of institutional rules. Court decisions percolate throughout the judicial system and create the impetus for subsequent cases that are brought with the intent of clarifying, expanding, or limiting past decisions in that area. In a broad sense, the dynamics of the agenda can impede the emergence of new issues. These dynamics also serve to introduce an inertia that will keep existing issues on the agenda. Thus, these dynamics are influential in agenda change across time. The evidence suggests that these agenda dynamics were particularly important in early periods. As a result, the dynamics may have constrained initial rates of agenda change, but ultimately abetted the accelerated pace of Civil Liberties growth. Thus, the dynamics introduce situations and conditions that can impede or assist agenda change.

The pace of agenda change, however, is not simply a function of the mix of cases brought to the Court. The responsibility for the construction of policy is shared between the Court and litigants. As noted, the Court has three institutional mechanisms to signal litigants and encourage or discourage further litigation: the patterns of case selection, the nature of the decisions on the merits, and the language of the Court's opinions in those areas. These factors were particularly important in the period of agenda transformation and served to structure the growth of the Civil Liberties agenda.

First, the Court's case selection policies send messages to litigants. Repeat players monitor the cases the Court accepts and rejects and respond to those cues. The success of the Jehovah's Witnesses in having their cases accepted encouraged their legal staff to continue to submit petitions despite the fact that they lost a number of early cases on the merits. The NAACP had similar success having its cases accepted and increased its output as a result.[19] In addition, groups pay attention to the Court's rationale for accepting the cases. Cases accepted to settle lower court conflicts normally carry different messages than cases accepted on policy grounds.

Filing cases, however, is a means to an end. The ultimate goal is victory on the merits of the cases. As a result, the pattern of the Court's substantive decisions sends important messages to groups who attempt to litigate strategically.[20] The legal arm of the Jehovah's Witnesses stepped up its efforts in the wake of unprecedented success in the 1942 term. The American Civil Liberties Union (ACLU) reduced its litigation efforts in what was termed a period of expedience when the Court was perceived as less sympathetic to its causes and its cases.[21]

Finally, the legal experts for groups pay close attention to the actual language of opinions that affect their interests. The tone of the Court's opinion, dicta, and any concurring and dissenting opinions carry a variety of messages. In fact, the language of opinions is a clear indication of the Court's position on a number of Civil Liberties issues. For instance, there were stark contrasts in the language of First Amendment decisions across time. The First Amendment cases decided in the 1937-1942 period were marked by forceful language supporting a broad view of free speech. As the cases became more difficult, the Court tempered the language of its decisions.[22] The Equality decisions were more tentative expressions than the post-1937 free speech decisions. Rather than axiomatic statements supporting the tenets of free expression, the civil rights decisions were authored in measured tones. In response, the NAACP took a slow deliberate pace in its litigation strategies seeking relatively small but safe advances.

In the early stages of the conversion to a civil liberties agenda, proper conditions were not prevalent. Neither the Court nor most organized groups were particularly effective at constructing coherent, consistent policy furthering individual rights.[23] Groups were forming litigation arms and struggling to develop strategies that would maximize their policy goals and reflect the emerging doctrine on the Court.[24] The Court was trying to cope with a series of new issues and its own evolving conception of its new role.

Empirically, levels of support for individual rights fluctuated dramatically in the 1938-1952 period. Judicial support for Civil Liberties dropped from almost 60 percent in the 1938-1947 decade to 36 percent in the 1948-1952 period. This was particularly acute in Substantive Rights, where levels of support dropped from 53 percent in the first decade to 22 percent in the 1950s. This reflects the notion of issue evolution. As the cases get more difficult, support levels are bound to decline. These levels of fluctuation have consequences for the dynamics of the agenda. Inconsistencies in levels of support limit the ability of the Court to cultivate its external resources. Litigants are uncertain of the trends of the Court's decisions. This chills their behavior in bringing subsequent rounds of cases. As a consequence, the cases the Court desired may not have been available at the appropriate time.

An analysis of the cases the Court refused to accept in the 1947-1956 period showed that demand, or lack thereof, was a critical problem. The Court received few civil liberties cases at the very time it seemed to be searching for such cases. In these ten terms, the Court refused five First Amendment and five freedom-of-the-press cases and twenty-three Equality petitions. In virtually all of these thirty-three cases, the Court's refusal to accept the cases left intact liberal lower court rulings. In addition, the Court denied eleven First Amendment religion petitions, some of which were narrow battles between rival sects within a church--controversies the Court has typically sidestepped. The Court refused to hear eleven obscenity and seventeen libel cases, which were not considered to be within the ambit of the First Amendment during this period.

This dearth of cases apparently affected the pace of agenda change. Indeed, the Court received only a trickle of significant individual rights cases into the mid-1950s. The Court's work in specific policy subareas has occasionally been slowed by the need to wait for a case to fill an abyss in the emerging doctrine. The upshot is that when the Court revises policy, whether in a wholesale fashion or in a constrained area, the Court's agenda will reflect the change slowly. At the other end, the agenda may continue to be populated by such cases long after the Court has shifted its focus or attempted to restrict access to the policy area in question. Once litigants provided the cases, the agenda space allocated to Civil Liberties cases grew rapidly.

The effects attributable to the process labeled the dynamics of the agenda were initially compounded by the novelty of the Civil Liberties issues. The emergence and evolution of First Amendment issues, beyond those concerned with free speech, and equal protection constrained agenda change at the outset. The greatest effects of the novel issues on agenda change were time bound and were manifested for over a decade.

The Novelty of the Issues

The agenda tends to be inhospitable to new issues. Despite the goals of the justices and the Court, situations and conditions can block the emergence or sudden growth of a new issue. Wholly new issues do not suddenly appear on the agenda; rather "new issues" tend to be recombinations of old issues. This supports the influence of situations and conditions on judicial decisionmaking and, by implication, agenda building. New issues tend to emerge from other related issues that are found at later stages of development. In fact, this expectation is met at the broadest levels. The standards and tests the Court used to confront and evaluate Substantive Rights issues such as "void for vagueness," "overbreadth," "least restrictive means," and the scrutiny tests developed to resolve equal protection issues were borrowed directly from economic tests and doctrines.[25]

Although the dynamics of the agenda would normally constrain the initial pace of agenda change, when that factor is coupled with the emergence of a series of new issues that arrive simultaneously, the effects are even more dramatic. These issues had to emerge and develop their own identity. That process normally takes a while to unfold. Because these issues had few analogues, the problem was compounded.

Once the new issues reach the agenda, they lay claim to future agenda space as they begin to move through their individual evolutionary cycles. As a result, significant agenda change is manifested a few terms after the seminal decision opens the new area. The effects of these processes were particularly important during the period in which Civil

Liberties issues were making their first significant appearance on the agenda.

The 1937-1947 period has not been categorized as a creative judicial period and the Court in this era was seen as cautious.[26] Part of the reason for the tentative expansion of rights was that the Court was having to settle new issues while attempting to construct theory that would underpin the emerging doctrine. This was complicated by the fact that many of the early Civil Liberties cases came from other issue domains. In particular, a number of individual rights cases emerged from wartime restrictions, governmental regulations, and economic disputes.[27]

This process is consistent with notions of policy emergence and evolution. A new issue area often arises at a later stage of an existing issue area. If there is sufficient Supreme Court interest or the multidimensional issues are significantly different from one another, then the Court will separate the issues. The result is that the original issue returns to its doctrinal development while the new issue is considered on its own terms. The fundamentally different nature of the individual rights issues from the wartime restrictions, government regulation, and economic issues that spawned them convinced justices that different standards of decision were necessary. As a consequence, the Court had to separate the Civil Liberties issues and evaluate them differently.

Although Civil Liberties cases were growing in agenda prominence, such issues did not capture a significant percentage of the Court's agenda space for over a decade and did not reach a consistent level of 30 percent until 1957. There is also weighty individual- and institutional-level evidence to suggest that the emergence and evolution of issues structured agenda change.

On the individual level, studies of decisionmaking find an important amount of fluidity (individual vote changing) in voting on the merits during the period of the initial ascension of Civil Liberties.[28] Some of that fluidity may be attributed to the novelty of the issues and a lack of established voting patterns in these areas.[29] A study of a later period, once Civil Liberties had established their claim to agenda space, reported a marked decrease in fluidity[30] that may be due to the fact that the individual rights issues had become regular agenda items.

Similarly, research concerned with this early period and biographies of the justices who served during this period demonstrate that the voting patterns of these members in the realm of civil liberties were inconsistent and still evolving.[31] Even libertarian justices like Douglas and Black were hardly consistent protectors of individual rights in the early periods of Civil Liberties growth. Studies of recent terms found that this "freshman effect" had diminished.[32] The rise of new, unprecedented issues apparently contributed to this freshman effect. What may have compounded the inconsistency is the fact that there was a substantial amount of membership turnover during this period. Furthermore, many of the new justices came to the Supreme Court without prior judicial experience. For instance, Douglas came from the Securities and Exchange Commission, Black from the Senate, and Frankfurter from the halls of academia. Thrust onto the High Court, the new members were confronted with unprecedented issues while learning the nuances of judicial procedures and new roles in a legal environment.[33]

On the institutional level, the effects of the emergence and evolution of new issues were also evident. Space on the agenda may expand or contract although there are finite limits. Space expands when the issues are routine and have been before the justices for years. Solutions are handy and predilections well established. Consequently, decisions requires less time. Often the Court is deciding one narrow issue in the case for the sole purpose of resolving a conflict between lower courts. As a result, the justices can accept more cases, meaning that space on the agenda expands. The Court possesses other tools that expand the size of the agenda to a degree. The Court often accepts a series of similar cases at the same time. When it does so, the Court typically chooses one of the cases as a vehicle for its major precedent and then briefly addresses parallel cases, urging lower courts to pay particular attention to the major precedents. The Court also appears to take additional cases that it is uncertain about. Rather than extensively review the case, the Court vacates and remands it again with reference to the case that got the full opinion.

New policy areas and issues, on the other hand, contract the agenda. There are start-up costs, decision patterns have not been established, and the novelty of the issues require more preparation and research by justices and clerks. Justices attempt to tie new issues to existing issues to provide a frame of reference and a set of standards that might be adapted. Over time, however, notions of policy evolution suggest that the new issue cannot be neatly subsumed under the rubric of an existing policy area. If the issues are separated, a new area results and costs more agenda resources than existing issues with well-established standards.

The evidence seems to substantiate the existence of these properties. As these processes began to unfold and Civil Liberties cases were increasingly gaining the agenda space formerly reserved for Economic matters, the number of cases decidedly shrunk (from normal levels of 130 to 150 cases to less than 100 per term in the 1947-1956 period), reaching a low of 75 in 1953. This occurred despite the fact that the number of petitions filed in the Court did not decline.

The growth of Civil Liberties can be described as steady, but incremental for two decades and quite dramatic thereafter. The early dialectic battle created inconsistencies in precedents and a lack of doctrine. The novelty of the issues affected the dynamics of the agenda, which in turn was responsible for the pace of agenda change until the 1950s. Once issues had accumulated a judicial history and the construction of the nascent doctrine was under way, large-scale agenda growth could occur. At that point, the dynamics of the agenda create the impetus that keeps these issues viable and a central concern of the Court.

LATER AGENDA CHANGE:
THE CONFLUENCE OF FACTORS

Membership changes eventually promoted proponents of the preferred position doctrine to primacy. A majority was able to construct doctrine to guide decisions in individual rights cases. Further membership changes in the later Warren Court galvanized the Court's liberal wing, abetted the development of individual rights, and further stimulated the Civil Liberties agenda. The goals of the individual members and the collective Court turned even more decisively toward individual liberties. The effects of this change were significant in that the goals of the Court could overcome some of the constraints imposed by rules and situations.

Symbolically and practically, the *Brown* decision had enormous consequences. The decision to desegregate the schools was accomplished through the radical extension of a common law remedy, equity. The role of the Court in requiring positive action to combat discrimination was also unprecedented on such a grand scale. The *Brown* decision encouraged judicial activism in a variety of other areas, confirming notions of the expansion of concerns. In addition, it ushered in a form of egalitarianism as a substantive response to liberalism.[34] The decision also alerted groups to the values and possibilities of further litigation efforts.

The influence of groups with experience in planned litigation provided the justices with the appropriate cases at important junctures of doctrinal development. Thus, the conditions and situations needed to continue the process of agenda change and policy construction could proceed. The ability of justices and litigants to marshall and combine resources is consistent with notions of agenda dynamics and issue evolution. Additional agenda space was available for Civil Liberties because Economic cases and the exigent agenda had been pared to their lowest levels. In this fashion, the Court was able to adapt the institutional rules so that their interference with the goals of members was significantly reduced.

Issue evolution led litigants to bring cases raising new, more difficult issues involving *de facto* discrimination, affirmative action, and gender discrimination. This continued the growth of the Civil Liberties agenda through the Burger Court. On other sets of issues, most notably Due Process, the Burger Court refused to extend many rights and retreated from Warren Court doctrines in other areas. This retreat coincided with the emergence and proliferation of conservative groups who used the judiciary systematically for the first time. Such changes kept the agenda open as litigants seeking to halt or reverse the expansion of individual rights probed to determine where evolving doctrine would eventually lead. A classic example of this is evident in the criminal procedure area. The agenda flourished with the broad protections of the Warren Court. Defendants who lost in the lower courts had a core of sympathetic justices. During the Burger Court, however, the state found a favorable venue when a lower court reversed a conviction on procedural grounds. Although dispositions changed and policy evolved, the agenda did not reflect wholesale changes. Criminal procedure cases retained a significant, but diminished, hold on agenda space.[35]

The need for extra volitional agenda space for Civil Liberties was met in two ways. First, the Court would settle lower court disputes only after they had existed for a while. Rather than settle conflicts as soon as they arose, the Supreme Court would wait for conflicts in Internal Revenue and Economic cases to reach a number of lower courts before expending valuable, finite agenda space to resolve them. Second, the Court moved U.S. Regulation cases to the exigent agenda and reduced the agenda space available to such issues.

In general, large-scale changes in the Court's ideological composition are expected to have a significant impact on the nature of Court doctrine. The effect on the agenda is less pronounced. Three factors explain what seems to be counterintuitive. First, if new justices have shifted the Court's ideological balance, they may want to alter the Court's doctrine in some areas, which requires taking the same kinds of cases in order to reverse or distinguish previous precedents. Thus, the Burger and Rehnquist courts, presumably more hostile to individual rights, have actually expanded the Civil Liberties agenda. Second, the judicial role requires the "new" Court to continue filling in the gaps left by its predecessors. Finally, changes in doctrine are bound to yield inconsistencies between lower courts, which will ultimately keep issues on the agenda in order to settle these disputes. Lower court judges will recognize the fact that doctrinal changes are under way, but may be unable to determine the eventual extent of such revision.

A number of factors limited the pace of change in the early period, but eventually the introduction of a new dynamic abetted the later growth of Civil Liberties and the concurrent change in the nature of the agenda. The patterns of change contain important procedural and substantive elements of rationality. The use of the recrudescent agendas is the procedural component of the change and demonstrates the purposive nature of the Court's agenda building. The expansion of concerns and the dispersion of attention represent the substantive components of the change and demonstrate the important linkage between agenda building and policymaking. Each of these substantive patterns resulted from the recrudescent agendas. The Court's policymaking designs had to be implemented through the selection of cases and the longer-term, broader process of agenda building.

DYNAMICS OF RECRUDESCENT AGENDAS: THE PROCEDURAL STRUCTURE OF CHANGE

The periodic recrudescent agenda represents a significant change from normal agenda patterns. Such recrudescent agendas do not emerge full blown, but result from dynamics set in motion earlier, particularly from landmark decisions and policy windows. Periodically, the Court is able to resolve enough questions from its exigent agenda that it has accrued agenda resources to continue the doctrinal construction initiated by earlier landmark decisions. Such landmarks are invitations to groups concerned with that issue and related areas. Litigants respond to landmark decisions and bring the next round of cases. A sudden expansion of agenda space for Civil Liberties also sends a message to the legal community and encourages groups to bring additional cases. The Court clears agenda space, most of the costs being borne by Economic cases from the exigent agenda, to continue the doctrinal construction initiated by the landmark decision.

Theoretically and procedurally, the notion of a recrudescent agenda makes sense. The dynamics of the agenda and the need to attend to the exigent agenda have two effects on change. During most terms, these factors dampen the pace of change because the Court must continue to address some issues, notably Economic cases, for the sole purpose of settling disputes. If Economic issues are sufficiently settled for the time being, the volitional agenda can be expanded. Thus, the situation becomes appropriate for broader-scale changes in the agenda.

Periodically, the dynamics are responsible for an acceleration of agenda change reflected in the recrudescent agenda. Landmark decisions set new issues, often involving individual rights, into motion. The Court must attend to these policy areas by fleshing out doctrine and answering questions left in the wake of the original decision. A policy window opens the agenda and lays a claim to future resources.

The Court has some ability to concentrate its resources by pairing similar cases. The Court often accepts and decides a significant case in an area and takes other similar cases at the same time. This conserves agenda space and the Court's time because the ancillary cases are decided with specific reference to the important decision. The division of the Court in the lesser cases tends to mirror the central case. The additional decisions tend to be authored by the same justice who wrote the foundation case or are unsigned *per curiam* opinions that apply the holding of the basic case.[36] The number of paired cases is significantly greater during the recrudescent agendas than during normal periods. The Court uses almost three times more paired cases during recrudescent agenda terms (an average of fourteen cases per term) than during normal terms (five cases per term). The number of *per curiam* decisions that tend to be basic applications of existing precedents were also greater during recrudescent agendas. The marked rise in the use of *per curiam* opinions (7 percent of the cases as opposed to 2 percent in regular terms) helped alter the pace of agenda change. These differences are magnified during the early recrudescent agendas. In this way, the justices can modify the institutional rules and constraints to achieve their policy goals.

This method of joining similar cases may reflect a broader process as well. The empirical investigation of the agenda shows that portions of the Court's agenda demonstrate the existence of an on-off cycle in case selection. The Court marshalls agenda resources by limiting its consideration of some issues in order to attend to others. These are not structural changes, but a short-term expansion of the agenda space allocated to some areas and corresponding reductions in other areas. Subsequently, the Court reverses the process, reconsidering areas that lay fallow at the expense of the recent beneficiaries of agenda space. The existence of on-off cycles in both the broader areas and the subareas lends credence to the hypothesized rationality underlying recrudescent agendas.

There is conclusive evidence of an on-off cycle. On the broadest level, there are clear growth trends in the Due Process, Substantive Rights, and Equality areas. Even within unmistakable trends, there is an oscillating cycle in which an area receives additional attention one year and significantly less during a following term. The periodicity of oscillations varies over time. During the nascent stages of Civil Liberties issues, there were period four oscillations (one "on" term and three "off" terms) that were reduced in stages, ultimately to a period one oscillation ("on" then "off") as Civil Liberties flourished. Oscillations are particularly pronounced during the periods surrounding a recrudescent agenda. The average increase in agenda space granted Civil Liberties in a recrudescent term is 13 percent (compared to a 0.8 percent increase in normal terms). Oscillations in Due Process cases were prevalent until the late 1960s. Substantive Rights and Equality have more recent on-off cycles.

Although on-off cycles should exist throughout, they exhibit different characteristics during recrudescent terms. During normal terms, gains by one area of Civil Liberties come at the expense of other individual rights issues. For instance, an increase in Due Process would be balanced by a decline in Substantive Rights and/or Equality, rather than at the expense of Economic or U.S. Regulation. By contrast, the cost of the expansion of Civil Liberties during a recrudescent agenda was borne by Economic, U.S. Regulation, and, in early terms, by Federalism (an average decline of 14 percent).

The existence of an on-off cycle and the use of paired cases and *per curiam* opinions have significant implications for agenda change.

Such patterns provide some rationality in constructing the agenda. Taking similar or paired cases allows justices to answer a series of questions simultaneously. More significantly, they allow the Court to construct policy more thoroughly by extending doctrine to different fact situations simultaneously. This provides the opportunity to impose consistency on the decisions, guide lower courts, and suggest further directions for litigation.

Neglecting other issues for a term provides agenda resources to accomplish this. These processes reinforce the transition to a Civil Liberties agenda. Increasing the agenda space allocated to Civil Liberties sows the seeds of future expansion. In the wake of a recrudescent agenda, exigent space must be reserved to resolve unsettled questions. The volitional agenda will be affected if the issue spreads into other related policy domains of interest. Such cycles are also concessions to the judicial policy process. The Court's decisions have the opportunity to percolate through the system and beget the next round of litigation. The Court could later turn its attention to those areas.

The recrudescent agenda tends to be derivative of previous agendas and policy windows opened earlier. Many cases represent narrow questions left unresolved by previous precedents, gross violations the Court feels compelled to correct,[37] or result from lower court conflicts. Occasionally lost in the numbers, however, are some very significant landmark decisions that occur during a recrudescent agenda. *Mapp v. Ohio* and *Monroe v. Pape*, major landmarks that continue to have profound effects a generation later, were decided during the 1960 recrudescent agenda.

Most importantly, recrudescent terms alter agenda dynamics. In such a term, the agenda space allocated to Civil Liberties grows dramatically. In the following term, Civil Liberties receive reduced Court attention, but the new level is greater than that achieved prior to the recrudescent agenda. In subsequent terms, the Court entrenches Civil Liberties at this level and enhances that position slightly. Thus, the most significant advances in Civil Liberties and corresponding declines in Economic and U.S. Regulation occur during recrudescent agendas. The cycle continues when the next recrudescent agenda moves Civil Liberties to another level of growth and establishes new dynamics or reinforces the existing dynamics.

The existence of significant numbers of paired cases and oscillating cycles is an element that marks each recrudescent agenda. In terms of general policies, recrudescent agendas were marked by significant reductions in the agenda space allocated to Economic cases during the early periods and Regulation cases more recently. The available space was transferred to Civil Liberties. The findings demonstrate empirical dimensions to the patterns of change, but do not reveal much about the substance of agenda change. The notion of spillovers, the means by which one or more issues evolve from a related issue, is critical in understanding the dynamics and substantive importance of agenda change.

THE SUBSTANTIVE NATURE
OF AGENDA CHANGE

The successful opening of a policy window often creates spillovers into related areas. When an institution commits itself to the consideration of one issue, it may, in effect, commit to a series of related issues. In terms of the theory of decisionmaking, this means that the appropriate situations or conditions for agenda building and policy change exist. Given the attempts at both rational and purposive behavior by litigants and justices, it is not surprising that judicial policymaking would exhibit these traits. Spillovers may occur during any term, but due to the availability of additional resources, recrudescent terms are particularly important vehicles.

Empirically, such spillovers can be found when the Court expands its nets to cover related issues. In addition to filling interstices left in the wake of landmark decisions, the Court may graft tested constitutional principles to related issues. The evidence bears this out on two levels. There were notable spillovers in each of the recrudescent agendas, but the form and structure of these phenomena have varied over time. The early recrudescent agendas follow a process labeled the "expansion of concerns" and are a consequence of the novelty of Civil Liberties issues at the time. During this period, the success in one summary area like Substantive Rights can be transplanted to another broad area like Equality. The later recrudescent agendas occurred in the context of an agenda already populated with individual rights cases and take a different form. The dispersion of attention is the means by which later recrudescent agendas unfolded. At this level, the decisions in one narrow area within Due Process, Substantive Rights, or Equality can be used to open or decide the cases in adjacent subareas.

THE EARLY RECRUDESCENT AGENDAS:
THE EXPANSION OF CONCERNS

The agenda literature suggests that there are rational connections between related issues. The phenomenon identified as the expansion of concerns confirms the proposition that an institution that deals with a collective issue (Due Process) will turn to other collective issues (Substantive Rights and Equality). The rise of an issue can create a recognition among justices and litigants that other areas merit attention. Initial success causes the most powerful spillovers. Entrepreneurs are encouraged to rush to the next issue while the momentum of the success in opening a policy window is still present.[38] Litigants who support the Court's landmark decision are interested in having the precedent extended to other areas of law. Justices who have used the landmark decision to achieve their policy goals should also be interested in broadening the impact by transplanting similar doctrine to related areas. Certainly, this seems evident in the earliest Civil Liberties policies. Once again, it emphasizes the influence of situations and conditions that enhance the emergence of new issues and the growth of the Civil Liberties agenda.

Procedurally, related issues can succeed if the coalition that constructed the initial program can be reformed. Policy change establishes new principles that entrepreneurs can use to assist other items. This is particularly relevant in the Supreme Court, where constitutional protections create precedents that various policy entrepreneurs hope can be adapted to their issues. The early recrudescent agendas occurred in the context of an agenda bereft of individual rights cases, but with a cadre of justices that were increasingly responsive to the general ideals, if not specific applications, of Civil Liberties. The justices had not constructed full-blown theoretical principles or specific legal doctrines, but there was some movement in this direction and an increasing concern with Civil Liberties issues. Empirically, the early recrudescent agendas (1942, 1947, and 1951) demonstrate similar spillover effects. The ascension of an individual area seemed to create the environment or conditions for the next area. Interest in Due Process spread first to Substantive Rights, and later into Equality. Footnote 4 and its first manifestations encouraged those interested in extending Civil Liberties. This horizontal type of spillover describes the expansion of concerns. Figure 6.5 illustrates this process, which governed the early recrudescent agendas and the early growth of the Civil Liberties agenda.

FIGURE 6.5

Expansion of Concerns:
Horizontal Spillovers

Substantive Rights	→	Due Process	→	Equality
Gitlow v. New York		*Palko v. Connecticut*		*Smith v. Allwright*
Cantwell v. Connecticut		*Adamson v. California*		*Shelley v. Kraemer*
Everson v. Bd. of Education		*Wolf v. Colorado*		*Brown v. Bd. of Education*

The expansion of concerns explains the structure of the early recrudescent agendas. The 1942 term, the first recrudescent agenda, resulted from growth in Due Process, which had an established claim to agenda space, and Substantive Rights, which was making its first significant appearance. The Jehovah's Witnesses were responsible for the proliferation of Substantive Rights cases, having six petitions accepted. The religious group had some success in having its cases accepted, mixed success on the merits of the cases, and increasing support of policy entrepreneurs on the Court and in the legal community.[39] They were successful in extending the issue in their cases from narrow arrests to free-expression and free-exercise claims that raised constitutional issues. More significantly, the Jehovah's Witnesses created an environment for future group litigation, particularly in the Equality area.

A surge in Equality cases was behind the 1947 recrudescent agenda. Another repeat player, the NAACP, was responsible. The Court continued to carve out narrow exceptions to *Plessy v. Ferguson* to open graduate and professional schools to black students. The Court also addressed the issue of segregated accommodations and the exclusion of blacks from juries, which were Due Process cases. The one landmark decision, *Shelley v. Kraemer* (housing), was a significant milestone on the road leading to *Brown v. Board of Education*.

The recrudescent agenda of 1951 was marked by each of the three Civil Liberties areas simultaneously reaching another level. The 1951 term involved precursors of issues that would become significant. *Beauharnais v. Illinois* 343 U.S. 250 (1951 term) raised the issue of libel a decade before it received constitutional recognition. The case involved alleged group libel against racial minorities. The Court had an early opportunity to end school segregation but suggested that further proceedings were necessary. Five cases raised the issue of incorporation of the criminal procedure amendments to the states. The incorporation issue was transplanted from the Substantive Rights domain. Decades earlier, the Court incorporated free speech, and in the preceding decade, the two religion clauses. The Court, however, was unwilling to nationalize the Due Process amendments at this time. The inability to specify clear standards was the impetus for a number of Due Process cases. The general "fair trial" standard and the specific "special circumstances" used for right-to-counsel cases induced the Court to decide a number of cases.

The evidence supports the existence of the expansion of concerns. The Court was encouraging litigants to bring a variety of Civil Liberties issues but had not constructed coherent constitutional theory as a guide. The opening of subsequent policy windows was marked by a coupling of similar solutions to emerging problems. The evolution of the tests used in the Equality area parallels the previous development of tests used in First Amendment freedom-of-expression cases.[40] Studies of judicial decisionmaking also lend credence to the notions of spillovers. During the early development of these issues, the major areas (criminal procedure and First Amendment issues, in particular) shared a common civil liberties dimension and received consistent levels of support from the same justices.[41]

The cross-pollination of doctrine from one area to another is not surprising considering the role of external policy entrepreneurs. The best-known repeat players of the time were often involved in a variety of policy areas. The NAACP and the Legal Defense Fund are best known for their attacks on discrimination in housing, education, and employment under the Fourteenth Amendment. They were also active in protecting the freedom-of-association rights of their members and have had extensive involvement in the Due Process area, seeking to end all-white juries and attacking the imposition of the death penalty on the grounds that it is applied in a racially discriminatory fashion.[42] The ACLU,[43] various conservative groups,[44] and the solicitor general[45] litigate or submit *amici* briefs in the Due Process, Equality, and Substantive Rights areas. Often new issues are framed in the language of past decisions and litigants seek remedies used in other cases. Success in one area spawns attempts to translate that success to other domains. The ability of groups to achieve the decision agenda and win on the merits is not a lesson lost on other groups. Policy entrepreneurs perceiving a problem have available a variety of alternatives and solutions that have been used elsewhere.

The incorporation of the two religion clauses of the First Amendment to the states created external pressure from groups and internal sympathy among some justices to extend protections to Due Process.[46] The work of groups like the Jehovah's Witnesses in Substantive Rights was critical in laying a foundation for Equality litigation.[47] The early cases sensitized the justices to further extensions of individual rights that were not confined to narrow domains due to their novelty.

These spillovers were a function of the transformation of the Court's role. The Court began to fulfill the promise of Footnote 4 by expanding its agenda across a variety of areas. In turn, the decisions, particularly in the Equality area, were laying a foundation for a transformation in American social policy, and the Court would be a leading actor in that endeavor.

LATER RECRUDESCENT AGENDAS: THE DISPERSION OF ATTENTION

At the next level, the connections are even more direct. Justices begin work in one subarea and spread their attention to related domains. As noted, the rise of specific issues tends to trigger other specific issues, reinforcing notions that there are elements of rationality to agenda change and conditions or situations are appropriate. For instance, once the Court incorporated the exclusionary rule to the states, pressure to extend incorporation to the Fifth and Sixth Amendments and beyond was felt. Exercise-of-religion decisions led litigants and the Court into the Establishment cases.[48] In the Equality area, the success of the NAACP in attacking enforced segregation in housing and education led to its efforts to combat discrimination in accommodations and employment.

The influx of new members raised the number of liberal justices to a critical mass that could pursue goals and develop theoretical and doctrinal principles. Increasingly, the Court was able to stamp a consistent imprint on Civil Liberties. The incorporation of provisions of the Bill of Rights restructured the relationship between the states and the individuals. Further, the Court began a process of practical elimination of the traditional exceptions to freedom of expression.[49] Although the Court continued to maintain that obscenity and libel were unprotected, it narrowed the bases on which these types of exceptions could be found. In scope, the Warren Court, which presided over the explosive growth of Civil Liberties, continued to adopt complementary principles of libertarianism in civil liberties and egalitarianism in civil rights cases.[50]

The later recrudescent agendas demonstrate a distinctive type of spillover effect, the dispersion of attention. The context for these later agendas (1957, 1960, 1967-68, 1976) was very different from the earlier recrudescent agendas. First, each of the major areas had already established claims to the agenda. Second, Civil Liberties increasingly dominated the Court's agenda. The new recrudescent agendas reinforced and enhanced this supremacy. The structure of agenda change in later recrudescent agendas has been more likely to occur within each substantive area, rather than between them. In a sense, then, the spillovers have been vertical, as Figure 6.6 suggests.

The 1957 and 1960 agendas represent transitional recrudescent terms combining remnants of the expansion of concerns with the advent of the dispersion of attention spillovers. During these terms, the Court accepted a variety of cases involving alleged Communists, spanning the Equality, Due Process, and Substantive Rights areas. These cases involved criminal procedure, deportation, loss of citizenship, freedom of association, job dismissal, and the authority of the House on Un-American Activities Committee. The preponderance of the spillovers involved the dispersion of attention. The 1960 recrudescent term reopened the agenda to free-exercise-of-religion cases through a series of cases involving Sunday closing laws. Minority rights spread across a variety of subareas involving elections, accommodations, employment, and freedom of association.

The 1967-1968 terms represent the next level of individual rights growth. Due to the proliferation of Civil Liberties cases, the Court may have needed two terms to pursue institutional and individual goals and attend to various subareas. The Court extended the incorporation process to cover jury trials (*Duncan v. Louisiana* 391 U.S. 145 (1967 term)) and double jeopardy (*Benton v. Maryland* 395 U.S. 784 (1968 term)). Search and seizure and self-incrimination raised more complex questions with decisions like *Terry v. Ohio* (patdown searches), *Marchetti v. United States* 390 U.S. 39 (1967 term) (declaring illegal gains on tax forms), and *Alderman v. United States* 394 U.S. 165 (1968 term) (wiretapping and search and seizure).

In the Substantive Rights area, a variety of notable cases represent the dispersion of attention during the 1967-1968 terms. Two cases that defined "symbolic speech"--draft card burning to protest the Vietnam War in *United States v. O'Brien* 391 U.S. 367 (1967 term) and students wearing antiwar armbands in *Tinker v. Des Moines School District* 393 U.S. 503 (1968 term)--evolved from "purer" forms of expression. The first comprehensive parochaid case (state aid to Catholic schools) and a case involving the teaching of evolution were decided during these terms.

While cases alleging racial discrimination continued to attract agenda space across a variety of areas, the most significant Equality decision during this recrudescent agenda was *Levy v. Louisiana* 391 U.S. 68 (1967 term). This decision expanded the net of equal protection to cover illegitimate children. This was important because it served to connect previous standards used for race and national origin to

188

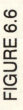

FIGURE 6.6

Dispersion of Attention:
Vertical Spillovers

Equality

Race Discrimination
Brown v. Bd. Of Education
→
Illegitimacy
Levy v. Louisiana
→
Gender
Reed v. Reed
→
Age
Massachusetts v. Murgia

Due Process

Search and Seizure
Mapp v. Ohio
→
Right to Counsel
Gideon v. Wainwright
→
Self-Incrimination
Miranda v. Arizona
→
Jury
Duncan v. Louisiana
→
Double Jeopardy
Benton v. Maryland

Substantive Rights

Artistic (Obscenity)
Roth v. United States
→
Free Press (Libel)
New York Times v. Sullivan
→
Speech Plus Conduct
Edwards v. South Carolina
→
Symbolic Speech
United States v. O'Brien

subsequent applications for gender issues and the disabled, even though the Court soon effectively rescinded this decision.

The 1976 term was also marked by the dispersion of attention and was the result of landmark decisions from previous terms. In the Substantive Rights area, the next generation of abortion cases was accepted and included questions of government funding. In addition, the Court moved decisively into a recently opened area: commercial speech. An establishment case that combined elements from previous parochaid cases, *Wolman v. Walter* 433 U.S. 229 (1976 term), also reached the decision agenda.

Equality cases also spread into new terrain. Gender discrimination cases raised a variation on the existing themes. These new cases involved a different type of gender discrimination—programs favoring women, which presented the Court with a dilemma, whether to allow benign programs to compensate for past inequalities or to apply the scrutiny standards rigidly. The Court also continued to address the issue of school desegregation in northern schools.

Due Process has undergone a very different type of transformation due to ideological changes on the Court. The increasingly conservative Court began to limit, reverse, or refuse to extend protections the Warren Court granted the accused. The recent willingness to create exceptions to the exclusionary rule and search-and-seizure protections brought successful petitions to create similar exceptions to the *Miranda* rule and double jeopardy protections during the 1976 term.[51]

Spillovers during later recrudescent agendas can be more directly traced to the policy windows. Justices begin work in a subarea and spread their concerns to proximate subareas. The dispersion of attention is evident in each area. For example, the *Mapp* decision created pressures to incorporate the Fifth and Sixth Amendments to the states. As noted, exceptions to the exclusionary rule have spilled over to other areas. In Substantive Rights, attempts have been made to extend protections granted political expression to commercial, artistic, and symbolic speech. The Equality area is the clearest indication of this process. Successful attacks on enforced segregation in education and housing led to efforts to combat discrimination in accommodations and employment. Such success was noted by women's groups, the elderly, and the disabled who sought constitutional protection.[52]

Both external and internal policy entrepreneurs see the connections and attempt to couple similar solutions to related problems. The Court cleared agenda space to resolve questions in the wake of previous landmarks and to shift attention to related issues. Thus, policy streams are re-created to open proximate policy windows. In effect, justices and litigants recognize the existence of the proper situation in order to pursue their goals.

The spillovers that define the dispersion of attention reflect the transformation of the Court's role and American politics. The Warren Court assumed the role of protecting rights and liberties. The agenda policies permitted the Court to accomplish its goals. The increasingly hostile reception of the elected branches to the scope of the Warren Court's decisions led to changes in the Court. The Burger and Rehnquist courts expanded the Civil Liberties agenda through the dispersion of attention. The goal was to reverse or limit the past policies that had fallen into disfavor. Such a reversal may portend a transformation in the Supreme Court's role.

CONCLUSION

The transformation of American politics created a virtual revolution in the Supreme Court's role. The transformation of the Court's role was reflected in dynamics that would alter the agenda and the nature of theory and doctrine over time. The growth and changes in Civil Liberties were at the heart of the Court's transformation. The early individual rights cases broke new constitutional ground and prepared the agenda for future growth.

Though a majority of the Supreme Court was interested in pursuing individual rights, the existing dynamics of the agenda served to limit any immediate change. Institutional norms and informal rules require the Court to set aside exigent agenda space that might be used to fill members' goals. The judicial role kept the venerable agenda items on the Court's docket. The exigent agenda continued to shrink over the next two decades as the volitional agenda increasingly gained prominence. Situations and conditions change over time and can enhance or constrain the goals of the members. The novelty of the new Civil Liberties issues consumed some of the volitional agenda space and pared the numbers of Civil Liberties cases the Court could accept at the outset. Gradually, the Court was able to overcome the retarding effects of these factors and the growth of Civil Liberties was accelerated.

The emergence of new issues should always affect the nature of agenda change. When a number of new issues arise simultaneously and the Court must create a philosophical and doctrinal foundation for their consideration, the impact is multiplied. The Court drifted during the early stages of Civil Liberties growth. The mandate of Footnote 4 captured majority support and represented a new brand of liberalism. National security priorities interrupted the construction of doctrine. Ultimately, when conditions allowed, the Court had more experience with Civil Liberties issues and the influx of new members strengthened the Court's majority. By the 1960s, the goals of the Court were established, the situation was propitious for the further development of individual rights, and the Court was adapting institutional norms to permit the increased attention to Civil Liberties issues.

There are strong theoretical and empirical reasons to believe such a dynamic process exists. Policy windows set various agenda dynamics in motion or alter existing dynamics. Many of the issues that emerge through a policy window are initially part of the volitional agenda. Once that window has been opened, the issue lays claim to agenda space for the foreseeable future. Lower courts will disagree about the scope of the original precedent and litigants will seek to extend or limit previous decisions. These cases may move the issue to the exigent agenda.

The periodicity of recrudescent agendas does not imply a purposiveness to the Court that does not exist but instead is a function of the Court's need to stabilize doctrine. It takes the Court a few terms to attend to the Economic issues to the point that the issue can be put aside to expand the individual rights agenda. The recrudescent agenda also provides the opportunity to attack unresolved Civil Liberties issues in a more systematic fashion. During the recrudescent agenda terms, the institutional rules and norms and the situation facing the Court reinforce the goals of the members of the Court.

The successful opening of a policy window pushes that specific issue on to the decision agenda. Perhaps more significantly, it may serve as the impetus for other policy windows that will introduce related issues to the decision agenda. In general, this process resembles issue evolution. A decision of the Court spawns related cases, often more difficult and complex and requiring the drawing of finer lines. Empirically, spillovers can be found in the recrudescent agendas when the Court expands its nets to cover a series of related issues. In addition to filling interstices left in the wake of landmark decisions, the Court may use tested constitutional principles to settle related issues. The periodic process structured and hastened the transformation of Civil Liberties and the transformation of the Court's agenda.

The results of the analysis suggest some significant implications. On the broadest level, the results of this analysis confirm the proposition that a diachronic institutional perspective is a valuable supplement to individual-level research. This neoinstitutional study suggests that processes of agenda change exhibit elements of rationality and have a defined structure. The institutional perspective emphasizes the connection between the agenda-building and policymaking stages of the judicial process.

The existence of important elements of rationality in processes of agenda building and policy construction is not meant to impute too much rationality to the Court as a unitary actor. The trends are incremental, but there is a bounded rationality underpinning the process. Policy entrepreneurs supplement both the incrementalism and rationality of the policy process. Advocates have the incentive to bring a range of cases to refine existing precedents; thus, issues tend to remain on the agenda. Groups are also responsible for structuring policy change by sequencing the cases brought before the Court. Entrepreneurs can advance their specific issue or may turn their attention to related areas.

Members of the Court are also important entrepreneurs with policy goals derived from their values and attitudes. Justices use case selection and the agenda-building process to pursue these goals. The judicial role orientation of members restrains the unrestricted use of values and attitudes. The judicial role also contributes to the incremental trends, but in a rational manner. Once issues achieve the agenda, the Court must allocate exigent agenda space to resolve lower court disputes and continue the construction of doctrine. Although this slows the pace of change, it is designed to achieve rational purposes: consistency in the law.

7

The Rehnquist Court and the Future of the Court's Agenda

The selection of Justice David Souter continues a process that began with the nomination of Chief Justice Warren Burger. The Supreme Court continues to move to the right on the ideological spectrum with the prospect that the conservatives on the Court are reaching a critical mass. Those prospects were enhanced by the resignation of Justice Thurgood Marshall. The increasing strength of this wing of the Court provides the potential numbers to control case selection and decisions on the merits. More importantly, membership changes have provided a margin that increasingly allows the conservatives to write more forceful opinions. With a closely divided Court, the conservatives could win their share of the cases, but the tone of the opinions would need to be moderated to retain a majority. With the advanced ages of the few remaining liberal justices, the prospects are that further changes in the membership of the Court are imminent. The question is, will these changes structurally alter the composition of the Supreme Court's agenda?

Figure 7.1 reviews the trends in agenda allocation to the major issue areas over the past half-century. The issues that form the Economic dimension have reached their effective nadirs and show no sign of rebirth. Federalism has demonstrated recent growth that is expected to continue. Many individual issues within the U.S. Regulation policy area have declined in agenda allocation. External forces and internal agenda dynamics may reinvigorate these issues and move some of them back to the volitional agenda. Civil Liberties remain the most significant consumer of agenda space. The lofty agenda status of Civil Liberties suggests that changes in agenda priorities will come at the expense of such issues. Growth in an area like Equality may come at the expense of other Civil Liberties areas, like Due Process, and mask underlying changes in the overall area.

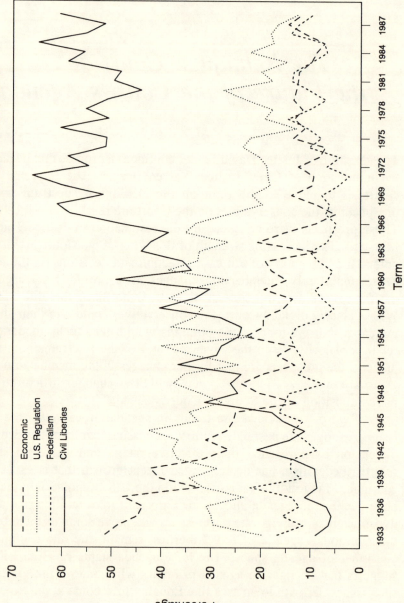

FIGURE 7.1

Trends in the Allocation of Agenda Space to Four Major Areas, 1933-1988 Terms

Economic
U.S. Regulation
Federalism
Civil Liberties

In terms of the theory of decisionmaking that has guided this analysis of the transformation of the Court's agenda, it is clear that the goals, rules, and situations have changed to a degree. The selections of Justices Kennedy and Souter and the retirement of Justice Brennan have altered the goals of the institution. Marshall's resignation should continue that process. Changes in some of the case screening procedures, which have eliminated large numbers of mandatory appeals and may reduce the *in forma pauperis* petitions, have altered some of the rules of the institution. Furthermore, the broad use of the cert pool and the increased number of justices involved have affected the institutional rules and dynamics of the process. Finally, the rise of conservative interest groups, the presumed politicization of the solicitor general's office,[1] and a less hospitable external environment for civil liberties and civil rights have created a situation for potential changes.

THE PROSPECTS FOR AGENDA CHANGE

The decisions of the Rehnquist Court have begun to demonstrate some evidence of change. In the aggregate, the decisions are somewhat more conservative than those of the later Burger Court. Perhaps more importantly, significant changes in the underlying philosophy of the Court have begun to emerge. Such philosophies have not captured majority support on the Court, but they have had the effect of altering the tenor of debate. The impact of policy entrepreneurs can be felt in direct and indirect ways. If a cadre of entrepreneurs has the votes to control decisions, they can dominate the specification of alternatives. Lacking a majority, such entrepreneurs may still have the ability to introduce different perspectives to the debate and force opponents to deal with the substantive and philosophical nature of their positions.

A number of justices on the Burger and Rehnquist courts could be described as conservative by their judicial behavior, but a few have grounded their decisions in an abiding theoretical and philosophical framework. On the current Court, William Rehnquist[2] and Antonin Scalia[3] propound relatively coherent judicial philosophies that structure their decisions. The effect of membership changes and the introduction of new aggressive philosophical precepts may ultimately change the nature of the theory that has underpinned judicial decisions since the "switch in time" and the mandate of Footnote 4.

The "new" philosophy, which represents a practical return to past doctrines in some senses, advocates attention to the original intent of the framers of the Constitution and a stricter construction of the document. This theory is complemented by an increased willingness to defer to elected branches in civil liberties and civil rights, thus rejecting the twentieth-century liberalism that has guided Court decisions and policymaking in individual rights cases. Even as the Burger Court undermined many precedents that came from the Warren Court, the nature of debate occurred within the context of the theoretical framework that had been in place since the ascension of the "preferred position" doctrine. The changes that might accompany the rejection of this theory would have the effect of altering the nature of debate and the standards of decisionmaking.

Some effects of the changing goals have been evident for the last decade and could be accelerated by recent changes in the Court. One of the basic assumptions underlying this study is that the judicial policy is the result of an interactive process between litigants and justices. Changes in the goals of the Court have demonstrated visible changes in the strategies of litigants and groups. The number of conservative groups using the courts has increased and these groups are more aggressive in using the judiciary. By the same token, liberal groups, who used the courts so successfully in past decades, have adopted other strategies. Liberal groups have sought to enhance their visibility in the elected branches of government, have adopted defensive strategies in using the courts, and have increasingly shifted their attention to the state courts and state constitutional protections.[4]

Concurrently, the Court begins to show signs of reopening parts of the Federalism and economic agendas, particularly in some areas of U.S. Regulation. Membership changes have elevated a majority that would recast the doctrine of intergovernmental relations. The changes in doctrine, which had exposure in the *National League of Cities* decision, reflect a retreat from national supremacy and a renewal of a form of dual federalism. David O'Brien claims that "at no time in the last half-century have there been stronger defenders of states' sovereignty on the U.S. Supreme Court"[5] than Rehnquist and Sandra Day O'Connor. If Rehnquist's prophecy in his dissent in *Garcia* comes to fruition, the changes in doctrine would alter the dynamics of the agenda in this area.

With the scope of federal activity, a change in Federalism doctrine would trigger a spate of cases and stake a renewed claim to significant agenda space. Empirically, given the growth of allocation of agenda space over the past decade, such a process appears to be under way. The dynamics of the agenda reveal that a sustained pattern of growth normally gains momentum and leads to even further expansion of agenda space.

The transformation of Federalism might have spillover effects on two other areas. First, unleashing state authority would give rise to new regulatory schemes. Once Federalism questions were resolved during the New Deal, U.S. Regulation flourished. State Regulation cases should expand their share of agenda space if changes in Federalism remove barriers to state authority. If regulations proliferate, cases challenging their scope and effects should reach the dockets in larger numbers. State courts would be responsible for deciding most of these cases, but if a broad deregulation attitude swept the Supreme Court, justices might limit the effects of state regulatory policies. Changes in Federalism might reinvigorate Court concern with U.S. Regulation. Limits on congressional authority under a new doctrine of dual federalism might necessitate a rewriting of regulations that would require some Court attention.

Changes in Federalism doctrine may have more wide-ranging spillover effects as well. If the Court advances a coherent, broadly based constitutional philosophy that supports the exercise of state prerogatives across a variety of domains, the effects may be felt outside the economic realm. Most notably, the Court could reverse some of the incorporation decisions and permit broader latitude for state police power in individual rights cases. Justices O'Connor[6] and Kennedy[7] have advocated a loosening of restraints on states in such matters, particularly criminal procedure. For different reasons, because they are seen as a potentially more favorable forum, some proponents of individual rights support use of the state courts to protect civil liberties. The Warren Court extended nationalization of the law from economic to civil liberties. A reversal of Federalism doctrine might encourage a similar process, changing the nature of individual rights as well.

For Regulation, a propitious situation--an open policy window--has been provided by the policies of deregulation. A policy entrepreneur, Justice Scalia, has the institutional position to pursue his philosophies. A hint of the impact of these changes is already visible and may portend additional changes. There is evidence that the ideological divisions defining an issue as part of the Court's volitional agenda are reemerging in Regulation cases. Fewer cases are accepted for the sole reason of resolving circuit conflicts, and fewer are decided unanimously. Individual justices are increasingly consistent in their decisions. If these changes are structural and enduring, rather than a temporary aberration, then some areas of Regulation policy will probably remain or migrate back to the volitional portion of the agenda. If that occurs, it is probably due to some revisions in the underlying philosophy that governs such decisions. Although a return to the theoretical principles that placed the Court in jeopardy in 1937 is unlikely, the new philosophy would undoubtedly provide greater freedom for businesses and allow fewer governmental restrictions. In this respect, it would represent a turn away from the twentieth-century liberalism born of the New Deal and eventually buttressed by the Supreme Court. If there is a change in the underlying nature of the Regulation cases, one effect will be apparent: a decline in the allocation of agenda space to Civil Liberties cases. Such a change could be the first overt signal of a transformation in the Supreme Court's agenda.

There is empirical evidence of some differences in the case selection policies of the Rehnquist Court, but whether that portends a revision of the agenda-building priorities of the Court remains to be seen. On the broadest level, the Rehnquist Court marginally, but significantly, cut the number of cases accepted in the 1987 and 1988 terms. Part of this may be attributable to the battles over Robert Bork's nomination and the occasional health problems that left the Court without a full complement of justices. Under such circumstances, the Court may defer judgment on controversial issues until all nine justices are present.

More significantly, the Rehnquist Court appears to be converting its institutional agenda in fundamental ways. In the 1987 and 1988 terms, across each of the policy domains including Civil Liberties, case selection was dominated by petitions that raised lower court conflicts. In a sense, the Court appeared to be reducing the volitional portion of its agenda and expanding exigent agenda space. This is in marked contrast to the agenda-building policies of the Court that had been in force, unabated, since 1937. Proponents have often argued that the Court should concentrate on settling problems in the lower courts and paying attention to the judicial role rather than pushing the individual policy dispositions of the dominant majority. Even though the members of the Court could certainly pursue ideological designs through the exigent agenda, it was more difficult and less efficient than having the discretion provided by the volitional agenda.

The 1989 term suggests that any thoughts of long-term structural changes in the rules may be premature. The exigent and volitional portions of the agenda returned to their previous relationship. Cases, particularly those involving Civil Liberties, no longer had to have a lower court conflict to reach the institutional agenda. In addition, the numbers of cases accepted rose to previous levels.

It is easy to assume that the 1987 and 1988 terms were temporary aberrations brought about by the fact that the Court was undergoing some changes in membership. Perhaps both the liberal and conservative wings were risk-averse in a period of Court drift. In the 1986 term, Chief Justice Rehnquist did not react particularly well to the new mantle of leadership. He continued to vote his conscience in many cases, disdaining the potential that went along with the new position. As a consequence, Justice Brennan was to assign opinions when Rehnquist dissented, enhancing his influence. Perhaps the uneasy ideological balance of the Court prompted both wings to move slowly. The occasional appearance of a Court vacancy may have led the justices to attend to the less controversial items on the exigent agenda and hold the volitional agenda issues in abeyance until the wrangling over the appointment process was completed.

On the other hand, the changes in the goals of the institution and the situation facing the Court suggest that the 1987 and 1988 terms may be the beginning of a transformation of the Court's agenda. If the goals and rules are effectively changed, then they will induce a change in the rules of the institution: a reformulation of the volitional and exigent portions of the agenda. In one sense, some transition is virtually guaranteed. Levels of agenda allocation to Civil Liberties cases have reached an effective ceiling. The dimensions of such a change might not be profound in any broad empirical sense. Not every subarea of Due Process, Substantive Rights, and Equality would be moved to the exigent agenda. More likely, the transition would resemble the process of transformation in U.S. Regulation cases during the Burger Court. Some subareas, like labor relations and antitrust, continued to hold space on the volitional agenda, while most subareas of Regulation exhibited the tendencies seen in exigent agenda cases.

Individual subareas within the Civil Liberties domain might begin to migrate to exigent agenda while others stay at the center of the Court's concerns. The most likely candidates for such a transformation would probably come from the Due Process area, particularly the criminal procedure areas. Some of the Substantive Rights areas might be the next to move. For a variety of reasons, Equality might be the last issue area to devolve. If such patterns follow this hypothesized process of transformation, then they would represent a trend similar to the initial growth of Civil Liberties. Although the patterns are not deterministic, the first area to stake a claim to the volitional agenda might be the first to forfeit that claim as well, and that process would probably not be completely coincidental. The process of spillovers governs the growth of agenda space. In other areas, in the past, the reduction of agenda space took a similar form.

The Due Process decisions of the Burger Court halted and in some cases effectively reversed the expansion of the rights of the accused. The Rehnquist Court has continued this trend. Few of the seminal decisions of the Warren Court have been overturned, but certainly major exceptions to the protections have been created. The Court has increasingly deferred to the judgment of police, prosecutors, and judges. It is a mark of the exigent agenda issues that decisions tend to be consistent. If the intent is to move the Due Process issues, the first stages may be in progress. These trends are most evident in the criminal procedure cases, which have declined significantly in the last decade. The rise of civil due process and prisoner rights cases have masked the decline of the criminal procedure cases.

One potentially troubling Due Process issue appears to have moved from the center of the Court's concerns: death penalty cases. The Supreme Court did not accept every individual challenge to capital punishment, but most of the justices claimed that such petitions earned very close scrutiny due to the ultimate nature of the punishment. In the last decade, however, the Court has been considerably more likely to respect the judgment of the jury if the proper procedures have been followed. Search-and-seizure cases may have begun similar trends. Increasingly, the Court accepts these cases to resolve an important issue in the administration of justice. Although those case selection policies certainly could qualify as part of the volitional agenda, they could be interpreted as related to the judicial role.

One decision in the 1990 term and a rules change may have an impact in altering the dynamics of the agenda. In *Arizona v. Fulminante* 111 S.Ct. 1246 (1990 term), a majority of the Court extended the "harmless error" standard to the admission of involuntary confessions. In other criminal procedure decisions, the Court has tolerated procedural irregularities if they resulted in such a harmless error. The effect is to grant greater latitude to state enforcement officials, giving them the opportunity in court to defend their procedures. The increasingly broad sweep and application of the harmless error standard continues to resemble the vague fair trial standard abandoned by the Warren Court. The immediate effect of the *Fulminante* decision on the agenda may not be evident. The Court will continue to accept such cases because the harmless error standard is unclear and states will encourage the Supreme Court to expand the discretion granted officials.

Over three dissents, Supreme Court Rule 39 was amended to permit the Court to deny "frivolous or malicious" *in forma pauperis* filings. Justice Marshall penned the most pointed dissent, claiming that the Court's tradition will now read: "All men and women are entitled to their day in Court only if they have the *means* and the *money*."[8] Though the practical effects of the amended Rule 39 and the *Fulminante* decision may be unclear, the symbolic message is testimony to the ideological changes in the Court's membership.

In the area of Substantive Rights, related processes of decisionmaking are under way. The Burger and Rehnquist courts have been more conservative than their predecessor, but the retreats have not been as pronounced. Advances in some areas and inconsistency in establishing standards in other areas keep these items current, although levels of allocation have declined. The failure to specify clear standards in free-expression, religion, libel, and abortion decisions virtually guarantee that these issues will remain on the agenda. Even if the Court decides to move these issues to the exigent agenda, they will remain important because lower courts will undoubtedly disagree about interpretations. Some evidence of change in a few subareas is available. Cases involving obscenity were shifted to the exigent agenda after the *Miller v. California* decision. The Supreme Court turned the decisions in obscenity cases over to local communities and normally accepted their judgments by refusing to review lower court decisions. A significant proportion of the decline in Substantive Rights can be attributed to the decline in obscenity decisions. Recent freedom-of-religion decisions that permit local authorities a great deal of discretion may lead to some measure of judicial abdication.

The Equality area should be the last to be moved from the exigent agenda. Because the area was the last to stake a claim to agenda space, it is still evolving. In addition, the dispersion of attention occurred later in the Equality cases and is still unfolding. The Court has more questions to consider before it can provide guidance and delegate authority over such issues to other actors. Indeed, while Due Process and Substantive Rights have declined, Equality cases have increased their share of the agenda space. Equality cases have been responsible for keeping Civil Liberties at its past levels.

In general, significant changes may be under way but may not be visible at the aggregate level. In other words, the Court may systematically move some subareas off the volitional agenda while it continues to address other subareas within the broader domain. As a result, the agenda space granted to Civil Liberties overall may not decline even though important substantive changes may be occurring. In fact, if the Court was interested in removing certain issues from its agenda, in the short term justices may need to address additional cases from that area to establish some consistency and provide guidance for lower courts. If such a process is currently unfolding, it will take a while for its full manifestation.

THE IMPLICATIONS OF
FUTURE AGENDA CHANGE

To undertake agenda change of the magnitude suggested would have important consequences for the role of the Supreme Court, the nature of public policy, and the rights of individuals. The surest manifestation of agenda change would be sharp, long-term reductions in the percentage of agenda space allocated to Civil Liberties. To abdicate its responsibilities in the various areas of individual rights would be akin to the Court's retreat from economic matters in 1937. At that time, the Court had an outlet: civil liberties and civil rights. What would fill the vacuum that would be left if Civil Liberties issues were delegated to other political actors is uncertain. The Court could delve back into the economic areas, but it would be on turf claimed by other actors. This would leave the Court in an interstitial, secondary role. The Court could rewrite Federalism doctrine. Redrawing the lines between the levels could take a number of years to implement and could require the expenditure of significant agenda resources.

The more likely alternative would be that the Court would follow the direction that the Rehnquist Court seemed to take in the 1987 and 1988 terms. Under this scenario, the Court would confine its case selection to those petitions demonstrating clear lower court conflict that had spread to a number of circuits. This practice has important costs for the Court as a policymaker. Cases that arrive from the exigent agenda are significantly less likely to be structured. This case selection strategy could also take a measure of coherence and rationality out of the construction of policy and doctrine.

In the volitional cases, justices and litigants often have the ability to gauge the broad direction of doctrinal construction. This affords them the opportunity to be relatively systematic in bringing to the Court the types of cases that will be logical extensions of the recent decisions. The Court can be somewhat proactive in selecting those cases that fit the next stage of development. The justices also have the opportunity to manipulate the petitions. Exigent agenda cases, however, force the Court into a more reactive stance. The cases are selected not because they are the next questions to be addressed but because lower courts have disagreed about the interpretation of similar fact situations. Although coherent policymaking would not be impossible, it would be more difficult.

Such a transformation of the agenda and the Court's role would affect the Court's agenda-building and policymaking capacity. The reactive stance that would result from these changes would undermine the nature of agenda building. In effect, the agenda would be reduced to the mere selection of cases. The interrelationships between current and subsequent agendas and between policy areas competing for agenda space would be reduced significantly.

Changing the role of the Court would have significant implications for notions of pluralism. Since 1937, insular minorities and unpopular groups have had a forum in the Supreme Court. If this avenue were foreclosed, it might mean the systematic disenfranchisement of a number of groups. One remaining point of access would be the state courts, which might create a patchwork of protections that would vary from state to state or region to region. The vast expansion of the Civil Liberties agenda was a result of the Warren Court's attempts to standardize the law through the incorporation of the Bill of Rights to the states and an expansive interpretation of the Fourteenth Amendment.

The systematic disenfranchisement of Civil Liberties from the Court's agenda seems unlikely, but such a move is a logical implication of a pure philosophy that emphasizes judicial restraint and deference to the elected branches of government. Despite the fact that justices who espouse such views are increasingly being nominated to the Court, this decrease would represent an extreme change in institutional rules and goals. Even if such a transformation were conceived, it would take a while to be implemented.

FORCES CONSTRAINING AGENDA CHANGE

Assessing the potential for agenda change in the Rehnquist Court affords the opportunity to summarize the most significant findings of this study. If there is one overriding generalization to be gleaned from the analysis, it is that there are important forces retarding rapid widespread agenda change. Even if the Rehnquist Court desires to move away from the agenda priorities of the last half-century, it is bound by the agenda policies and the doctrine of its predecessors.

The judicial role mandates that justices prepare the policy community before they begin to abdicate a policy area. With the vast array of Civil Liberties issues on the agenda, it would take the Court a long period of time to "settle" or begin resolving this large a number of issues. The dynamics of the agenda, the process by which cases are decided, reverberate through the system and beget subsequent cases. The process of closing the agenda takes a somewhat different set of dynamics. The intent of the Court is to condition demand and to signal litigants and lower courts, which requires a consistent line of decisions.

The process by which policies evolve from simpler to more complex forms also implies a process of devolution. The Court seldom directly overturns a previous precedent, particularly a landmark decision, without some prior warning.[9] A Court that changes its ideological goals is likely to take the same types of cases and issues as its predecessors in order to limit their decisions and to keep the specific issues viable and prominent on the Court's agenda.

Reverse processes of the expansion of concerns and the dispersion of attention would be expected to dominate the agenda and the policies of the Court under these circumstances. Judicial retreat in one area would be a signal to interested litigants to seek similar decisions in other domains or related areas of law. Indeed, since the Burger Court, these types of spillovers have occurred. When the Court began to pare protections in some areas of Due Process, pressure formed to reduce other rights in criminal procedure. In addition, once the Court showed signs of retrenchment in Due Process, litigants interested in restraining Substantive Rights and Equality sought access to the Court. Thus, even if the justices intended to move away from Civil Liberties, the number of policy areas requiring attention would guarantee that such issues would remain on the agenda. The dynamics of the agenda restrain the pace of agenda change.

Perhaps most significantly, Civil Liberties cases raise constitutional issues and mean that the Supreme Court must be the ultimate arbiter of such concerns. The Court could reverse the incorporation decisions and make the states largely responsible for civil liberties and civil rights within their jurisdictions, thus placing some broad limits on the size of the Civil Liberties agenda because many of the cases arise from state policies on individual rights and liberties. The Court could also adopt the position of Chief Justice Rehnquist and Justice Scalia and significantly limit the reach of the Fourteenth Amendment to *de jure* discrimination that is racially motivated. Denying access to a number of groups seeking the protections of the equal protection clause would sharply reduce the numbers of cases coming to the Court.

CONCLUSION

In the immediate future, it is unlikely that the Rehnquist Court can reverse the agenda priorities that dominated the Court since the ascension of the principles enunciated in Footnote 4. That footnote did not change the agenda overnight, but it did alter the dynamics that would eventually lead Civil Liberties to primacy. Similarly, if the Rehnquist Court is pursuing a different set of agenda priorities, the effects of its work will not be visible for a number of terms. Given the ideological predilections of the members of the Court, it is likely that Civil Liberties issues will remain an important component of their volitional agenda. The Rehnquist Court may have a significant amount of doctrine to rewrite before it vacates the area, if indeed that is the ultimate goal of the Court.

When future scholars and analysts map agenda and doctrinal trends, they may compare the influence of Ronald Reagan to Franklin Roosevelt a half-century earlier. The Nixon appointees changed the ideological goals of the Court, but some of the long-term effects were muted. The influence of past justices and existing doctrine limited the impact of the changes in the goals. In addition, the Burger Court faced a well-entrenched paradigm and a series of existing standards. Its work in slowing some of the Warren Court's advances and reversing law in other areas was the important spadework needed to initiate more significant structural changes that would transform the institution and its role.

The Reagan administration, representing an external situation for judicial policy change, filled a consequential role in what may ultimately be a transformation in the Court. A transformation that George Bush appears poised to complete. First, through his selections, Reagan was able to enhance the station of the conservative wing of the Court, not only by replacing moderates with conservatives, but by replacing an older conservative with a much younger ideologue. These actions provided additional conservative votes, which would translate into a higher percentage of victories and increasingly more forceful decisions.[10]

What may be more important, if the Court is beginning to adopt a new role, are the philosophies of the justices, particularly Rehnquist and Scalia. Reagan provided Rehnquist with the institutional position to pursue the new chief justice's judicial philosophy and ideological goals. Not only did Rehnquist have additional votes, he had the authority to construct the discuss list, to structure debate by speaking first in conference, and to assign the writing of the majority opinions. Adding Scalia provided intellectual and philosophical support as well as a vote. Had Robert Bork survived the nomination process, the theoretical and philosophical foundation would have been strengthened even further.

Although Justices Kennedy and Souter[11] do not appear to share the constrained value systems of Rehnquist and Scalia, they may, with Justices White and O'Connor, help to provide a comfortable majority for conservative decisions. The nature of debate and the opinions of the Court may increasingly come to reflect philosophical designs that may trigger a new paradigm. Such a transformation would change institutional rules and the role of the post-New Deal Supreme Court. Historical precedent suggests that the effects of such a transformation could be felt for well over a generation, perhaps for the next half-century.

Appendix 1:
Inclusion of Cases and Composition of Policy Areas

The decision was made to include all cases that received an opinion of one page or more in *The United States Reports*. This decision was based on the need to exclude relatively trivial cases. This rule yielded 7,688 cases in the 1933-1988 period, of which 7,682 fit one of the fourteen policy area categories. The tables that show the trends in five-year increments use the 1933-1987 period to create eleven five-year periods. The cases in the 1988 term did not differ markedly from those in the 1983-1987 terms in number or percentage.

The policy area is the most important variable under consideration. *The Supreme Court Reporter*, published by West, has its "key" system that labels the policy areas. These were used in the present study in the clearest cases, when all the keys listed the same policy area as controlling. In cases with multiple codings, the decisions were read quickly in order to prioritize the issue areas. The case was ultimately coded in terms of the most important issue or policy area (the original codings preserved the three most important issues, but for purposes of analysis, the single most significant issue was used). The categories are a mixture of substantive policy areas and legal concepts or rights. A few comments are necessary to describe the taxonomy of cases.

Due Process includes primarily, but not exclusively, criminal procedure cases. Among the areas are search and seizure, self-incrimination, death penalty, right to counsel, jury procedure, and double jeopardy. In addition, due process considerations in administrative proceedings are included.

Criminal Law involves cases that turned on a substantive interpretation of a criminal statute by the Court.

Substantive Rights is primarily composed of First Amendment cases. This harbors a variety of modes of expression, association rights, freedom of the press, as well as the exercise and establishment of religion. Individual rights to an abortion, rights of privacy, and cases involving conscientious objectors and alleged Communists are also included.

Government as Provider involves cases arising from the post-New Deal expansion of governmental power. Most involve social security and welfare questions. Most are substantive questions and statutory in emphasis.

Equality cases are often characterized as civil rights and involve alleged discrimination on the basis of race, gender, age, disability, or similar factors.

U.S. Regulation involves economic regulation of private industries by the central government. The major areas include labor relations, securities regulation, commerce, environmental concerns, patents and copyrights, bank regulation, food and drug regulation, and antitrust questions. The issues tend to involve administrative and regulatory agencies such as the National Labor Relations Board, Securities and Exchange Commission, Food and Drug Administration, and the Interstate Commerce Commission, among others.

State Regulation similarly involves economic regulation of private industries by state governments. Many of the same issues, such as labor relations, energy regulation, and environmental concerns, are involved in state regulatory schemes. State taxation is also included in this category.

Internal Revenue is concerned with cases involving interpretation of tax codes and Internal Revenue Service policies.

United States as Litigant involves disputes concerning government contracts and United States liability for, or immunity from, certain actions.

State as Litigant includes boundary disputes between two states, navigable waters cases, and state liability for certain actions.

Federalism revolves around the boundaries between federal and subnational authority. This includes questions involving the authority of the central government under the interstate commerce clause. Another class of cases involves disputes between the central government and individual states over waterways or navigable waters.

Ordinary Economic Litigation houses a series of miscellaneous cases with a common economic denominator. The cases typically involve the allocation of a good or service between competing litigants. Often the cases involve personal injuries and represent a suit by an individual against a company. The majority of the disputes arise from injuries or alleged wrongful death actions against companies by railroad workers or sailors. Some of the cases involve losses in shipping. Later cases, reflecting changes in technology, involve injury and wrongful death tort actions in airplane mishaps. Many of these cases ultimately turn on jurisdictional issues of which courts have the authority or the type of judgments the lower courts can utilize in deciding the dispute.

Foreign Affairs includes cases involving governmental power in international affairs. Many of the issues involve treaties and Trading With the Enemy Act.

Separation of Powers involves the Supreme Court's attempts to regulate the boundaries between the judiciary and the other branches of government or between the legislative and executive branches. Some of the questions involve the province of the judiciary, but most are attempts to delineate congressional and presidential power.

An analysis of the policy areas reveals that some of the fourteen areas share common elements that suggest that they fit a broader dimension. Due Process, Substantive Rights, and Equality form a *Civil Liberties* dimension. The Internal Revenue, State Regulation, United States as Litigant, State as Litigant, and Ordinary Economic areas share a common *Economic* dimension. Part of the analysis focuses on these broader Civil Liberties and Economic dimensions.

Appendix 2:
Tenure of Chief Justices
of the United States

1789-1794	Jay Court	The Supreme Court was considered insignificant and did not even convene one term.
1795	Rutledge Court	Appointed in recess, Rutledge's nomination was defeated.
1796-1800	Ellsworth Court	Court lacked "energy, weight,...dignity."
1801-1835	Marshall Court	Infused the Court with power of judicial review, breathed life into the central government, and defined nation/state relations.
1836-1863	Taney Court	Redefined federalism, but is best remembered for *Dred Scott* decision that precipitated Civil War.
1864-1873	Chase Court	Upheld the authority of the central government in economic matters and reconstruction.
1874-1887	Waite Court	Sharply limited the protections of privileges and immunities clause, 13th, 14th, and 15th Amendments.
1888-1909	Fuller Court	The Court sided with business against federal power and organized labor.

1910-1920	White Court	Continued economic policies of its predecessors and placed early limits on free speech.
1921-1929	Taft Court	Allowed some governmental regulation and began the process of incorporating the Bill of Rights to the states in *Gitlow v. New York.*
1930-1940	Hughes Court	Rejection of the New Deal hurt Court's legitimacy and led to a new role: protecting individual liberties and deferring in economic matters to the elected branches.
1941-1945	Stone Court	Continued to allow central government regulatory authority, but protection of individual liberties was limited by World War II.
1946-1952	Vinson Court	Generally considered a conservative tribunal, some of its restrictive decisions can be attributed to the complexity of unprecedented civil liberties cases.
1953-1969	Warren Court	Engineered a constitutional revolution in civil rights and civil liberties, interposing federal authority in economic and individual rights areas.
1969-1986	Burger Court	Marked retreat in some civil liberties areas, but advances in abortion and gender equality defy conservative categorization.
1986-	Rehnquist Court	Has continued retrenchment of Burger Court and portends an acceleration of the retreat as the conservatives reach a critical mass.

Appendix 3:
Supreme Court Decisions Cited

Adamson v. California 332 U.S. 146 (1947 term)
Alderman v. United States 394 U.S. 165 (1968 term)
Arizona v. Fulminante 111 S.Ct. 1246 (1990 term)
Atkins v. Children's Hospital (261 U.S. 525) (1923)
Baker v. Carr 369 U.S. 186 (1961 term)
Beauharnais v. Illinois 343 U.S. 250 (1951 term)
Benton v. Maryland 395 U.S. 784 (1968 term)
Bivens v. Six Unknown Named Federal Narcotics Agents 403 U.S. 388
    (1970 term)
Bowsher v. Synar 478 U.S. 714 (1985 term)
Brown v. Board of Education 347 U.S. 483 (1953 term)
Burns Baking Company v. Bryan 264 U.S. 504 (1924)
Camara v. Municipal Court 387 U.S. 523 (1967 term)
Cantwell v. Connecticut 310 U.S. 296 (1939 term)
Carter v. Carter Coal Co. 298 U.S. 238 (1935 term)
Chappell v. Wallace 462 U.S. 296 (1981 term)
Connally v. General Construction (269 U.S. 385)
Cooley v. Board of Wardens 12 Howard 299 (1852)
Dennis v. United States 339 U.S. 162 (1950 term)
Employment Division Department of Human Resources of Oregon v. Smith
    110 S.Ct. 1595 (1989 term)
Dobson v. Commissioner of Internal Revenue 320 U.S. 489 (1943 term)
Duncan v. Louisiana 391 U.S. 145 (1967 term)
Edwards v. South Carolina 372 U.S. 229 (1962 term)
Equal Employment Opportunity Commission v. Wyoming 460 U.S. 226
    (1982 term)
Erie Railroad v. Tompkins 304 U.S. 64 (1937 term)
Everson v. Board of Education 330 U.S. 1 (1946 term)
Federal Energy Regulatory Commission v. Mississippi 456 U.S. 742 (1981 term)

Feres v. United States 340 U.S. 135 (1949 term)

Follett v. Town of McCormick 321 U.S. 573 (1943 term)

Garcia v. San Antonio Metropolitan Transit Authority 469 U.S. 528 (1984 term)

Gibbons v. Ogden 9 Wheaton 1 (1824)

Gideon v. Wainwright 372 U.S. 335 (1962 term)

Gitlow v. New York 268 U.S. 652 (1924 term)

Griswold v. Connecticut 381 U.S. 479 (1964 term)

Grosso v. United States 390 U.S. 62 (1967 term)

Hague v. C.I.O. 307 U.S. 496 (1938 term)

Haynes v. United States 390 U.S. 85 (1967 term)

Helvering v. Hallock 309 U.S. 106 (1939 term)

Immigration and Naturalization Service v. Chadha 462 U.S. 919 (1982 term)

Jones v. Opelika 316 U.S. 584 (1941 term)

Lemon v. Kurtzman 403 U.S. 602 (1971 term)

Levy v. Louisiana 391 U.S. 68 (1967 term)

Lochner v. New York 198 U.S. 45 (1905)

Maguire v. Commissioner of Internal Revenue 313 U.S. 1 (1940 term)

Mapp v. Ohio 367 U.S. 643 (1960 term)

Marbury v. Madison 1 Cranch 137 (1803)

Marchetti v. United States 390 U.S. 39 (1967 term)

Massachusetts Board of Retirement v. Murgia 427 U.S. 307 (1975 term)

McCulloch v. Maryland 4 Wheaton 316 (1819)

Milk Wagon Drivers Union v. Meadowmoor Dairies 312 U.S. 287 (1940 term)

Miller v. California 413 U.S. 15 (1972 term)

Minersville v. Gobitis 310 U.S. 586 (1939 term)

Miranda v. Arizona 384 U.S. 436 (1965 term)

Missouri ex rel Gaines v. Canada 305 U.S. 337 (1938 term)

Monroe v. Pape 365 U.S. 176 (1960 term)

Morrissey v. Commissioner of Internal Revenue 296 U.S. 344 (1935 term)

Murdoch v. Pennsylvania 319 U.S. 103 (1942 term)

National Labor Relations Board v. Jones & Laughlin Steel Company 301
     U.S. 1 (1936 term)

National League of Cities v. Usery 426 U.S. 833 (1975 term)

New York v. Miln 11 Peters 102 (1837)

New York Times v. Sullivan 376 U.S. 254 (1963 term)

Palko v. Connecticut 302 U.S. 319 (1937 term)

Pinellas Ice Company v. Commissioner of Internal Revenue 287 U.S. 462
     (1932 term)

Plessy v. Ferguson 163 U.S. 537 (1896)

Powell v. Alabama 287 U.S. 45 (1932)

Reed v. Reed 404 U.S. 71 (1971 term)

Roe v. Wade 410 U.S. 113 (1972 term)

Roth v. United States 354 U.S. 476 (1956 term)

Runyon v. McCrary 427 U.S. 160 (1975 term)

Schechter Poultry Corp. v. United States 295 U.S. 495 (1934 term)

Schneider v. Irvington 308 U.S. 147 (1939 term)

Screws v. United States 325 U.S. 91 (1944 term)

See v. Seattle 387 U.S. 541 (1966 term)

Shelley v. Kraemer 334 U.S. 1 (1947 term)

Smith v. Allwright 321 U.S. 649 (1943 term)

Smyth v. Ames 169 U.S. 466 (1898)

Stanton v. Stanton 421 U.S. 7 (1974 term)

Swift v. Tyson 16 Peters 1 (1842)

Terry v. Ohio 392 U.S. 1 (1967 term)

Texas v. Johnson 109 S.Ct. 2533 (1988 term)

Thomas v. Collins 323 U.S. 516 (1944 term)

Thornhill v. Alabama 310 U.S. 88 (1939 term)

Tinker v. Des Moines School District 393 U.S. 503 (1968 term)

United States v. Carolene Products 304 U.S. 144 (1937 term)

United States v. Darby Lumber Co. 312 U.S. 100 (1940 term)

United States v. Johnson 481 U.S. 681 (1986 term)

United States v. O'Brien 391 U.S. 367 (1967 term)

Valentine v. Chrestensen 316 U.S. 52 (1941 term)

Wesberry v. Sanders 376 U.S. 1 (1963 term)

West Virginia State Board of Education v. Barnette 319 U.S. 624 (1942 term)

Wolf v. Colorado 338 U.S. 25 (1948 term)

Wolman v. Walter 433 U.S. 229 (1976 term)

Zurcher v. Stanford Daily 436 U.S. 547 (1977 term)

Appendix 4:
Digest of Important Cases

Adamson v. California 332 U.S. 146 (1947 term): Important because of the concurring and dissenting opinions concerned with the nature of incorporation.

Baker v. Carr 369 U.S. 186 (1961 term): The landmark decision that said that legislative districts must be reapportioned. This occurred during the liberal period of the Warren Court and opened the agenda to similar issues.

Benton v. Maryland 395 U.S. 784 (1968 term): Incorporated the protections against double jeopardy to the states. One of the final provisions to be incorporated.

Bowsher v. Synar 478 U.S. 714 (1985 term): Declared portions of the Gramm-Rudman-Hollings Budget Reduction Act unconstitutional as a violation of separation of powers.

Brown v. Board of Education 347 U.S 483 (1953 term): Ended "separate but equal" in education. Wide-scale use of equity; it served to open the agenda to a variety of groups and issues.

Camara v. Municipal Court 387 U.S. 523 (1967 term): An extension of Fourth Amendment provisions to administrative, civil searches. Fueled a growth in the agenda space allocated to Due Process.

Cantwell v. Connecticut 310 U.S. 296 (1939 term): Case that combined freedom-of-expression and -religion considerations. Incorporated free-exercise provision of the First Amendment and opened the Substantive Rights agenda. Also signaled the influence of the Jehovah's Witnesses, a group litigant.

Carter v. Carter Coal Co. 298 U.S. 238 (1935 term): Invalidated federal coal regulations. The case, an important Federalism decision, served to narrow the authority of the central government under the commerce clause and contributed to the conflict between the president and the Court.

Cooley v. Board of Wardens 12 Howard 299 (1852): Federalism decision during the Taney Court that created "selective exclusiveness," giving some power to the central government under the commerce clause, while reserving other authority to the states. Part of the "dual federalism" theory.

Department of Human Resources of Oregon v. Smith 110 S.Ct. 1595 (1989 term): A decision that may reflect a change in the standards the Court uses for evaluating free-exercise cases and could portend changes in the agenda.

Erie Railroad v. Tompkins 304 U.S. 64 (1937 term): Critical landmark decision that closed the agenda to a category of economic issues.

Feres v. United States 340 U.S. 135 (1949 term): Important decision that restricted torts claims against the U.S. government.

Garcia v. San Antonio Metropolitan Transit Authority 469 U.S. 528 (1984 term): Signaled a return to the federalism decisions of the previous decades, reversing the *National League of Cities v. Usery* decision.

Gibbons v. Ogden 9 Wheaton 1 (1824): Marshall Court decision that served as the basis of federalism doctrine. The Court upheld the authority of the central government to regulate waterways under the interstate commerce clause.

Gideon v. Wainwright 372 U.S. 335 (1962 term): Case that incorporated the right-to-counsel provision of the Sixth Amendment to the states and abetted the growth of the Due Process agenda.

Griswold v. Connecticut 381 U.S. 479 (1964 term): The creation of the right to privacy, a basis for abortion rights. Signaled the willingness of the Warren Court to advance rights and open the agenda.

Immigration and Naturalization Service v. Chadha 462 U.S. 919 (1982 term): Significant separation of powers decision that invalidated over a hundred legislative veto provisions.

Lemon v. Kurtzman 403 U.S. 602 (1971 term): The decision that created the standard used to evaluate Establishment of Religion cases. The decision was a result and cause of the growth of the Substantive Rights agenda.

Levy v. Louisiana 391 U.S. 68 (1967 term): Extended equal protection doctrine to illegitimate children. Though this was reversed within a few years, it signaled the Court's intent to go beyond race and served as a bridge to other groups seeking equal protection. This helped expand the Equality agenda.

Lochner v. New York 198 U.S. 45 (1905): Struck down state regulations on bakers' hours. An example of the Court's substantive due process decisions upholding the prerogatives of business.

Mapp v. Ohio 367 U.S. 643 (1960 term): Critical case that began the process of incorporation of the criminal procedure amendments and dramatically altered the Due Process agenda.

Marbury v. Madison 1 Cranch 137 (1803): Arguably the most important Court decision, it created the power of judicial review.

McCulloch v. Maryland 4 Wheaton 316 (1819): Marshall Court landmark that expanded the elastic clause of Article I Section 8 and strengthened the power of Congress and the central government.

Miller v. California 413 U.S. 15 (1972 term): Obscenity landmark that changed the standards of evaluation permitting local communities to determine what was obscene. In effect, this closed access to the Supreme Court's agenda to obscenity cases.

Minersville v. Gobitis 310 U.S. 586 (1939 term): Emblematic of the Court's early Civil Liberties decisions, it served to chill behavior and slow the growth of Substantive Rights cases on the agenda.

Miranda v. Arizona 384 U.S. 436 (1965 term): An example of the dispersion of attention, regarding the incorporation of a provision in the wake of *Mapp*.

Missouri ex rel Gaines v. Canada 305 U.S. 337 (1938 term): While the Court was unsympathetic to Substantive Rights and Due Process, early Equality decisions were sympathetic to minorities. Initial step on the road to *Brown*.

Monroe v. Pape 365 U.S. 176 (1960 term): Landmark decision that expanded Section 1983 of 42 U.S.C.A. to allow individuals whose civil rights have been violated to sue. Dramatically opened the agenda to these types of cases.

National Labor Relations Board v. Jones & Laughlin Steel Company 301 U.S. 1 (1936 term): Upholding the Wagner Act, the case occurred during the Court-packing plan. The decision served the dual purpose of legitimating a crucial portion of the New Deal and beginning the process of reorienting federal-state relations. The decision fueled the growth of the Regulation agenda and began to limit the space granted Federalism cases.

National League of Cities v. Usery 426 U.S. 833 (1975 term): Landmark decision that appeared to reverse four decades of Federalism decisions upholding the commerce clause. Led to a resurgence in the agenda space allocated such cases.

New York Times v. Sullivan 376 U.S. 254 (1963 term): Landmark freedom-of-the-press decision that attempted to define libel. This decision opened the agenda significantly to Substantive Rights cases.

Palko v. Connecticut 302 U.S. 319 (1937 term): Early Civil Liberties decision that raised the issue of incorporation. The Court's refusal to extend incorporation served to limit the growth of agenda in these areas.

Roe v. Wade 410 U.S. 113 (1972 term): Abortion decision that opened the agenda to further Substantive Rights cases and belies the image of a conservative Burger Court.

Roth v. United States 354 U.S. 476 (1956 term): Early, nonrestrictive obscenity decision that was responsible for a growth in the proportion of agenda space allocated to Substantive Rights.

Schechter Poultry Corp. v. United States 295 U.S. 495 (1934 term): Declared the National Recovery Act, a core of the New Deal, unconstitutional. The decision helped precipitate the battle between the president and the Court.

Screws v. United States 325 U.S. 91 (1944 term): Determined that a state official can be tried under federal law for violation of the civil rights of individuals. Helped begin process of opening the Equality agenda.

See v. Seattle 387 U.S. 541 (1966 term): Another administrative search-and-seizure cases decided with *Camara* case.

Shelley v. Kraemer 334 U.S. 1 (1947 term): Banned courts from upholding restrictive covenants in housing. Part of an early recrudescent agenda, it signaled the beginning of broader remedies for blacks.

Smyth v. Ames 169 U.S. 466 (1898): An early decision justifying substantive due process and requiring the Court to examine the reasonableness of the law in question. A foundation for the decisions striking down New Deal programs.

Swift v. Tyson 16 Peters 1 (1842): Allowed the federal courts to substitute their judgment in common law for state law in categories of economic cases. The reversal of this decision was necessary to alter the dynamics of the agenda and pare the cases accepted in the Ordinary Economic area.

Terry v. Ohio 392 U.S. 1 (1967 term): Case involving "patdown" searches. This signaled a retreat in criminal procedure cases that would continue during the Burger and Rehnquist courts and led to the growth of the agenda in this area.

United States v. Carolene Products 304 U.S. 144 (1937 term): Relatively minor regulation case known for a footnote that suggested that civil liberties be accorded a "preferred position."

United States v. Darby Lumber Co. 312 U.S. 100 (1940 term): Upheld the Fair Labor Standards Act to expand the agenda space granted Labor Relations and Regulation and expanded the power of the central government under the commerce clause at the expense of the states.

West Virginia State Board of Education v. Barnette 319 U.S. 624 (1942 term): Overturned flag salute decision in *Minersville v. Gobitis*. The case is symbolic of the novelty and confusion of the Court in Civil Liberties issues.

Notes

CHAPTER 1

1. *The Federalist Papers* (New York: New American Library, 1961), p. 465.

2. Alexis de Tocqueville, *Democracy in America* (New York: New American Library, 1956), pp. 72-75.

3. The definition of agenda setting is gathered from a variety of sources including Roger Cobb and Charles Elder, *Participation in American Politics: The Dynamics of Agenda Building*, 2nd ed. (Baltimore: Johns Hopkins University Press, 1983) and Robert Eyestone, *From Social Issues to Public Policy* (New York: John Wiley & Sons, 1978). The notions of the "decision agenda" and the "institutional agenda" are derived from John Kingdon, *Agendas, Alternatives, and Public Policies* (Boston: Little, Brown & Co., 1984), pp. 3-4, 85-88.

4. A number of traditional doctrinal analyses of the Court's decisions exist. The most notable include Robert McCloskey, *The American Supreme Court* (Chicago: University of Chicago Press, 1960) and Alpheus Thomas Mason, *The Supreme Court from Taft to Burger* (Baton Rouge: Louisiana State University Press, 1979). More recent doctrinal analyses include C. Herman Pritchett, *Constitutional Civil Liberties* (Englewood Cliffs, NJ: Prentice-Hall, 1984) and C. Herman Pritchett, *Constitutional Law of the Federal System* (Englewood Cliffs, NJ: Prentice-Hall, 1984).

5. Gerhard Casper and Richard Posner, *The Workload of the Supreme Court* (Chicago: American Bar Federation, 1976).

6. The discussion of the writs of certiorari and appeals relies on Lawrence Baum, *The Supreme Court*, 3rd ed. (Washington, D.C.: Congressional Quarterly, 1989), pp. 11-13; Doris Marie Provine, *Case Selection in the United States Supreme Court* (Chicago: University of Chicago Press, 1980), pp. 1-7; David M. O'Brien, *Storm Center*, 2nd ed. (New York: W. W. Norton, 1990), pp. 184-187.

7. Baum, *The Supreme Court*, pp. 92-105.

8. David Danelski, "The Influence of the Chief Justice in the Decisional Process of the Supreme Court," in *American Court Systems*, 2nd ed., Sheldon Goldman and Austin Sarat (New York: Longman, 1989), pp. 488-489.

9. O'Brien, *Storm Center*, pp. 156-157.

10. Ibid., pp. 163-167.

11. Stephen Wasby, *The Supreme Court and the Federal Judicial System*, 3rd ed. (Chicago: Nelson Hall, 1989), pp. 193-194.

12. Joseph Tanenhaus, Marvin Schick, Matthew Muraskin, and Daniel Rosen, "The Supreme Court's Certiorari Jurisdiction: A Cue Theory," in *Judicial Decision-Making*, ed. Glendon Schubert (New York: The Free Press, 1963), pp. 111-132; H. W. Perry, "Deciding to Decide: Agenda Setting in the United States Supreme Court" (Ph.D. dissertation, University of Michigan, 1987) (to be published by the Harvard University Press).

13. Sheldon Goldman and Thomas Jahnige, *The Federal Courts as a Political System*, 3rd ed. (New York: Harper & Row, 1985), Chapter 5.

14. S. Sidney Ulmer, "The Decision to Grant Certiorari as an Indicator to Decision 'On the Merits'," *Polity* 4 (Summer 1972): 429-447; S. Sidney Ulmer, "Selecting Cases for Supreme Court Review: An Underdog Model," *American Political Science Review* 72 (September 1978): 902-910; Donald Songer, "Concern for Policy Outputs as a Cue for Supreme Court Decisions on Certiorari," *Journal of Politics* 41 (November 1979): 1185-1194.

15. Perry, "Deciding to Decide," pp. 322-327.

16. Glendon Schubert, "Policy Without Law: An Extension of the Certiorari Game," *Stanford Law Review* 14 (March 1962): 284-327.

17. Provine, *Case Selection*, pp. 161-168.

18. Perry, "Deciding to Decide," pp. 226-252.

19. Dorothy James, "Role Theory and the Supreme Court," *Journal of Politics* 30 (February 1968): 160-186; J. Woodford Howard, *Courts of Appeals in the Federal Judicial System* (Princeton, NJ: Princeton University Press, 1981), pp. 122-138.

20. S. Sidney Ulmer, "The Supreme Court's Certiorari Decisions: Conflict as a Predictive Variable," *American Political Science Review* 78 (December 1984): 901-911; Arthur Hellman, "The Supreme Court, the National Law and the Selection of Cases for the Plenary Docket," *University of Pittsburgh Law Review* 44 (Spring 1983): 521-634; Arthur Hellman, "Error Correction, Lawmaking, and the Supreme Court's Exercise of Discretionary Review," *University of Pittsburgh Law Review* 44 (Summer 1983): 795-877.

21. Perry, "Deciding to Decide," pp. 315-322.

22. Provine, *Case Selection*, pp. 114-125; James Gibson, "Judges' Role Orientations, Attitudes and Decisions: An Interactive Model," *American Political Science Review* 72 (September 1978): 911-924.

23. Provine, *Case Selection*, pp. 130-133.

24. A number of studies are representative of the institutional-level focus of the lower courts. Among them are Stanton Wheeler, Bliss Cartwright, Robert Kagan, and Lawrence Friedman, "Do the 'Haves' Come Out Ahead? Winning and Losing in State Supreme Courts," *Law & Society Review* 21 (1987): 403-446; Wayne McIntosh, "150 Years of Litigation and Dispute Settlement: A Court Tale," *Law & Society Review* 15 (1980-1981): 823-846; Joel Grossman and Austin Sarat, "Litigation in the Federal Courts: A Comparative Perspective," *Law & Society Review* 9 (Winter 1975): 322-343; Burton Atkins and Henry Glick, "Environmental and Structural Variables as Determinants of Issues in State Courts of Last Resort," *American Journal of Political Science* 20 (February 1976): 391-425.

25. Casper and Posner, *The Workload*, pp. 27-32.

26. Gregory Caldeira, "The United States Supreme Court and Criminal Cases: Alternative Models of Agenda-Building," *British Journal of Political Science* 11 (October 1981): 449-470.

27. Thomas Likens, "Agenda Setting by the High Court: Systematic Processes or Noise?" Paper prepared for the American Political Science Association meetings, 1979.

28. Samuel Estreicher and John Sexton, *Redefining the Supreme Court's Role* (New Haven, CT: Yale University Press, 1986). Their fuller study is found in *New York University Law Review* 59 (October 1984): 677-1004; *New York University Law Review* 59 (November 1984): 1005-1402; *New York University Law Review* 59 (December 1984): 1403-1929.

29. Representative of the most significant judicial behavior studies are: David Rohde and Harold Spaeth, *Supreme Court Decision Making* (San Francisco: W. H. Freeman, 1976); Glendon Schubert, "The 1960 Term of the Supreme Court: A Psychological Analysis," *American Political Science Review* 56 (March 1962): 90-107; J. Woodford Howard, "On the Fluidity of Judicial Choice," *American Political Science Review* 62 (March 1968): 43-57; Walter Murphy, *Elements of Judicial Strategy* (Chicago: University of Chicago Press, 1964); Jeffrey Segal, "Supreme Court Justices as Human Decision Makers: An Individual Level Analysis of Search and Seizure Cases," *Journal of Politics* 48 (November 1986): 938-955.

30. There are a number of important studies of case selection in the Supreme Court. A sample of these includes Provine, *Case Selection*; Ulmer, "The Decision to Grant Certiorari"; Tanenhaus et al., "The Supreme Court's Certiorari Jurisdiction"; Ulmer, "The Supreme Court's Certiorari Decisions"; Perry, "Deciding to Decide."

31. Included among the neoinstitutional studies of the Supreme Court are Lee Epstein, Thomas Walker, and William Dixon, "The Supreme Court and Criminal Justice Disputes: A Neo-Institutional Perspective," *American Journal of Political Science* 33 (November 1989): 825-841; David Barnum, "The Supreme Court and Public Opinion: Judicial Decision Making in the Post-New

Deal Period," *Journal of Politics* 47 (May 1985): 652-666; Jeffrey Segal, "Predicting Supreme Court Cases Probabilistically: The Search and Seizure Cases, 1962-1981," *American Political Science Review* 78 (December 1984): 891-900.

32. Included among the neoinstitutional studies of Congress are Joseph Cooper and David Brady, "Toward a Diachronic Analysis of Congress," *American Political Science Review* 75 (December 1981): 988-1006; Barbara Deckard Sinclair, "Party Realignment and the Transformation of the Political Agenda: The House of Representatives," *American Political Science Review* 71 (September 1977): 940-953; Barbara Deckard Sinclair, *The Transformation of the U.S. Senate* (Baltimore: Johns Hopkins University, 1989).

33. Thomas Hammond and Gary Miller, "A Social Choice Perspective on Expertise and Authority in Bureaucracy," *American Journal of Political Science* 29 (February 1985): 1-28.

34. Melinda Gann Hall and Paul Brace, "Order in the Courts: A Neo-Institutional Approach to Judicial Consensus," *Western Political Quarterly* 42 (1989): 391-407; Paul Brace and Melinda Gann Hall, "Neo-Institutionalism and Dissent in State Supreme Courts," *Journal of Politics* 52 (February 1990): 54-70.

35. Richard Funston, *A Vital National Seminar: The Supreme Court in American Political Life* (Palo Alto, CA: Mayfield, 1978); William Louthan, *The United States Supreme Court: Lawmaking in the Third Branch of Government* (Englewood Cliffs, NJ: Prentice-Hall, 1991); Charles Franklin and Liane Kosaki, "Republican Schoolmaster: The U.S. Supreme Court, Public Opinion, and Abortion," *American Political Science Review* 83 (September 1989): 751-771.

36. Theodore Lowi, *The End of Liberalism*, 2nd ed. (New York: Norton, 1979).

37. Rogers Smith, *Liberalism and American Constitutional Law* (Cambridge: Harvard University Press, 1985), Chapter 1.

38. Gregory Caldeira and John Wright, "Organized Interests and Agenda Setting in the U.S. Supreme Court," *American Political Science Review* 82 (December 1988): 1109-1128.

39. Rohde and Spaeth, *Supreme Court Decision Making*.

40. Schubert, "The 1960 Term."

41. The Supreme Court Judicial Data Base was collected under the auspices of Professor Harold Spaeth. The data base covers the cases decided during the Warren, Burger, and Rehnquist courts (up to the 1988 term). Among the most important variables in the data base are the types of litigants, the existence of lower court dissensus, the reason for granting certiorari, the form of the decision, the legal provisions considered by the Court, the authority for the decision, the issue, the direction of the decision (liberal or conservative), the

winning party, the vote in the case, the opinions and interagreements between the justices.

42. Because the time frame for this study of the Court's agenda includes two additional decades (1933-1952) not included in the Supreme Court Data Base, I collected some supplementary evidence. Many of the variables contained in the Supreme Court Data Base are not needed for this analysis. Among the variables I collected are the type of issue, the direction of the decision, whether the lower court decision was reversed or affirmed, the reason for granting certiorari, the vote in the case, and the votes of the individual justices. There are potential sources of inconsistencies between the data base and my codings. One discrepancy is in the coding of the issue. I have followed my own coding rules because my data set was collected prior to the Supreme Court Data Base. The coding of civil liberties and regulation cases is reliable. There may be some discrepancy in the coding of Economic cases. My coding rules focus on the substantive issue, while the Supreme Court Data Base is more concerned with the jurisdictional issue, which is often involved in these types of cases. In coding the reasons for granting certiorari, one item merits attention. Jurisdictional decisions that are accepted to "consider an important question in judicial administration" appear to be closer to the notion of the judicial role and lower court dissensus than the policy values normally defined in decisions as "due to the importance of the issue." For the Economic cases in the 1953-1988 period, cases that were coded as accepted due to their importance were examined to see if the administration of the lower courts was behind the grant.

CHAPTER 2

1. Alice Fleetwood Bartee, *Cases Lost, Causes Won* (New York: St. Martin's Press, 1984), pp. 1-9.

2. Charles Johnson and Bradley Canon, *Judicial Policies: Implementation and Impact* (Washington, D.C.: Congressional Quarterly, 1984).

3. Linda Greenhouse, "Of Tents with Wheels and Houses with Oars," *New York Times*, May 16, 1985, p. 12.

4. David Rohde and Harold Spaeth, *Supreme Court Decision Making* (San Francisco: Freeman, 1976), chapter 4.

5. Robert McCloskey, *The American Supreme Court* (Chicago: University of Chicago Press, 1960); Arthur Selwyn Miller, *The Supreme Court and American Capitalism* (New York: The Free Press, 1968).

6. Although this may seem to be the vestige of a bygone era, recent nominees have paid verbal homage to the notion of nonpartisanship. The testimony of Sandra Day O'Connor, Antonin Scalia, Anthony Kennedy, and David Souter before the Senate Judiciary Committee was filled with allusions to their open-mindedness and the fact that none of the four brought any agenda to

the Court. See Elder Witt, *A Different Justice* (Washington, D.C.: Congressional Quarterly, 1985.

7. The Court has a number of means of avoiding cases. If the Court already accepted the case, it has rules of access that it could enforce to rid itself of troublesome cases. The Court could find that a litigant lacked standing or the case was either "moot" or was not "ripe" for judicial determination. In some cases, the Court can refuse to hear the case because it is a "political question" and should be decided by the other branches of government.

8. James Simon, *Independent Journey: The Life of William O. Douglas* (New York: Harper & Row, 1980); McCloskey, *The American Supreme Court*, p. 201.

9. Alexander Bickel, *The Least Dangerous Branch: The Supreme Court at the Bar of Politics* (Indianapolis: Bobbs-Merrill, 1968).

10. Arthur S. Miller, *Toward Increased Judicial Activism* (Westport, CT: Greenwood Press, 1982); John Hart Ely, *Democracy and Distrust: A Theory of Judicial Review* (Cambridge: Harvard University Press, 1980).

11. Sheldon Goldman and Thomas Jahnige, *The Federal Courts as a Political System*, 3rd ed. (New York: Harper & Row, 1985), chapter 5.

12. Wallace Mendelson, "Mr. Justice Frankfurter and the Distribution of Judicial Power in the United States," *Midwest Journal of Political Science* 2 (February 1958): 40-51; Mark Silverstein, *Constitutional Faiths* (Ithaca, NY: Cornell University Press, 1983).

13. James Gibson, "Judges' Role Orientations, Attitudes and Decisions: An Interactive Model," *American Political Science Review* 72 (September 1978): 911-924.

14. Silverstein, *Constitutional Faiths*, pp. 141-142; Gerald T. Dunne, *Hugo Black and the Judicial Revolution* (New York: Simon & Schuster, 1977).

15. David Songer, "Concern for Policy Outputs as a Cue for Supreme Court Decisions on Certiorari," *Journal of Politics* 41 (November 1979): 1186-1190; Glendon Schubert, "Policy Without Law: An Extension of the Certiorari Game," *Stanford Law Review* 14 (March 1962): 290-296.

16. Justices White and Blackmun frequently dissent from denials of certiorari when a circuit conflict is alleged.

17. S. Sidney Ulmer, "The Supreme Court's Certiorari Decisions: Conflict as a Predictive Variable," *American Political Science Review* 78 (December 1984): 901-911; H. W. Perry, "Deciding to Decide."

18. Sheldon Goldman, "Voting Behavior on the United States Courts of Appeals Revisited," *American Political Science Review* 69 (June 1975): 493-495.

19. Perry, "Deciding to Decide," has labeled this the outcome mode of the case selection process. The jurisprudence mode is his description of case selection based on the need to fulfill the judicial role. Samuel Estreicher and John Sexton conceptualize the agenda as composed of different segments that resemble the exigent and volitional components posited in this study. These

authors advocate a new role for the Court that would settle more of the intercircuit conflicts that they think adversely affect the judicial system.

20. By implication, some justices lend additional credence to this conception of the Court's agenda as bifurcated: exigent and volitional. Proponents of a National Court of Appeals frequently call for that proposed court to have the authority to settle disputes between lower courts or reverse misinterpretations of Supreme Court precedents. See Samuel Estreicher and John Sexton, *Redefining the Supreme Court's Role* (New Haven, CT: Yale University Press, 1986), p. 26. Such a court's work would shrink the Supreme Court's exigent agenda and allow its volitional agenda to grow.

21. Craig Ducat and Robert Dudley, "Dimensions Underlying Economic Policy-Making in the Early and Later Burger Courts," *Journal of Politics* 49 (May 1987): 521-539; Robert Dudley and Craig Ducat, "The Burger Court and Economic Liberalism," *Western Political Quarterly* 39 (June 1986): 236-249.

22. In *The Federalist Papers* (New York: New American Library, 1961), no. 10, James Madison's views of factions, the need to tolerate them, and possible means of coping with these groups are given.

23. Theodore Lowi, *The End of Liberalism*, 2nd ed. (New York: Norton, 1979), pp. 50-63.

24. Lee Epstein, *Conservatives in Court* (Knoxville: University of Tennessee Press, 1985), pp. 147-148; Susan Olson, "The Political Evolution of Interest Group Litigation," in *Governing Through Courts*, ed. Richard Gambitta, Marilyn May, and James Foster (Beverly Hills, CA: Sage, 1981), pp. 234-249.

25. Policy entrepreneurs have incentives to get a range of cases to the docket to advance policy designs and fill interstices in the law; see Epstein, *Conservatives in Court*, pp. 148-150; Gregory Caldeira and John Wright, "Organized Interests and Agenda Setting in the U.S. Supreme Court," *American Political Science Review* 82 (December 1988): 1109-1128; Marc Galanter, "Why the Haves Come Out Ahead: Speculations on the Limits of Legal Change," *Law & Society Review* 8 (Fall 1974): 105-116; Robert Scigliano, *The Supreme Court and the Presidency* (New York: The Free Press, 1971), pp. 173-195; William Donahue, *The Politics of the American Civil Liberties Union* (New Brunswick, NJ: Transaction Press, 1985); Samuel Walker, *In Defense of American Liberties*: *A History of the ACLU* (New York: Oxford University Press, 1990); Milton Konvitz, *Expanding Liberties* (New York: Viking Press, 1966), pp. 11-15. Studies implicitly or explicitly (Doris Marie Provine, *Case Selection in the United States Supreme Court* (Chicago: University of Chicago Press, 1980), pp. 86-94) note that organized litigants pay careful attention to Court decisions, and their success is a function of their ability to bring the cases the Court is seeking at the proper time. Groups may opt for narrower strategies. The disability rights movement focused on remedies, rather than broad principles (Olson, "The Political Evolution," pp. 241-244). Conservative groups often join cases to

counteract liberal groups rather than litigate offensively (Epstein, *Conservatives in Court*, pp. 147-149).

26. Frank Sorauf, *The Wall of Separation* (Princeton, NJ: Princeton University Press, 1976), pp. 344-346.

27. Stephen Wasby, Anthony D'Amato, and Rosemary Metrailer, *Desegregation from Brown to Alexander* (Carbondale: Southern Illinois University Press, 1977). C. Herman Pritchett, *Constitutional Civil Liberties* (Englewood Cliffs, NJ: Prentice-Hall, 1984), pp. 258-264.

28. Stephen Wasby, "How Planned Is 'Planned Litigation'?" *American Bar Foundation Research Journal* 32 (1984): 83-138. Wasby argued that planned litigation is much more difficult now than it was before the 1980s. This statement is consistent with the thesis of this study. The proliferation of interest groups and their expanding concerns have made the process of monitoring a variety of areas of law almost insuperable.

29. This is a two-way process. Repeat players earn a reputation over time and those who are trusted by the Court are more likely to have their petitions treated seriously. Identity of the petitioner is a significant cue for justices in case selection; see Joseph Tanenhaus et al., "The Supreme Court's Certiorari Jurisdiction: A Cue Theory" in *Judicial Decision-Making*, ed. Glendon Schubert (New York: The Free Press, 1963, pp. 122-123); Provine, *Case Selection*, pp. 10-22; Perry, "Deciding to Decide," Chapter 3.

30. In *Gideon v. Wainwright*, *amici* briefs requested from the states were overwhelming in favor of Gideon. See Richard Cortner, *The Supreme Court and the Second Bill of Rights* (Madison: University of Wisconsin Press, 1981), p. 196. In *Mapp v. Ohio*, the *amicus* filed by the ACLU urged the Court to turn the issue, ostensibly obscenity, into search and seizure and was successful (Cortner, p. 181). The use of *amici* briefs has grown dramatically, affecting over half the cases the Court decides. See Karen O'Connor and Lee Epstein, "The Role of Interest Groups in Supreme Court Policy Formation," in *Public Policy Formation*, ed. Robert Eyestone (Greenwich, CT: JAI Press, 1984), pp. 70-71.

31. Kay Lehman Schlozman and John Tierney, *Organized Interests and American Democracy* (New York: Harper & Row, 1986), pp. 290-301.

32. Caldeira and Wright, "Organized Interests," pp. 1119-1122.

33. The solicitor general and the Court possess checks over each other. The solicitor general can flood the Court with petitions if he is unhappy with the Court's past policies. The Court can refuse large numbers of the petitions or deal the government a large number of losses on the merits. Scigliano, *The Supreme Court*, Chapter 6; Lincoln Caplan, *The Tenth Justice* (New York: Vintage Books, 1987). Thus, the solicitor general needs to litigate strategically and often does so very successfully; see Provine, *Case Selection*, pp. 87-92.

34. Gerald T. Dunne, *Hugo Black and the Judicial Revolution* (New York: Simon & Schuster, 1977), pp. 261-264.

35. Silverstein, *Constitutional Faiths*, p. 191.

36. Sue Davis, *Justice Rehnquist and the Constitution* (Princeton, NJ: Princeton University Press, 1989), pp. 24-32.

37. S. Sidney Ulmer, "Issue Fluidity in the United States Supreme Court," in *Supreme Court Activism and Restraint*, ed. Stephen Halpern and Charles Lamb (Lexington, MA: D.C. Heath, 1982), pp. 322-323.

38. Ulmer, "Issue Fluidity," p. 323; Cortner, *The Supreme Court*, p. 195.

39. Lawrence Baum, "Measuring Policy Change in the U.S. Supreme Court," *American Political Science Review* 82 (September 1988): 905-912.

40. Wasby, "How Planned Is 'Planned Litigation'?" pp. 83-138.

41. John Kingdon, *Agendas, Alternatives, and Public Policies* (Boston: Little, Brown & Co.), pp. 128-131.

42. Richard Pacelle and Roberta Herzberg, "Altering the Balance: The Impact of Membership Change upon Voting Alignments in the United States Supreme Court, 1966-1985." Paper prepared for the Midwest Political Science Association meetings, 1988.

43. Kingdon, *Agendas*, pp. 138-139; Jack Walker, "Setting the Agenda in the U.S. Senate: A Theory of Problem Selection," *British Journal of Political Science* 7 (October 1977): 423-445.

44. Kingdon, *Agendas*, pp. 174-181.

45. Arthur Hellman, "Case Selection in the Burger Court: A Preliminary Inquiry," *Notre Dame Law Review* 60 (Fall 1985): 1006-1007.

46. Kingdon, *Agendas*, pp. 200-204.

47. Matthew Crenson, *The Unpolitics of Air Pollution* (Baltimore: Johns Hopkins University Press, 1971), p. 173.

48. Ibid., p. 170.

49. Ibid., p. 172.

CHAPTER 3

1. Richard Neustadt, *Presidential Power: The Politics of Leadership from F.D.R. to Carter* (New York: John Wiley & Sons, 1980), pp. 192-195.

2. V.O. Key, "A Theory of Critical Elections," *Journal of Politics* 17 (February 1955): 245-265.

3. James Sundquist, *Dynamics of the Party System* (Washington, D.C.: The Brookings Institution, 1973), pp. 26-39.

4. Gerald Pomper and Susan Lederman, *Elections in America*, 2nd ed. (New York: Longman's, 1980), pp. 210-225.

5. Robert Dahl, "Decision Making in a Democracy: The Supreme Court and National Policy Making," *Journal of Public Law* 6 (Fall 1957):

279-295; Richard Funston, "The Supreme Court and Critical Elections," *American Political Science Review* 69 (September 1975): 795-811.

6. Jonathan Casper, "The Supreme Court and National Policy-Making," *American Political Science Review* 70 (March 1976): 50-63; David Adamany, "Realigning Elections and the Supreme Court," *Wisconsin Law Review* 57 (1973): 790-846; John Gates, *The Supreme Court and Partisan Realignment* (Boulder: Westview Press, forthcoming).

7. Robert McCloskey, *The American Supreme Court* (Chicago: University of Chicago Press, 1960), pp. 180-181.

8. Gerald Dunne, *Hugo Black and the Judicial Revolution* (New York: Simon & Schuster, 1977), pp. 181-183.

9. Alpheus Thomas Mason, *Harlan Fiske Stone: Pillar of the Law* (New York: Viking Press, 1956), pp. 513-517.

10. Dunne, *Hugo Black*, p. 184.

11. The discussion of the justices and their ideological dispositions is based on Henry Abraham, *Justices and Presidents: A Political History of Appointments to the Supreme Court*, 2nd ed. (New York: Oxford University Press, 1985) and Jeffrey Segal and Albert Cover, "Ideological Values and Votes of U.S. Supreme Court Justices," *American Political Science Review* 83 (August 1989): 557-565.

12. Jae-On Kim and Charles Mueller, *Introduction to Factor Analysis* (Beverly Hills, CA: Sage, 1978) and Jae-On Kim and Charles Mueller, *Factor Analysis: Statistical Methods and Practical Issues* (Beverly Hills, CA: Sage, 1978).

13. Time series analyses using the shares of agenda space as the unit of analysis or using the raw numbers of cases accepted (with controls introduced for a ten-year period when the raw numbers of cases declined or with the period treated as an interruption in the series) substantiate the relationships between the issues in their competition for the finite agenda space. Ultimately, factor analysis was utilized because it was easier to interpret and it yielded a graphic representation (Figure 3.1).

14. "Recrudesce" means to break out after an inactive period; a new outbreak after a period of abatement.

CHAPTER 4

1. Grant Gilmore, *The Ages of American Law* (New Haven, CT: Yale University Press, 1977), pp. 33-34.

2. Rogers Smith, *Liberalism and American Constitutional Law* (Cambridge: Harvard University Press, 1985), pp. 14-17.

3. Robert McCloskey, *The American Supreme Court* (Chicago: University of Chicago Press, 1960), p. 181.

4. Martin Sklar, *The Corporate Reconstruction of American Capitalism* (Cambridge: Cambridge University Press, 1988), pp. 33-37.

5. S. Sidney Ulmer, "Issue Fluidity in the United States Supreme Court," in *Supreme Court Activism and Restraint*, ed. Stephen Halpern and Charles Lamb (Lexington, MA: D.C. Heath, 1982), pp. 321-323; Richard Cortner, *The Supreme Court and the Second Bill of Rights* (Madison: University of Wisconsin Press, 1981), pp. 195-217.

6. Melvin Urofsky, *A March of Liberty: A Constitutional History of the United States*, Volume 2: *Since 1965* (New York: Knopf, 1988), p. 698.

7. Kermit Hall, *The Magic Mirror: Law in American History* (New York: Oxford University Press, 1989), p. 283.

8. Urofsky, *A March of Liberty*, p. 698.

9. Gerald Casper and Richard Posner, *The Workload of the Supreme Court* (Chicago: American Bar Federation, 1976), pp. 29-31; Joel Grossman and Austin Sarat, "Litigation in the Federal Courts: A Comparative Perspective," *Law & Society Review* 9 (Winter 1975): 321-345; Austin Sarat and Joel Grossman, Courts and Conflict Resolution: Problems in the Mobilization of Adjudication" *American Political Science Review* 69 (December 1975): 1200-1217.

10. Sarat and Grossman, "Courts and Conflict Resolution."

11. Urofsky, *A March of Liberty*, pp. 698-699.

12. C. Herman Pritchett, *Constitutional Law of the Federal System* (Englewood Cliffs, NJ: Prentice-Hall, 1984), p. 136, quoting Justice Harlan; see also Hall, *The Magic Mirror*, p. 283 and Urofsky, *A March of Liberty*, pp. 698-699.

13. Gilmore, *The Ages of American Law*, pp. 93-95.

14. Pritchett, *Constitutional Law*, p. 136.

15. Peter Schuck, *Suing Government: Citizen Remedies for Official Wrongs* (New Haven, CT: Yale University Press, 1983), pp. 40-43.

16. *Monroe v. Pape* was certainly a major case involving the tort liability of governmental officials, but it is categorized under the Equality cases due to the substantive nature of the facts of the case. The *Monroe* case expanded the use of the Civil Rights Acts, particularly Section 1983, which had long been dormant. See Schuck, *Suing Government*, pp. 47-51, for a broader historical and doctrinal discussion of Section 1983 and the context of the *Monroe* decision.

17. Howard Ball, "The United States Supreme Court's Glossing of the Federal Torts Claims Act: Statutory Construction and Veterans' Tort Actions," *Western Political Quarterly* 41 (September 1988): 529-552.

18. Stephen Wasby, *The Supreme Court in the Federal Judicial System*, 3rd ed. (Chicago: Nelson-Hall, 1988), p. 54.

19. There were some important decisions in the Internal Revenue area, but none that might qualify as landmark decisions. The coding of the agenda data base included noting the precedents the Court cited as the basis for its

decisions in the current cases, whether the decision was followed, distinguished, or overruled. On that basis, a few Internal Revenue cases received an unusual number of citations in later cases. *Pinellas Ice Company v. Commissioner of Internal Revenue* 287 U.S. 462 (1932 term), involving corporate taxes from mergers and reorganization, appeared to spawn a number of subsequent cases that sought to refine this precedent. *Morrissey v. Commissioner of Internal Revenue* 296 U.S. 344 (1935 term) extended the *Pinellas* decision and was controlling precedent for a number of cases. Three cases, *Helvering v. Hallock* 309 U.S. 106 (1939 term), *Maguire v. Commissioner of Internal Revenue* 313 U.S. 1 (1940 term), and *Dobson v. Commissioner of Internal Revenue* 320 U.S. 489 (1943 term), serve as a bridge between the Internal Revenue Codes of 1939 and 1954. They are the last Internal Revenue decisions to receive extensive, systematic citation in later Court decisions.

20. Harold Dubroff, *The United States Tax Court: An Historical Analysis* (Chicago: Commerce Clearing House, 1979), p. 177.

21. Charles Johnson and Bradley Canon, *Judicial Policies: Implementation and Impact* (Washington, D.C.: Congressional Quarterly, 1984).

22. Estreicher and Sexton confirm the existence of this trend and urge its extension.

23. A number of analysts have identified the Court as increasingly a forum for constitutional issues. See Casper and Posner, *The Workload*, pp. 50-51; Baum, *The Supreme Court*, 3rd. ed. (Washington, D.C.: Congressional Quarterly, 1989), p. 27; David M. O'Brien, *Storm Center*, 2nd ed. (New York: Norton, 1990), pp. 244-249. Still other analysts implicitly or explicitly refer to certain cues, indices, or signals that make acceptance of a case more likely (H. W. Perry, "Deciding to Decide: Agenda Setting in the United States Supreme Court," Ph.D. dissertation, University of Michigan, 1987 (to be published by Harvard University Press), pp. 333-351; see footnotes 27 and 28 infra). The existence of a constitutional issue is one such signal or cue.

24. Constitutional issues are identified by the "keys" found in the *Supreme Court Reporter*. The key "Constitutional Law" was used to identify cases that raised such questions. In many of these cases, the Court used issue suppression to limit or dismiss the constitutional question.

25. The Supreme Court Data Base was used as the basis for determining whether decisions were liberal or conservative. The Supreme Court Data Base relied on the typology established in Sheldon Goldman, "Voting Behavior on the United States Courts of Appeals, 1961-1964," *American Political Science Review* 60 (June 1966): 374-383. A number of analysts have discussed the problems of determining what is liberal and what is conservative in economic cases. Lawrence Baum as well as Craig Ducat and Robert Dudley note that scholars have trouble determining ideological directions in such cases, and justices may have similar problems as well. See Lawrence Baum, "Measuring Policy Change in the U.S. Supreme Court," *American Political Science Review* 82 (September

1988): 905-912; Craig Ducat and Robert Dudley, "The Burger Court and Economic Liberalism," *Western Political Quarterly* 39 (June 1986): 236-249.

26. James Sundquist, *The Dynamics of the Party System* (Washington, D.C.: Brookings Institution, 1973).

27. Perry, "Deciding to Decide," pp. 321-322.

28. Tanenhaus et al., "The Supreme Court's Certiorari Jurisdiction: A Cue Theory," In *Judicial Decision-Making*, ed. Glendon Schubert (New York: the Free Press, 1963), pp. 111-132; Perry, "Deciding to Decide," pp. 333-351.

CHAPTER 5

1. R. Kent Newmyer, *The Supreme Court Under Marshall and Taney* (New York: Crowell, 1968).

2. Robert McCloskey, *The American Supreme Court* (Chicago: University of Chicago Press, 1960), pp. 136-139.

3. Ibid., pp. 126-127.

4. Rogers Smith, *Liberalism and American Constitutional Law* (Cambridge: Harvard University Press, 1985), pp. 153-154.

5. McCloskey, *The American Supreme Court*, p. 132.

6. C. Herman Pritchett, *Constitutional Civil Liberties* (Englewood Cliffs, NJ: Prentice Hall, 1984), pp. 298-306.

7. John Nowak, Ronald Rotunda, and J. Nelson Young, *Constitutional Law*, 3rd ed. (Minneapolis: West Publishing, 1986), pp. 343-345.

8. Jack Walker, "The Diffusion of Innovations Among the States," *American Political Science Review* 63 (September 1969): 880-899; Bradley Canon and Lawrence Baum, "Patterns of Adoption of Tort Law Innovations: An Application of Diffusion Theory to Judicial Decisions," *American Political Science Review* 75 (December 1981): 975-987.

9. Edward Carmines and James Stimson, *Issue Evolution: Race and the Transformation of American Politics* (Princeton, NJ: Princeton University Press, 1989), pp. 9-10.

10. Robert Dahl, "Decision-Making in a Democracy: The Supreme Court and National Policy Making," *Journal of Public Law* 6 (Fall 1957): 279-295. See also Casper, "The Supreme Court and National Policy Making," *American Political Science Review* 70 (March 1976): 50-63.

11. James Sundquist, *The Dynamics of the Party System* (Washington D.C.: Brookings Institution, 1973).

12. McCloskey, *The American Supreme Court*, pp. 169-177.

13. Sheldon Goldman, *Constitutional Law: Cases and Essays*, 2nd ed. (New York: Harper Collins, 1991), p. 267.

14. The rise of these issues was largely accidental. Disputes between the central government and states over water resources or lands do not arise

systematically. The Court has a very limited ability to affect these cases. A very consistent line of decisions can stop a recurring dispute between the United States and an individual state from coming back to the Supreme Court. In the recent periods, there was some rationality to the selection of these cases. The Court accepted a number of these disputes simultaneously to issue some consistent decisions and guide the lower courts and the states.

15. Pritchett, *Constitutional Law of the Federal System*, p. 235.

16. See, for example, *Federal Energy Regulatory Commission v. Mississippi* 456 U.S. 742 and *E.E.O.C. v. Wyoming* 460 U.S. 226.

17. *Garcia v. San Antonio Metropolitan Transit Authority* 469 U.S. 528 (1984 term).

18. Richard Cortner, *The Supreme Court and the Second Bill of Rights*, (Madison: University of Wisconsin Press, 1981).

19. Louis Fisher, *Constitutional Dialogues: Interpretation as Political Process* (Princeton, NJ: Princeton University Press, 1988), p. 260.

20. Martin Shapiro, *The Supreme Court and Administrative Agencies* (New York: The Free Press, 1968), pp. 18-36.

21. Kingdon, *Agendas,* p. 203.

22. David Brady with Joseph Stewart, "Congressional Party Realignment and Transformation of Public Policy in Three Realignment Eras," *American Journal of Political Science* 26 (May 1982): 333-360.

23. Jack Walker, "Setting the Agenda in the U.S. Senate: A Theory of Problem Selection," *British Journal of Political Science* 7 (October 1977): 423-445.

24. John Kingdon, *Agendas, Alternatives, and Public Policies* (Boston: Little, Brown, 1984), p. 195.

25. McCloskey, *The American Supreme Court*, pp. 126-128.

26. Donald Crowley, "Judicial Review of Administrative Agencies: Does the Type of Agency Matter?" *Western Political Quarterly* 40 (June 1987): 265-283.

27. Ibid., 271-280.

28. Robert Dudley and Craig Ducat, "The Burger Court and Economic Liberalism," *Western Political Quarterly* 39 (June 1986): 236-249.

29. Lee Epstein, *Conservatives in Court* (Knoxville: University of Tennessee Press), p. 30.

30. Glendon Schubert, *The Judicial Mind: The Attitudes and Ideologies of Supreme Court Justices 1946-1963* (Evanston, IL: Northwestern University Press, 1965), pp. 127-150; Glendon Schubert, *The Judicial Mind Revisited* (New York: Oxford University Press, 1974), pp. 43-48.

31. David Rohde and Harold Spaeth, *Supreme Court Decision Making* (San Francisco: Freeman, 1976), pp. 157-160.

32. Stephen Wasby, *The Supreme Court and the Federal Judicial System*, 3rd ed. (Chicago: Nelson Hall, 1989), pp. 332-333.

33. R. S. Malkovits, "The Burger Court, Antitrust, and Economic Analysis," in *The Burger Court: The Counter-Revolution That Wasn't*, ed. Vincent Blasi (New Haven, CT: Yale University Press, 1983), pp. 182-183.

34. Wasby, *The Supreme Court*, p. 333.

35. Arthur Fox, "Showing Workers Who's Boss," in *The Burger Court: Rights and Wrongs in the Supreme Court 1969-1986*, ed. Herman Schwartz (New York: Penguin Books, 1987), pp. 229-231.

36. David Silberman, "The Burger Court and Labor-Management Relations," in *The Burger Court*: *Rights and Wrongs in the Supreme Court 1969-1986*, ed. Herman Schwartz (New York: Penguin Books, 1987), pp. 221; Fox, "Showing Workers," pp. 229-231

37. R. S. Malkovits, "The Burger Court, Antitrust, and Economic Analysis," p. 182.

38. Donald Crowley, "Judicial Review," pp. 265-283.

39. Donald Songer, "The Impact of the Supreme Court on Trends in Economic Policy Making in the United States Courts of Appeals," *Journal of Politics* 49 (August 1987): 830-844.

40. Ducat and Dudley use a somewhat different mix of cases, including some issues categorized in this study as Ordinary Economic. The results, however, are largely consistent when these cases are eliminated from the analysis. Ducat and Dudley, "The Burger Court," pp. 521-539.

41. Henry Abraham, *Justices and Presidents, A Political History of Appointments to the Supreme Court*, 2nd ed. (New York: Oxford University Press, 1985), p. 210.

42. Ibid., pp. 294-295, 334.

CHAPTER 6

1. Henry Abraham, *Freedom and the Court: Civil Rights and Liberties in the United States*, 5th ed. (New York: Oxford University Press, 1988), pp. 21-37; Richard Funston, *A Vital National Seminar: The Supreme Court in American Political Life* (Palo Alto, CA: Mayfield, 1978), pp. 200-206; Paul Murphy, *World War I and the Origin of Civil Liberties* (New York: W. W. Norton, 1979).

2. R. Jeffrey Lustig, *Corporate Liberalism: The Origins of Modern American Political Theory, 1890-1920* (Berkeley: University of California Press, 1982), Chapter 1; Stephen Skowronek, *Building a New American State: The Expansion of National Administrative Capacities, 1877-1928* (New York: Cambridge University Press, 1983), Chapter 1.

3. Smith, *Liberalism and American Constitutional Law* (Cambridge: Harvard University Press, 1985), pp. 14-15.

4. For example, see Robert McCloskey, *The American Supreme Court* (Chicago: University of Chicago Press, 1960); C. Herman Pritchett, *Civil Liberties and the Vinson Court* (Chicago: University of Chicago Press, 1954).

5. Smith, *Liberalism*, pp. 77-78.

6. Baum, "Measuring Policy Change in the U.S. Supreme Court," *American Political Science Review* 82 (September 1988): 905-912.

7. Lee Epstein, *Conservatives in the Court* (Knoxville: University of Tennessee Press, 1985), pp. 120-125.

8. Richard Cortner, *The Supreme Court and the Second Bill of Rights* (Madison: University of Wisconsin Press, 1981), pp. 278-283.

9. Pritchett, *Civil Liberties*," p. 4.

10. Joseph Kobylka, "A Court-Related Context for Group Litigation: Libertarian Groups and Obscenity," *Journal of Politics* 49 (November 1987): 1061-1079.

11. William Brennan, "State Constitutions and the Protection of Individual Rights," *Harvard Law Review* 90 (January 1977): 489-504.

12. Gary McDowell, *Equity and the Constitution* (Chicago: University of Chicago Press, 1982), pp. 3-4.

13. Smith, *Liberalism*, p. 99; John Brigham, *Civil Liberties & American Democracy* (Washington, D.C.: Congressional Quarterly, 1984), pp. 42-43.

14. Thomas Kuhn, *The Structure of Scientific Revolutions*, 2nd ed. enlarged (Chicago: University of Chicago Press, 1970), pp. 23-34. Jack Walker, "The Diffusion of Knowledge, Policy Communities and Agenda Setting: The Relationship of Knowledge and Power," in *New Strategic Perspectives on Social Policy*, ed. John E. Tropman, Milan Dluhy, and Roger M. Lind (New York: Pergamon Press, 1981), pp. 80-82, uses the concept of a paradigm to explain agenda innovation as a part of the policy literature. Funston, *A Vital National Seminar*, considers the Court the functional equivalent of modern philosophers composing evolving democratic theories. The analogy of a paradigm is relevant in this respect as well.

15. Gerald T. Dunne, *Hugo Black and the Judicial Revolution* (New York: Simon & Schuster, 1977), pp. 256-264; William O. Douglas, *The Court Years* (New York: Random House, 1980), pp. 43-56; Cortner, p. 137.

16. Mark Silverstein, *Constitutional Faiths* (Ithaca, NY: Cornell University Press, 1983), p. 191. Helen Shirley Thomas, *Felix Frankfurter: Scholar on the Bench* (Baltimore: Johns Hopkins University Press, 1960).

17. Robert McCloskey, "Deeds Without Doctrines: Civil Rights in the 1960 Term of the Supreme Court," *American Political Science Review* 56 (March 1962): 71-89; Walter Murphy, "Deeds Under a Doctrine: Civil Liberties in the 1963 Term," *American Political Science Review* 59 (March 1965): 64-79.

18. Smith, *Liberalism*, pp. 106-107.

19. Milton Konvitz, *Expanding Liberties* (New York: Viking Press, 1966), pp. 11-16, 235-244.

20. A number of studies suggest that interest groups are responsive to the ideological balance of the Court and the state of doctrinal development. Joseph Kobylka discusses the exit of the ACLU from obscenity litigation in the wake of unfavorable Court decisions. Lee Epstein attributes the rise of conservative litigants to the favorable environment created by the Burger Court. Lincoln Caplan maintains that the solicitor general became much more politicized and conservative in response to the environment created by President Reagan and the Burger Court. For Kobylka, see Note 10, above; for Epstein, see Note 7; Lincoln Caplan, *The Tenth Justice* (New York: Vintage Books, 1987).

21. William Donahue, *The Politics of the American Civil Liberties Union* (New Brunswick, NJ: Transaction Press, 1985), p. 15.

22. Early cases such as *Hague v. Committee for Industrial Organization* (307 U.S. 496) expressed strong support for individual rights. Footnote 1 in Stone's concurring opinion is particularly forceful. In *Thornhill v. Alabama*, Justice Murphy eloquently defended free expression and advocated a further expansion of civil liberties (310 U.S. at 102-106). Justice Rutledge reinforced the preferred position doctrine in *Thomas v. Collins* (323 U.S. 516). On the negative side, in *Milk Wagon Drivers Union v. Meadowmoor Dairies* (312 U.S. 287), Justice Frankfurter restricted expression due to violence. This served as a cue for the state in later cases. In a number of cases, justices in the majority and the dissenting opinions disagreed about the nature of the alleged violence or whether it existed. World War II and the cold war led to ambivalent decisions from a Court seeking to protect expression but concerned with national security. Dicta played a role in cases like *Schneider v. Irvington* (308 U.S. 147), where the Court purposely left open questions of the protection afforded commercial speech. A few terms later, *Valentine v. Chrestensen* (316 U.S. 52) afforded the Court the opportunity to resolve this issue. In *Follett v. Town of McCormick* (321 U.S. 573), a free-exercise case, the dicta and the dissent raised the issue of the Establishment Clause, portend of a very troubling issue. Stone's dissent in *Minersville School District v. Gobitis* (310 U.S. 586) and the favorable commentary supporting it gave aid and comfort to the Jehovah's Witnesses, strengthening their resolve.

23. Donahue, *The Politics*, pp. 14-15; Cortner, *The Supreme Court*, pp. 100-108.

24. The Jehovah's Witnesses began to approach the Supreme Court in 1938. From 1938-1946, the Court decided fifteen cases brought by the Jehovah's Witnesses, more than the total number of religion cases in the previous 150 years (Konvitz, *Expanding Liberties*, p. 12). The NAACP had a presence prior to 1937, but it expanded activities as a result of the post-1937 changes and the more propitious opportunities it offered; see Stephen Wasby, Anthony D'Amato, and Rosemary Metrailer, *Desegregation from Brown to Alexander* (Carbondale: Southern Illinois University Press, 1977), p. 31. The ACLU expanded activities after the Great Depression in a climate that economically and philosophically

was more conducive (Donahue, *The Politics*, p. 17). Although as noted, World War II, national security fears, and the emergence of more difficult issues discouraged the ACLU from pursuing civil liberties vigorously and led to a period of retrenchment. Soon after, the Court reduced the jurisdictional limits required to bring cases in equity and began to expand this form of relief (McDowell, *Equity*, p. 103).

25. Supreme Court tests like "the reasonable man" (*Lochner v. New York* 198 U.S. 45) (Pritchett, *Constitutional Civil Liberties*, p. 22); "overbreadth" (*Adkins v. Children's Hospital* 261 U.S. 525); "least restrictive means" (*Burns Baking Company v. Bryan* 264 U.S. 504); see Jack Balkin, "Ideology and Counterideology from *Lochner* to *Garcia*," *UMKC Law Review* 54 (Winter 1985): 185; and "void for vagueness" (*Connally v. General Construction* 269 U.S. 385) (Pritchett, *Constitutional Civil Liberties*, p. 228) were originally tests and standards used in economic areas, and later adapted to First Amendment cases, primarily freedom-of-expression cases. The Court also used "strict" and "minimum" scrutiny as Economic tests in *Lochner*; see Martha Field, "Comment: *Garcia v. San Antonio Metropolitan Transit Authority*: The Demise of a Misguided Doctrine," *Harvard Law Review* 99 (November 1985): 114.

26. Robert Steamer, *The Supreme Court in Crisis* (Amherst: University of Massachusetts Press, 1971).

27. Many of the "new" civil liberties issues were recombinations of older, often unrelated issues. A significant proportion of the criminal procedure cases came from Internal Revenue cases raising questions of due process and search and seizure. The preponderance of speech cases in the 1938-1947 period involved labor disputes. The majority of equal protection cases involved immigration in wartime or discrimination against citizens of other states. The growth of government and regulatory activities spawned litigation crossing policy lines.

28. J. Woodford Howard, "On the Fluidity of Judicial Choice," *American Political Science Review* 62 (March 1962): 43-57.

29. Pritchett, *Civil Liberties*, p. 4; C. Herman Pritchett, *The Roosevelt Court* (Chicago: Quadrangle Books, 1948), pp. 96-102.

30. Saul Brenner, "Fluidity on the Supreme Court: 1956-1967," *American Journal of Political Science* 26 (May 1982): 388-390.

31. Eloise Snyder, "The Supreme Court as a Small Group," *Social Forces* 36 (March 1958): 232-236; S. Sidney Ulmer, "Toward a Theory of Sub-Group Formation in the United States Supreme Court," *Journal of Politics* 27 (February 1965): 133-152. Mary Francis Berry, *Stability, Security, and Continuity* (Westport, CT: Greenwood Press, 1978), p. 50; J. Woodford Howard, *Mr. Justice Murphy: A Political Biography* (Princeton: Princeton University Press, 1968), pp. 236-237; Joseph Lash, *From the Diaries of Felix Frankfurter* (New York: W. W. Norton, 1975), p. 264. Douglas, *The Court*

Years, pp. 43-45; James Simon, *Independent Journey: The Life of William O. Douglas* (New York: Harper & Row, 1980).

32. Edward Heck and Melinda Gann Hall, "Bloc Voting and the Freshman Justice Revisited," *Journal of Politics* 43 (August 1981): 852-860; Richard Pacelle and Patricia Pauly, "The Evolving Behavior of New Justices: A New Freshman Effect?" Paper prepared for the Midwest Political Science meetings, April 5-7, 1990, Chicago, Illinois.

33. Henry Abraham, *Justices and Presidents: A Political History of Appointments to the Supreme Court*, 2nd ed. (New York: Oxford University Press, 1988), pp. 210-211.

34. Smith, *Liberalism*, p. 85.

35. Arthur Hellman, "The Supreme Court, the National Law, and the Selection of Cases for the Plenary Docket," *University of Pittsburgh Law Review* 44 (Spring 1983): 435-444.

36. There are many examples of paired cases. A number of reapportionment cases accompanied the "name" case, *Wesberry v. Sanders* 376 U.S. 1 (1963 term). *Grosso v. United States* 390 U.S. 62 and *Haynes v. United States* 390 U.S. 85 (1967 term) accompanied *Marchetti v. United States* 390 U.S. 39 (1967 term) involving refusal to pay taxes on the grounds that it constituted self-incrimination for ill-gotten gains. The most prominent of the *per curiam* decisions are the dozen that accompanied *Miller v. California*, the decision that redefined the standards of obscenity.

37. Many of the early civil liberties decisions were accepted because there were severe violations of rights. The Court acknowledged this in a series of cases involving the Jehovah's Witnesses that were decided after widespread persecution of the sect in the wake of the *Minersville School District v. Gobitis* (Konvitz, *Expanding Liberties*, p. 13). More recently, the Court had to accept *Stanton v. Stanton* 421 U.S. 7 (1974 term), a gender discrimination case involving different ages of majority for women and men, more than once because Oregon courts ignored the United States Supreme Court's decision (Richard Pacelle and Lawrence Baum, "Supreme Court Authority in the Judiciary: A Study of Remands," *American Politics Quarterly*, forthcoming.

38. Kingdon, *Agendas*, p. 203.

39. The 8 to 1 *Minersville* decision spawned volumes of comment, most of it favorable to Justice Stone, the lone dissenter; see Alice F. Bartee, *Cases Lost, Cases Won* (New York: St. Martin's Press, 1984), pp. 180-181. Within a few terms, a number of justices admitted their error in the case and were able to overturn the decision in *West Virginia State Board of Education v. Barnette*.

40. In First Amendment cases, the Court began using restrictive tests that upheld state police power, turned to the liberal "preferred position" doctrines, and finally to the moderate balancing tests, such as "time, place, and manner" restrictions (Pritchett, *Constitutional Civil Liberties*, pp. 20-32). A similar pattern of doctrinal evolution can be traced for Equality cases. "Ordinary" or

"minimum" scrutiny was too restrictive for all situations, so "strict" scrutiny was developed for some groups. Eventually, an intermediate level, "moderate" scrutiny was adopted; see Andrea Bonnicksen, *Civil Rights and Liberties* (Palo Alto, CA: Mayfield Publishing, 1982), pp. 150-160. The Court also used "strict" and "minimum" scrutiny as economic tests in *Lochner* and other cases (Field, "The Demise of a Misguided Doctrine," 114).

41. Schubert, "The 1960 Term of the Supreme Court."

42. Wasby, "How Planned Is 'Planned Litigation'?" pp. 102-106.

43. Donahue, *The Politics*, pp. 16-17; Samuel Walker, *In Defense of American Liberties*, chapter 11.

44. Epstein, *Conservatives*, chapter 5.

45. Caplan, *The Tenth Justice,* pp. 4-7; Robert Scigliano, *The Supreme Court and the Presidency* (New York: The Free Press, 1971), pp. 168-182.

46. Cortner, *The Supreme Court*, pp. 144-150.

47. Konvitz, *Expanding Liberties*, p. 13.

48. Pritchett, *Civil Liberties and the Vinson Court*, pp. 10-14.

49. Smith, *Liberalism*, p. 107.

50. Ibid., p. 65.

51. Arthur Hellman, "Case Selection in the Burger Court: A Preliminary Inquiry," *Notre Dame Law Review* 60 (Fall 1985): 976-978.

52. Susan Olson, "The Political Evolution of Interest Group Litigation," in *Governing Through Courts*, ed. Richard Gambitta, Marilyn May, and James Foster (Beverly Hills, CA: Sage, 1981), pp. 234-249.

CHAPTER 7

1. Lincoln Caplan, *The Tenth Justice* (New York: Vintage Books, 1987); James Cooper, "The Solicitor General and the Evolution of Activism," *Indiana Law Journal* 65 (Summer 1990): 675-696.

2. Sue Davis, *Justice Rehnquist and the Constitution* (Princeton, NJ: Princeton University Press, 1989); John Denvir, "Justice Rehnquist and Constitutional Interpretation," *Hastings Law Journal* 34 (May 1983): 1011-1053; Robert Riggs and Thomas Proffitt, "The Judicial Philosophy of Justice Rehnquist," *Akron Law Review* 16 (Spring 1983): 555-604; Thomas Kleven, "The Constitutional Philosophy of Justice William H. Rehnquist," *Vermont Law Review* 8 (Spring 1983): 1-54; Jeff Powell, "The Compleat Jeffersonian: Justice Rehnquist and Federalism," *Yale Law Journal* 91 (June 1982): 1317-1370.

3. Richard Brisbin, "The Conservatism of Antonin Scalia," *Political Science Quarterly* 105 (Spring 1990): 1-29; Jean Morgan Meaux, "Justice Scalia and Judicial Restraint: A Conservative Resolution of Conflict Between Individual and State," *Tulane Law Review* 62 (November 1987): 225-260; James Wyszynski, "In Praise of Judicial Restraint: The Jurisprudence of Justice

Antonin Scalia," *Detroit College of Law Review* (Spring 1989): 117-162; William Eskridge, "The New Textualism," *UCLA Law Review* 37 (April 1990): 621-691.

4. William Brennan, "State Constitutions and the Protections of Individual Rights," *Harvard Law Review* 90 (January 1977): 489-504; Larry Elison and Dennis Simmons, "Federalism and State Constitutions: The New Doctrine of Independent and Adequate State Grounds," *Montana Law Review* 45 (Summer 1984): 177-214.

5. David O'Brien, "Federalism as a Metaphor in the Constitutional Politics of Public Administration," *Public Administration Review* 49 (September/October 1989): 411.

6. Elder Witt, *A Different Justice* (Washington, D.C.: Congressional Quarterly, 1985); Richard Cordray and James Vrodelis, "The Emerging Jurisprudence of Justice O'Connor," *University of Chicago Law Review* 52 (Spring 1985): 389-459; Barbara Olson Bruckman, "Justice Sandra Day O'Connor: Trends Toward Judicial Restraint," *Washington and Lee Law Review* 42 (Fall 1985): 1185-1231.

7. Richard Carelli, "Opinions Portray Kennedy as Pragmatic Conservative," *Chicago Daily Law Bulletin* 133 (November 11, 1987): 3; Richard Reuben, "After One Year on Court, Justice Kennedy Still a Mystery Man," *Chicago Daily Law Bulletin* 135 (April 21, 1989): 1.

8. In re Amendment to Rule 39 III S.Ct. at 1574 (1991).

9. Howard Ball, *Judicial Craftsmanship or Fiat?* (Westport, CT: Greenwood Press, 1981), pp. 26-33; William Louthan, *The United States Supreme Court: Lawmaking in the Third Branch of Government* (Englewood Cliffs, NJ: Prentice-Hall, 1991), pp. 229-230.

10. Stephen Chapple and Donna Kraus, "Rehnquist-Scalia Combined Effect May Far Exceed Current Predictions," *National Law Journal* 9 (September 15, 1986): 24.

11. Charley Roberts, "Portrait of Souter Starts to Emerge; He's Conservative, but Some See a Moderate Streak; An 'Interpretationist'," *The Los Angeles Daily Journal* 103 (July 25, 1990): 1; Terence Moran, "Souter's Legal Faith: Process over Principle: A Purist at Heart," *Legal Times* 13 (August 27, 1990): 1; Charles Kelbey, "Jurisprudential Choices for Judge Souter," *New York Law Journal* 204 (September 13, 1990): 2.

Bibliography

Abraham, Henry. *Freedom and the Court: Civil Rights and Liberties in the United States.* 5th ed. New York: Oxford University Press, 1988.

_____. *Justices and Presidents: A Political History of Appointments to the Supreme Court.* 2nd ed. New York: Oxford University Press, 1985.

Adamany, David. "Realigning Elections and the Supreme Court." *Wisconsin Law Review* 57 (1973): 790-846.

Atkins, Burton, and Henry Glick. "Environmental and Structural Variables as Determinants of Issues in State Courts of Last Resort." *American Journal of Political Science* 20 (February 1976): 391-425.

Balkin, Jack. "Ideology and Counterideology from *Lochner to Garcia*." *UMKC Law Review* 54 (Winter 1985): 175-214.

Ball, Howard. *Judicial Craftsmanship or Fiat?* Westport, CT: Greenwood Press, 1981.

_____. "The United States Supreme Court's Glossing of the Federal Torts Claims Act: Statutory Construction and Veterans' Tort Actions." *Western Political Quarterly* 41 (September 1988): 529-552.

Barnum, David. "The Supreme Court and Public Opinion: Judicial Decision Making in the Post-New Deal Period." *Journal of Politics* 47 (May 1985): 652-666.

Bartee, Alice Fleetwood. *Cases Lost, Causes Won.* New York: St. Martin's Press, 1984.

Baum, Lawrence. "Measuring Policy Change in the U.S. Supreme Court." *American Political Science Review* 82 (September 1988): 905-912.

_____. *The Supreme Court.* 3rd ed. Washington, D.C.: Congressional Quarterly, 1989.

Berry, Mary Francis. *Stability, Security, and Continuity.* Westport, CT: Greenwood Press, 1978.

Bickel, Alexander. *The Least Dangerous Branch: The Supreme Court at the Bar of Politics.* Indianapolis: Bobbs-Merrill, 1968.

Bonnicksen, Andrea. *Civil Rights and Liberties.* Palo Alto, CA: Mayfield, 1982.

Brace, Paul, and Melinda Gann Hall. "Neo-Institutionalism and Dissent in State Supreme Courts." *Journal of Politics* 52 (February 1990): 54-70.

Brady, David, with Joseph Stewart. "Congressional Party Realignment and Transformation of Public Policy in Three Realignment Eras." *American Journal of Political Science* 26 (May 1982): 333-360.

Brennan, William. "State Constitutions and the Protection of Individual Rights." *Harvard Law Review* 90 (January 1977): 489-504.

Brenner, Saul. "Fluidity on the Supreme Court: 1956-1967." *American Journal of Political Science* 26 (May 1982): 388-390.

Brigham, John. *Civil Liberties & American Democracy.* Washington, D.C.: Congressional Quarterly, 1984.

Brisbin, Richard. "The Conservatism of Antonin Scalia." *Political Science Quarterly* 105 (Spring 1990): 1-29.

Bruckman, Barbara Olson. "Justice Sandra Day O'Connor: Trends Toward Judicial Restraint." *Washington and Lee Law Review* 42 (Fall 1985): 1185-1231.

Caldeira, Gregory. "The United States Supreme Court and Criminal Cases: Alternative Models of Agenda-Building." *British Journal of Political Science* 11 (October 1981): 449-470.

_____, and John Wright. "Organized Interests and Agenda Setting in the U.S. Supreme Court." *American Political Science Review* 82 (December 1988): 1109-1128.

Canon, Bradley, and Lawrence Baum. "Patterns of Adoption of Tort Law Innovations: An Application of Diffusion Theory to Judicial Decisions." *American Political Science Review* 75 (December 1981): 975-987.

Caplan, Lincoln. *The Tenth Justice.* New York: Vintage Books, 1987.

Carelli, Richard. "Opinions Portray Kennedy as Pragmatic Conservative." *Chicago Daily Law Bulletin* 133 (November 11, 1987): 3.

Carmines, Edward, and James Stimson. *Issue Evolution: Race and the Transformation of American Politics.* Princeton, NJ: Princeton University Press, 1989.

Casper, Gerhard, and Richard Posner. *The Workload of the Supreme Court.* Chicago: American Bar Federation, 1976.

Casper, Jonathan. "The Supreme Court and National Policy-Making." *American Political Science Review* 70 (March 1976): 50-63.

Chapple, Stephen, and Donna Kraus. "Rehnquist-Scalia Combined Effect May Far Exceed Current Predictions." *National Law Journal* 9 (September 15, 1986): 24.

Cobb, Roger, and Charles Elder. *Participation in American Politics: The Dynamics of Agenda Building.* 2nd ed. Baltimore: Johns Hopkins University Press, 1983.

Cooper, James. "The Solicitor General and the Evolution of Activism." *Indiana Law Journal* 65 (Summer 1990): 675-696.

Cooper, Joseph, and David Brady. "Toward a Diachronic Analysis of Congress." *American Political Science Review* 75 (December 1981): 988-1006.

Cordray, Richard, and James Vrodelis. "The Emerging Jurisprudence of Justice O'Connor." *University of Chicago Law Review* 52 (Spring 1985): 389-459.

Cortner, Richard. *The Supreme Court and the Second Bill of Rights*. Madison: University of Wisconsin Press, 1981.

Crenson, Matthew. *The Unpolitics of Air Pollution*. Baltimore: Johns Hopkins University Press, 1971.

Crowley, Donald. "Judicial Review of Administrative Agencies: Does the Type of Agency Matter?" *Western Political Quarterly* 40 (June 1987): 265-283.

Dahl, Robert. "Decision Making in a Democracy: The Supreme Court and National Policy Making." *Journal of Public Law* 6 (Fall 1957): 279-295.

Danelski, David. "The Influence of the Chief Justice in the Decisional Process of the Supreme Court." In *American Court Systems*, 2nd ed., edited by Sheldon Goldman and Austin Sarat, 486-499. New York: Longman, 1989.

Davis, Sue. *Justice Rehnquist and the Constitution*. Princeton, NJ: Princeton University Press, 1989.

Denvir, John. "Justice Rehnquist and Constitutional Interpretation." *Hastings Law Journal* 34 (May 1983): 1011-1053.

Donahue, William. *The Politics of the American Civil Liberties Union*. New Brunswick, NJ: Transaction Press, 1985.

Douglas, William O. *The Court Years*. New York: Random House, 1980.

Dubroff, Harold. *The United States Tax Court: An Historical Analysis*. Chicago: Commerce Clearing House, 1979.

Ducat, Craig, and Robert Dudley. "Dimensions Underlying Economic Policy-Making in the Early and Later Burger Courts." *Journal of Politics* 49 (May 1987): 521-539.

Dudley, Robert, and Craig Ducat. "The Burger Court and Economic Liberalism." *Western Political Quarterly* 39 (June 1986): 236-249.

Dunne, Gerald T. *Hugo Black and the Judicial Revolution*. New York: Simon & Schuster, 1977.

Elison, Larry, and Dennis Simmons. "Federalism and State Constitutions: The New Doctrine of Independent and Adequate State Grounds." *Montana Law Review* 45 (Summer 1984): 177-214.

Ely, John Hart. *Democracy and Distrust: A Theory of Judicial Review*. Cambridge: Harvard University Press, 1980.

Epstein, Lee. *Conservatives in Court*. Knoxville: University of Tennessee Press, 1985.

_____, Thomas Walker, and William Dixon. "The Supreme Court and Criminal Justice Disputes: A Neo-Institutional Perspective." *American Journal of Political Science* 33 (November 1989): 825-841.

Eskridge, William. "The New Textualism." *UCLA Law Review* 37 (April 1990): 621-691.

Estreicher, Samuel, and John Sexton. "New York University Supreme Court Project." *New York University Law Review* 59 (October 1984): 677-1004.

_____. "New York University Supreme Court Project." *New York University Law Review* 59 (November 1984): 1005-1402.

_____. "New York University Supreme Court Project." *New York University Law Review* 59 (December 1984): 1403-1929.

_____, and John Sexton. *Redefining the Supreme Court's Role.* New Haven, CT: Yale University Press, 1986.

Eyestone, Robert. *From Social Issues to Public Policy.* New York: John Wiley, 1978.

The Federalist Papers. New York: New American Library, 1961.

Field, Martha. "Comment: *Garcia v. San Antonio Metropolitan Transit Authority*: The Demise of a Misguided Doctrine." *Harvard Law Review* 99 (November 1985): 84-119.

Fisher, Louis. *Constitutional Dialogues: Interpretation as Political Process.* Princeton, NJ: Princeton University Press, 1988.

Fox, Arthur. "Showing Workers Who's Boss." In *The Burger Court: Rights and Wrongs in the Supreme Court 1969-1986,* edited by Herman Schwartz, 228-239. New York: Penguin Books, 1987.

Franklin, Charles, and Liane Kosaki. "Republican Schoolmaster: The U.S. Supreme Court, Public Opinion, and Abortion." *American Political Science Review* 83 (September 1989): 751-771.

Funston, Richard. "The Supreme Court and Critical Elections." *American Political Science Review* 69 (September 1975): 795-811.

_____. *A Vital National Seminar: The Supreme Court in American Political Life.* Palo Alto, CA: Mayfield, 1978.

Galanter, Marc. "Why the 'Haves' Come Out Ahead: Speculations on the Limits of Legal Change." *Law & Society Review* 8 (Fall 1974): 105-116.

Gates, John. *The Supreme Court and Partisan Realignment: A Macro- and Microlevel Perspective.* Boulder, CO: Westview Press, forthcoming.

Gibson, James. "Judges' Role Orientations, Attitudes and Decisions: An Interactive Model." *American Political Science Review* 72 (September 1978): 911-924.

Gilmore, Grant. *The Ages of American Law.* New Haven, CT: Yale University Press, 1977.

Goldman, Sheldon. *Constitutional Law: Cases and Essays.* 2nd ed. New York: Harper Collins, 1991.

_____. "Voting Behavior on the United States Courts of Appeals, 1961-1964." *American Political Science Review* 60 (June 1966): 374-383.

_____. "Voting Behavior on the United States Courts of Appeals Revisited." *American Political Science Review* 69 (June 1975): 493-495.

_____, and Thomas Jahnige. *The Federal Courts as a Political System*. 3rd ed. New York: Harper & Row, 1985.

Greenhouse, Linda. "Of Tents with Wheels and Houses with Oars." *New York Times* (May 16, 1985): 12.

Grossman, Joel, and Austin Sarat. "Litigation in the Federal Courts: A Comparative Perspective." *Law & Society Review* 9 (Winter 1975): 321-346.

Hall, Kermit. *The Magic Mirror: Law in American History*. New York: Oxford University Press, 1989.

Hall, Melinda Gann, and Paul Brace. "Order in the Courts: A Neo-Institutional Approach to Judicial Consensus." *Western Political Quarterly* 42 (September 1989): 391-407.

Hammond, Thomas, and Gary Miller. "A Social Choice Perspective on Expertise and Authority in Bureaucracy." *American Journal of Political Science* 29 (February 1985): 1-28.

Heck, Edward, and Melinda Gann Hall. "Bloc Voting and the Freshman Justice Revisited." *Journal of Politics* 43 (August 1981): 852-860.

Hellman, Arthur. "Case Selection in the Burger Court: A Preliminary Inquiry." *Notre Dame Law Review* 60 (Fall 1985): 947-1055.

_____. "Error Correction, Lawmaking, and the Supreme Court's Exercise of Discretionary Review." *University of Pittsburgh Law Review* 44 (Summer 1983): 795-877.

_____. "The Supreme Court, the National Law and the Selection of Cases for the Plenary Docket." *University of Pittsburgh Law Review* 44 (Spring 1983): 521-634.

Howard, J. Woodford. *Courts of Appeals in the Federal Judicial System*. Princeton, NJ: Princeton University Press, 1981.

_____. *Mr. Justice Murphy: A Political Biography*. Princeton, NJ: Princeton University Press, 1968.

_____. "On the Fluidity of Judicial Choice." *American Political Science Review* 62 (March 1968): 43-57.

James, Dorothy. "Role Theory and the Supreme Court." *Journal of Politics* 30 (February 1968): 160-186.

Johnson, Charles, and Bradley Canon. *Judicial Policies: Implementation and Impact*. Washington, D.C.: Congressional Quarterly, 1984.

Kelbey, Charles. "Jurisprudential Choices for Judge Souter." *New York Law Journal* 204 (September 13, 1990): 2.

Key, V.O. "A Theory of Critical Elections." *Journal of Politics* 17 (February 1955): 245-265.

Kim, Jae-On, and Charles Mueller. *Factor Analysis: Statistical Methods and Practical Issues*. Beverly Hills, CA: Sage, 1978.

_____. *Introduction to Factor Analysis*. Beverly Hills, CA: Sage, 1978.

Kingdon, John. *Agendas, Alternatives, and Public Policies*. Boston: Little, Brown, 1984.

Kleven, Thomas. "The Constitutional Philosophy of Justice William H. Rehnquist." *Vermont Law Review* 8 (Spring 1983): 1-54.

Kobylka, Joseph. "A Court-Related Context for Group Litigation: Libertarian Groups and Obscenity." *Journal of Politics* 49 (November 1987): 1061-1079.

Konvitz, Milton. *Expanding Liberties*. New York: Viking Press, 1966.

Kuhn, Thomas. *The Structure of Scientific Revolutions*. 2nd ed., enlarged. Chicago: University of Chicago Press, 1970.

Lash, Joseph. *From the Diaries of Felix Frankfurter*. New York: Norton, 1975.

Likens, Thomas. "Agenda Setting by the High Court: Systematic Processes or Noise?" Paper prepared for the American Political Science Association meetings, 1979.

Louthan, William. *The United States Supreme Court: Lawmaking in the Third Branch of Government*. Englewood Cliffs, NJ: Prentice-Hall, 1991.

Lowi, Theodore. *The End of Liberalism*. 2nd ed. New York: Norton, 1979.

Lustig, R. Jeffrey. *Corporate Liberalism: The Origins of Modern American Political Theory, 1890-1920*. Berkeley: University of California Press, 1982.

Malkovits, R. S. "The Burger Court, Antitrust, and Economic Analysis." In *The Burger Court: The Counter-Revolution That Wasn't*, edited by Vincent Blasi, 180-197. New Haven, CT: Yale University Press, 1983.

Mason, Alpheus Thomas. *Harlan Fiske Stone: Pillar of the Law*. New York: Viking Press, 1956.

_____. *The Supreme Court from Taft to Burger*. Baton Rouge: Louisiana State University Press, 1979.

McCloskey, Robert. "Deeds Without Doctrines: Civil Rights in the 1960 Term of the Supreme Court." *American Political Science Review* 56 (March 1962): 71-89.

_____. *The American Supreme Court*. Chicago: University of Chicago Press, 1960.

McDowell, Gary. *Equity and the Constitution*. Chicago: University of Chicago Press, 1982.

McIntosh, Wayne. "150 Years of Litigation and Dispute Settlement: A Court Tale." *Law & Society Review* 15 (1980-1981): 823-846.

Meaux, Jean Morgan. "Justice Scalia and Judicial Restraint: A Conservative Resolution of Conflict Between Individual and State." *Tulane Law Review* 62 (November 1987): 225-260.

Mendelson, Wallace. "Mr. Justice Frankfurter and the Distribution of Judicial Power in the United States." *Midwest Journal of Political Science* 2 (February 1958): 40-51.

Miller, Arthur Selwyn. *The Supreme Court and American Capitalism.* New York: The Free Press, 1968.

_____. *Toward Increased Judicial Activism.* Westport, CT: Greenwood Press, 1982.

Moran, Terence. "Souter's Legal Faith: Process over Principle: A Purist at Heart." *Legal Times* 13 (August 27, 1990): 1.

Murphy, Paul. *World War I and the Origin of Civil Liberties.* New York: Norton, 1979.

Murphy, Walter. "Deeds Under a Doctrine: Civil Liberties in the 1963 Term." *American Political Science Review* 59 (March 1965): 64-79.

_____. *Elements of Judicial Strategy.* Chicago: University of Chicago Press, 1964.

Neustadt, Richard. *Presidential Power: The Politics of Leadership from F.D.R. to Carter.* New York: Wiley, 1980.

Newmyer, R. Kent. *The Supreme Court Under Marshall and Taney.* New York: Crowell, 1968.

Nowak, John, Ronald Rotunda, and J. Nelson Young. *Constitutional Law.* 3rd ed. Minneapolis: West Publishing, 1986.

O'Brien, David M. "Federalism as a Metaphor in the Constitutional Politics of Public Administration." *Public Administration Review* 49 (September/October 1989): 411-419.

_____. *Storm Center.* 2nd ed. New York: Norton, 1990.

O'Connor, Karen, and Lee Epstein. "The Role of Interest Groups in Supreme Court Policy Formation." In *Public Policy Formation,* edited by Robert Eyestone, 63-81. Greenwich, CT: JAI Press, 1984.

Olson, Susan. "The Political Evolution of Interest Group Litigation." In *Governing Through Courts,* edited by Richard Gambitta, Marilyn May, and James Foster, 234-249. Beverly Hills, CA : Sage, 1981.

Pacelle, Richard, and Lawrence Baum. "Supreme Court Authority in the Judiciary: A Study of Remands." *American Politics Quarterly,* forthcoming.

_____, and Roberta Herzberg. "Altering the Balance: The Impact of Membership Change upon Voting Alignments in the United States Supreme Court, 1966-1985." Paper prepared for the Midwest Political Science Association meetings, 1988.

_____, and Patricia Pauly. "The Evolving Behavior of New Justices: A New Freshman Effect?" Paper prepared for the Midwest Political Science meetings, 1990.

Perry, H. W. "Deciding to Decide: Agenda Setting in the United States Supreme Court." Ph.D. dissertation, University of Michigan, 1987. (To be published by Harvard University Press.)

Pomper, Gerald, and Susan Lederman. *Elections in America*. 2nd ed. New York: Longman's, 1980.

Powell, Jeff. "The Compleat Jeffersonian: Justice Rehnquist and Federalism." *Yale Law Journal* 91 (June 1982): 1317-1370.

Pritchett, C. Herman. *Civil Liberties and the Vinson Court*. Chicago: University of Chicago Press, 1954.

_____. *Constitutional Civil Liberties*. Englewood Cliffs, NJ: Prentice-Hall, 1984.

_____. *Constitutional Law of the Federal System*. Englewood Cliffs, NJ: Prentice-Hall, 1984.

_____. *The Roosevelt Court*. Chicago: Quadrangle Books, 1948.

Provine, Doris Marie. *Case Selection in the United States Supreme Court*. Chicago: University of Chicago Press, 1980.

Reuben, Richard. "After One Year on Court, Justice Kennedy Still a Mystery Man." *Chicago Daily Law Bulletin* 135 (April 21, 1989): 1.

Riggs, Robert, and Thomas Proffitt. "The Judicial Philosophy of Justice Rehnquist." *Akron Law Review* 16 (Spring 1983): 555-604.

Roberts, Charley. "Portrait of Souter Starts to Emerge; He's Conservative, But Some See a Moderate Streak; An 'Interpretationist'." *The Los Angeles Daily Journal* 103 (July 25, 1990): 1.

Rohde, David, and Harold Spaeth. *Supreme Court Decision Making*. San Francisco: Freeman, 1976.

Sarat, Austin, and Joel Grossman. "Courts and Conflict Resolution: Problems in the Mobilization of Adjudication." *American Political Science Review* 69 (December 1975): 1200-1217.

Schlozman, Kay Lehman, and John Tierney. *Organized Interests and American Democracy*. New York: Harper & Row, 1986.

Schubert, Glendon. *The Judicial Mind Revisited*. New York: Oxford University Press, 1974.

_____. *The Judicial Mind: The Attitudes and Ideologies of Supreme Court Justices 1946-1963*. Evanston: Northwestern University Press, 1965.

_____. "Policy Without Law: An Extension of the Certiorari Game." *Stanford Law Review* 14 (March 1962): 284-327.

_____. The 1960 Term of the Supreme Court: A Psychological Analysis." *American Political Science Review* 56 (March 1962): 90-107.

Schuck, Peter. *Suing Government: Citizen Remedies for Official Wrongs*. New Haven: Yale University Press, 1983.

Scigliano, Robert. *The Supreme Court and the Presidency*. New York: The Free Press, 1971.

Segal, Jeffrey. "Predicting Supreme Court Cases Probabilistically: The Search and Seizure Cases, 1962-1981." *American Political Science Review* 78 (December 1984): 891-900.

_____. "Supreme Court Justices as Human Decision Makers: An Individual Level Analysis of Search and Seizure Cases." *Journal of Politics* 48 (November 1986): 938-955.

_____, and Albert Cover. "Ideological Values and Votes of U.S. Supreme Court Justices." *American Political Science Review* 83 (August 1989): 557-565.

Shapiro, Martin. *The Supreme Court and Administrative Agencies.* New York: The Free Press, 1968.

Silberman, David. "The Burger Court and Labor-Management Relations." In *The Burger Court: Rights and Wrongs in the Supreme Court 1969-1986,* edited by Herman Schwartz, 220-227. New York: Penguin Books, 1987.

Silverstein, Mark. *Constitutional Faiths.* Ithaca, NY: Cornell University Press, 1983.

Simon, James. *Independent Journey: The Life of William O. Douglas.* New York: Harper & Row, 1980.

Sinclair, Barbara Deckard. "Party Realignment and the Transformation of the Political Agenda: The House of Representatives." *American Political Science Review* 71 (September 1977): 940-953.

_____. *The Transformation of the U.S. Senate.* Baltimore: Johns Hopkins University Press, 1989.

Sklar, Martin. *The Corporate Reconstruction of American Capitalism.* Cambridge: Cambridge University Press, 1988.

Skowronek, Stephen. *Building a New American State: The Expansion of National Administrative Capacities, 1877-1928.* New York: Cambridge University Press, 1983.

Smith, Rogers. *Liberalism and American Constitutional Law.* Cambridge: Harvard University Press, 1985.

Snyder, Eloise. "The Supreme Court as a Small Group." *Social Forces* 36 (March 1958): 232-236.

Songer, Donald. "Concern for Policy Outputs as a Cue for Supreme Court Decisions on Certiorari." *Journal of Politics* 41 (November 1979): 1185-1194.

_____. "The Impact of the Supreme Court on Trends in Economic Policy Making in the United States Courts of Appeals." *Journal of Politics* 49 (August 1987): 830-844.

Sorauf, Frank. *The Wall of Separation.* Princeton, NJ: Princeton University Press, 1976.

Steamer, Robert. *The Supreme Court in Crisis.* Amherst: University of Massachusetts Press, 1971.

Sundquist, James. *The Dynamics of the Party System*. Washington, D.C.: Brookings Institution, 1973.

Tanenhaus, Joseph, Marvin Schick, Matthew Muraskin, and Daniel Rosen. "The Supreme Court's Certiorari Jurisdiction: A Cue Theory." In *Judicial Decision-Making*, edited by Glendon Schubert, 111-132. New York: The Free Press, 1963.

Thomas, Helen Shirley. *Felix Frankfurter: Scholar on the Bench*. Baltimore: Johns Hopkins University Press, 1960.

Tocqueville, Alexis de. *Democracy in America*. New York: New American Library, 1956.

Ulmer, S. Sidney. "The Decision to Grant Certiorari as an Indicator to Decision 'On the Merits.'" *Polity* 4 (Summer 1972): 429-447.

_____. "Issue Fluidity in the United States Supreme Court." In *Supreme Court Activism and Restraint*, edited by Stephen Halpern and Charles Lamb, 319-350. Lexington, MA: D.C. Heath, 1982.

_____. "Selecting Cases for Supreme Court Review: An Underdog Model." *American Political Science Review* 72 (September 1978): 902-910.

_____. "The Supreme Court's Certiorari Decisions: Conflict as a Predictive Variable." *American Political Science Review* 78 (December 1984): 901-911.

_____. "Toward a Theory of Sub-Group Formation in the United States Supreme Court." *Journal of Politics* 27 (February 1965): 133-152.

Urofsky, Melvin. *A March of Liberty: A Constitutional History of the United States*. Volume 2: *Since 1965*. New York: Knopf, 1988.

Walker, Jack. "The Diffusion of Innovations Among the States." *American Political Science Review* 63 (September 1969): 880-899.

_____. "The Diffusion of Knowledge, Policy Communities and Agenda Setting: The Relationship of Knowledge and Power." In *New Strategic Perspectives on Social Policy*, edited by John E. Tropman, Milan Dluhy, and Roger M. Lind, 75-96. New York: Pergamon Press, 1981.

_____. "Setting the Agenda in the U.S. Senate: A Theory of Problem Selection." *British Journal of Political Science* 7 (October 1977): 423-445.

Walker, Samuel. *In Defense of American Liberties*: *A History of the ACLU*. New York: Oxford University Press, 1990.

Wasby, Stephen. "How Planned is 'Planned Litigation'?" *American Bar Foundation Research Journal* 32 (1984): 83-138.

_____. *The Supreme Court and the Federal Judicial System*. 3rd ed. Chicago: Nelson Hall, 1989.

_____, Anthony D'Amato, and Rosemary Metrailer. *Desegregation from Brown to Alexander*. Carbondale: Southern Illinois University Press, 1977.

Wheeler, Stanton, Bliss Cartwright, Robert Kagan, and Lawrence Friedman. "Do the 'Haves' Come Out Ahead? Winning and Losing in State Supreme Courts." *Law & Society Review* 21 (1987): 403-446.

Witt, Elder. *A Different Justice.* Washington, D.C.: Congressional Quarterly, 1985.

Wyszynski, James. "In Praise of Judicial Restraint: The Jurisprudence of Justice Antonin Scalia." *Detroit College of Law Review* (Spring 1989): 117-162.

About the Book and Author

When we think of judicial activism—the Court's role in making public policy—we often focus on individuals: the Robert Borks or Thurgood Marshalls of the times. In this book, Richard Pacelle explores the *institutional* judicial activism of the Supreme Court through the dramatic changes in its agenda as it has evolved from 1933 to the present. Once dominated by economic issues, the Supreme Court's agenda is now populated largely by cases involving individual rights and liberties. This shift is hardly accidental, Pacelle argues, and he offers quantitative as well as qualitative assessments of the means and motivations for change. Over 7,500 cases serve as the basis of analysis, and the narrative is amplified by informative appendixes: an explanation of the author's case taxonomy, a chronology of the Court's chief justices, a list of cases cited, and a digest of key cases. The systematic framework provided for tracing historical changes in the Supreme Court's agenda is the first of its kind and is sure to be valuable in future analyses and projections of coming change beyond the Rehnquist Court.

Richard L. Pacelle, Jr., is assistant professor of political science at the University of Missouri–St. Louis.

Index